FORKHILL PROTESTANTS AND FORKHILL CATHOLICS, 1787–1858

McGILL-QUEEN'S STUDIES IN THE HISTORY OF RELIGION

Volumes in this series have been supported by the Jackman Foundation of Toronto.

SERIES TWO In memory of George Rawlyk
Donald Harman Akenson, Editor

1 Marguerite Bourgeoys and Montreal, 1640–1665
Patricia Simpson

2 Aspects of the Canadian Evangelical Experience
Edited by G.A. Rawlyk

3 Infinity, Faith, and Time
Christian Humanism and Renaissance Literature
John Spencer Hill

4 The Contribution of Presbyterianism to the Maritime Provinces of Canada
Edited by Charles H.H. Scobie and G.A Rawlyk

5 Labour, Love, and Prayer
Female Piety in Ulster Religious Literature, 1850–1914
Andrea Ebel Brozyna

6 The Waning of the Green
Catholics, the Irish, and Identity in Toronto, 1887–1922
Mark G. McGowan

7 Religion and Nationality in Western Ukraine
The Greek Catholic Church and the Ruthenian National Movement in Galicia, 1867–1900
John-Paul Himka

8 Good Citizens
British Missionaries and Imperial States, 1870–1918
James G. Greenlee and Charles M. Johnston

9 The Theology of the Oral Torah
Revealing the Justice of God
Jacob Neusner

10 Gentle Eminence
A Life of Cardinal Flahiff
P. Wallace Platt

11 Culture, Religion, and Demographic Behaviour
Catholics and Lutherans in Alsace, 1750–1870
Kevin McQuillan

12 Between Damnation and Starvation
Priests and Merchants in Newfoundland Politics, 1745–1855
John P. Greene

13 Martin Luther, German Saviour
German Evangelical Theological Factions and the Interpretation of Luther, 1917–1933
James M. Stayer

14 Modernity and the Dilemma of North American Anglican Identities, 1880–1950
William H. Katerberg

15 The Methodist Church on the Prairies, 1896–1914
George Emery

16 Christian Attitudes Towards the State of Israel
Paul Charles Merkley

17 A Social History of the Cloister
Daily Life in the Teaching Monasteries of the Old Regime
Elizabeth Rapley

18 Households of Faith
Family, Gender, and Community in Canada, 1760–1969
Edited by Nancy Christie

19 Blood Ground
Colonialism, Missions, and the Contest for Christianity in the Cape Colony and Britain, 1799–1853
Elizabeth Elbourne

20 A History of Canadian Catholics
Gallicanism, Romanism, and Canadianism
Terence J. Fay

21 The View from Rome
Archbishop Stagni's 1915 Reports on the Ontario Bilingual Schools Question
Edited and translated by John Zucchi

22 The Founding Moment
Church, Society, and the Construction of Trinity College
William Westfall

23 The Holocaust, Israel, and Canadian Protestant Churches
Haim Genizi

24 Governing Charities
Church and State in Toronto's Catholic Archdiocese, 1850–1950
Paula Maurutto

25 Anglicans and the Atlantic World
High Churchmen, Evangelicals, and the Quebec Connection
Richard W. Vaudry

26 Evangelicals and the Continental Divide
The Conservative Protestant Subculture in Canada and the United States
Sam Reimer

27 Christians in a Secular World
The Canadian Experience
Kurt Bowen

28 Anatomy of a Seance
A History of Spirit Communication in Central Canada
Stan McMullin

29 With Skilful Hand
The Story of King David
David T. Barnard

30 Faithful Intellect
Samuel S. Nelles and Victoria University
Neil Semple

31 W. Stanford Reid
An Evangelical Calvinist in the Academy
A. Donald MacLeod

32 A Long Eclipse
The Liberal Protestant Establishment and the Canadian University, 1920–1970
Catherine Gidney

33 Forkhill Protestants and Forkhill Catholics, 1787–1858
Kyla Madden

SERIES ONE
G.A. Rawlyk, Editor

1 Small Differences
Irish Catholics and Irish Protestants, 1815–1922
An International Perspective
Donald Harman Akenson

2 Two Worlds
The Protestant Culture of Nineteenth-Century Ontario
William Westfall

3 An Evangelical Mind
Nathanael Burwash and the Methodist Tradition in Canada, 1839–1918
Marguerite Van Die

4 The Dévotes
Women and Church in Seventeenth-Century France
Elizabeth Rapley

5 The Evangelical Century
College and Creed in English Canada from the Great Revival to the Great Depression
Michael Gauvreau

6 The German Peasants' War and Anabaptist Community of Goods
James M. Stayer

7 A World Mission
Canadian Protestantism and the Quest for a New International Order, 1918–1939
Robert Wright

8 Serving the Present Age
Revivalism, Progressivism, and the Methodist Tradition in Canada
Phyllis D. Airhart

9 A Sensitive Independence
Canadian Methodist Women Missionaries in Canada and the Orient, 1881–1925
Rosemary R. Gagan

10 God's Peoples
Covenant and Land in South Africa, Israel, and Ulster
Donald Harman Akenson

11 Creed and Culture
The Place of English-Speaking Catholics in Canadian Society, 1750–1930
Edited by Terrence Murphy and Gerald Stortz

12 Piety and Nationalism
Lay Voluntary Associations and the Creation of an Irish-Catholic Community in Toronto, 1850–1895
Brian P. Clarke

13 Amazing Grace
Studies in Evangelicalism in Australia, Britain, Canada, and the United States
Edited by George Rawlyk and Mark A. Noll

14 Children of Peace
W. John McIntyre

15 A Solitary Pillar
Montreal's Anglican Church and the Quiet Revolution
Joan Marshall

16 Padres in No Man's Land
Canadian Chaplains and the Great War
Duff Crerar

17 Christian Ethics and Political Economy in North America
A Critical Analysis of U.S. and Canadian Approaches
P. Travis Kroeker

18 Pilgrims in Lotus Land
Conservative Protestantism in British Columbia, 1917–1981
Robert K. Burkinshaw

19 Through Sunshine and Shadow
The Woman's Christian Temperance Union, Evangelicalism, and Reform in Ontario, 1874–1930
Sharon Cook

20 Church, College, and Clergy
A History of Theological Education at Knox College, Toronto, 1844–1994
Brian J. Fraser

21 The Lord's Dominion
The History of Canadian Methodism
Neil Semple

22 A Full-Orbed Christianity
The Protestant Churches and Social Welfare in Canada, 1900–1940
Nancy Christie and Michael Gauvreau

23 Evangelism and Apostasy
The Evolution and Impact of Evangelicals in Modern Mexico
Kurt Bowen

24 The Chignecto Covenanters
A Regional History of Reformed Presbyterianism in New Brunswick and Nova Scotia, 1827–1905
Eldon Hay

25 Methodists and Women's Education in Ontario, 1836–1925
Johanne Selles

26 Puritanism and Historical Controversy
William Lamont

Forkhill Protestants and Forkhill Catholics 1787–1858

KYLA MADDEN

McGill-Queen's University Press
Montreal & Kingston · London · Ithaca

ISBN 0-7735-2855-5 (cloth)
ISBN 0-7735-3060-6 (paper)

Legal deposit fourth quarter 2005
Bibliothèque nationale du Québec

This book has been published with the help of a grant from the Canadian Federation for the Humanities and Social Sciences, through the Aid to Scholarly Publications Programme, using funds provided by the Social Sciences and Humanities Research Council of Canada.

McGill-Queen's University Press acknowledges the support of the Canada Council for the Arts for our publishing program. We also acknowledge the financial support of the Government of Canada through the Book Publishing Industry Development Program (BPIDP) for our publishing activities.

National Library of Canada Cataloguing in Publication

Madden, Kyla, 1974–
Forkhill protestants and Forkhill catholics, 1787–1858 / Kyla Madden.
(McGill-Queen's studies in the history of religion; 33)
Includes bibliographical references and index.
ISBN 0-7735-2855-5 (bnd)
ISBN 0-7735-3060-6 (pbk)
1. Armagh (Northern Ireland : County) – History – 18th century.
2. Armagh (Northern Ireland : County) – History – 19th century.
3. Forkhill (Northern Ireland) – History – 18th century. 4. Forkhil (Northern Ireland) – History – 19th century. I. Title. II. Series.
DA995.F67M33 2005 941.6'6'081 C2004-906819-9

Typeset in Sabon 10/12
by Infoscan Collette, Quebec City

In memory of Eileen Garvey

Dá fhada an lá tagann an tráthnóna

Contents

Illustrations, Figures, and Maps xi

Acknowledgments xiii

1 The Sectarian Disease 3

2 Settlement and Resistance, 1787–1792 10

3 Rebellion, 1795–1798 28

4 Land and People, 1821 45

5 Education, 1790–1861 64

6 Outrage, 1832–1852 82

7 Famine, 1845–1850 121

8 Religion, 1846–1858 142

9 An Astronomy Lesson 156

Appendix: A Ribbon Oath 163

Notes 165

Bibliography 219

Index 235

Illustrations, Figures, and Maps

ILLUSTRATIONS

Portrait of Richard Jackson, Esq. 11
A page from the assize indictment book for Armagh, 1790 26
The boardroom of the trustees in Forkhill 132
The old Church of Ireland in Forkhill 151

FIGURES

1 Types of household, 1821 50
2 Types of household by denomination, 1821 50
3 Size distribution of farms, 1821 53
4 Size distribution of farms by denomination, 1821 53
5 Proportion of males in each age group who were heads of independent households, 1821 55
6 Occupations of males and females, 1821 57
7 Occupations of males by denomination, 1821 57
8 Occupations of females by denomination, 1821 58

MAPS

1 County Armagh xv
2 The civil parish of Forkhill showing townland boundaries xvi
3 The Forkhill estate, 1832 xvii

Acknowledgments

I have incurred many debts during the research and writing of this book. It's only now, sitting down to record them all, that I realize how many.

I owe my greatest debt to my thesis supervisor, Donald Harman Akenson. With characteristic generosity and wry humour, he shared his encyclopedic knowledge of nineteenth-century Ireland and his insights into the gulf that exists between the past and what we call history. I learned from him that historical writing requires two things above all: good scholarship and a good story. I hope this book goes some way to meeting his standard.

I owe an enormous debt to David Wilson, who introduced me to the study of Irish history at the University of Toronto. He is an exceptional scholar and inspiring teacher who encouraged me to pursue graduate work in Irish history when few saw any future in it. I will be forever grateful for that encouragement and for his friendship ever since.

To my family and friends in Ireland, north and south, I thank you with all my heart. In Belfast, Dr Desmond and Mary Olive Campbell gave me a home away from home. In Forkhill, my Aunt Nora McCoy, Padraig and Briege, and the Garvey family extended wonderful hospitality whenever I came to stay.

In south Armagh, I met many local historians who shared their knowledge generously, and always with a sense of humour. In particular, I am grateful to Pauline Loughran, for her countless stories and for pointing me in the direction of new research; to the Reverend Mervyn Kingston for his careful stewardship of the records of the Forkhill estate; to Master James Keating for sharing his work on local literary traditions; and to Kevin McMahon, whose pioneering work with archival sources has shed much light on the history of south Armagh.

When telling their stories, local historians like to point to the spot where an event is supposed to have taken place; to tell you that it happened *there*. I remember going for a walk one day through the townlands of Carriff and Mullaghbawn with a local history enthusiast named Mickey McGuigan. The walk took us seven hours, and Mickey never stopped telling stories, mainly about the rebels of 1798. *He was born there; he was captured there; he was hanged there.* I don't know if the stories were all true, but experiencing those moments of connection between past and present makes the study of local history a true joy.

Although I owe the local historians of south Armagh a great debt, I must add that the views that are expressed in the following pages are my own, and I bear sole responsibility for any errors in fact or interpretation.

I am grateful to the following institutions that kindly permitted me to consult their records during the course of my research: the Public Record Office of Northern Ireland, the Armagh Public Library, the Cardinal O'Fiaich Memorial Library and Archive, the Royal Irish Academy, the National Archives of Ireland, the National Library of Ireland, and the Department of Irish Folklore at University College, Dublin.

Once the writing was underway, I had help from many quarters. I am grateful to those who read the manuscript at various stages and offered their criticism and suggestions, particularly D.H. Akenson, David Wilson, Joan Harcourt, and the two anonymous readers appointed by McGill-Queen's; the manuscript has benefited immeasurably from their input. For assistance with maps and graphs, I am very grateful to Mike Pacey. For assistance with statistical analysis, I thank Emily Spencer. For the English translation of a poem in Irish, I am grateful to Seamus Cregg.

At McGill-Queen's University Press, Philip Cercone, John Zucchi, Joanne Pisano, Joan McGilvray, and Roger Martin could not have been more helpful and encouraging at every stage. Carlotta Lemieux edited the manuscript with a remarkable combination of precision and intuition; I was extremely fortunate to have her as my editor.

I am grateful to Father Edward Jackman whose interest in the dissemination of new scholarship encouraged him to endow the McGill-Queen's University Press Studies in the History of Religion series, of which this book is now a part. I thank him for his support of this project.

And I thank my family – Mom and Dad, and Nuala and Aileen – for their love and support, and also for their technical help: my mom read the manuscript at various stages, offering many helpful suggestions; my sister heroically proofread the 1821 census database. Most of the photographs were taken by my dad, whose love of Irish history has proved to be contagious. Above all, I thank my parents for taking us to Forkhill for our summer holidays year after year; it was there that this book began.

Finally, I dedicate this book to my grandmother, Eileen Garvey, who will always be Forkhill to me.

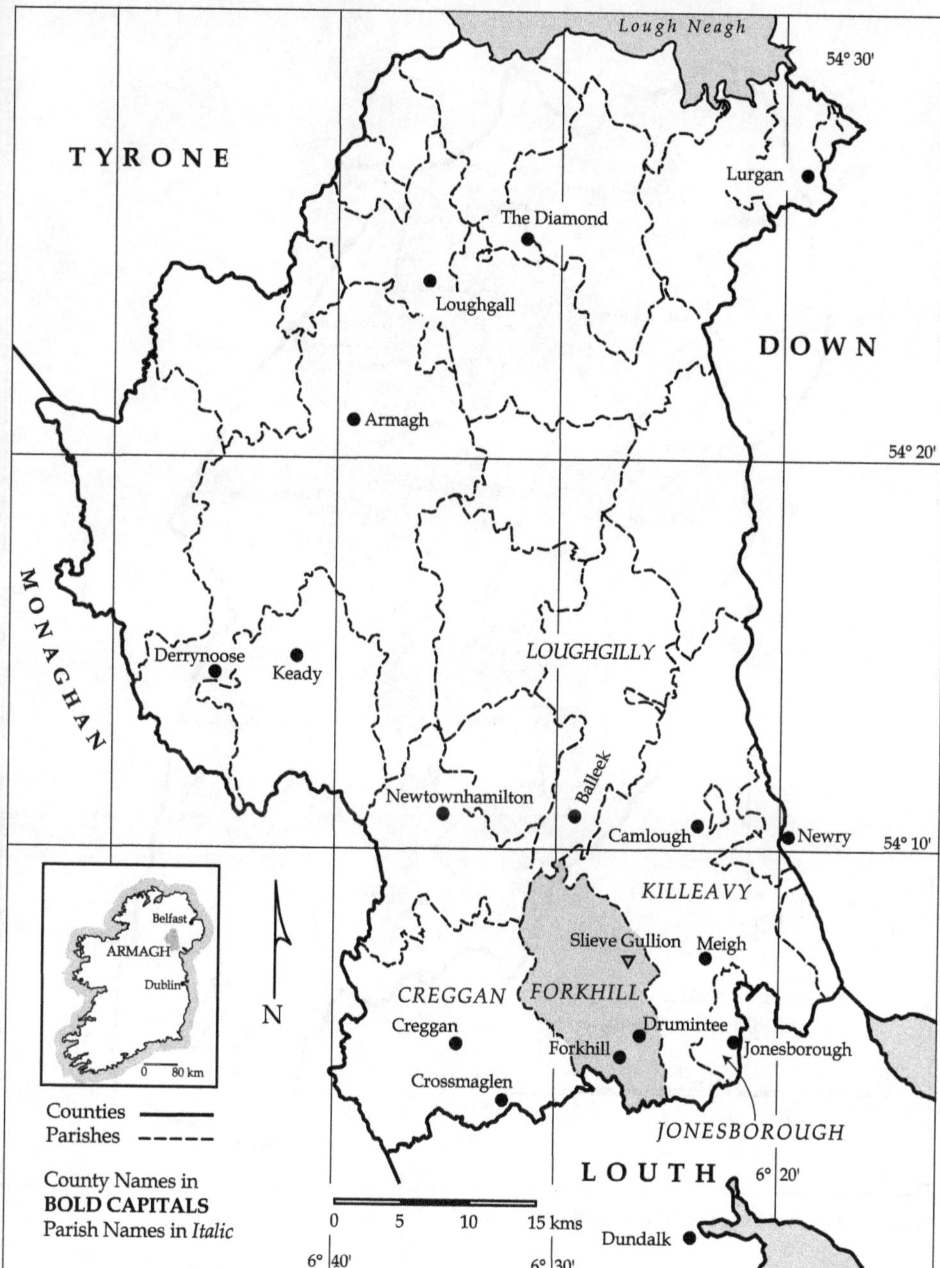

Map 1 County Armagh, showing Forkhill and neighbouring parishes

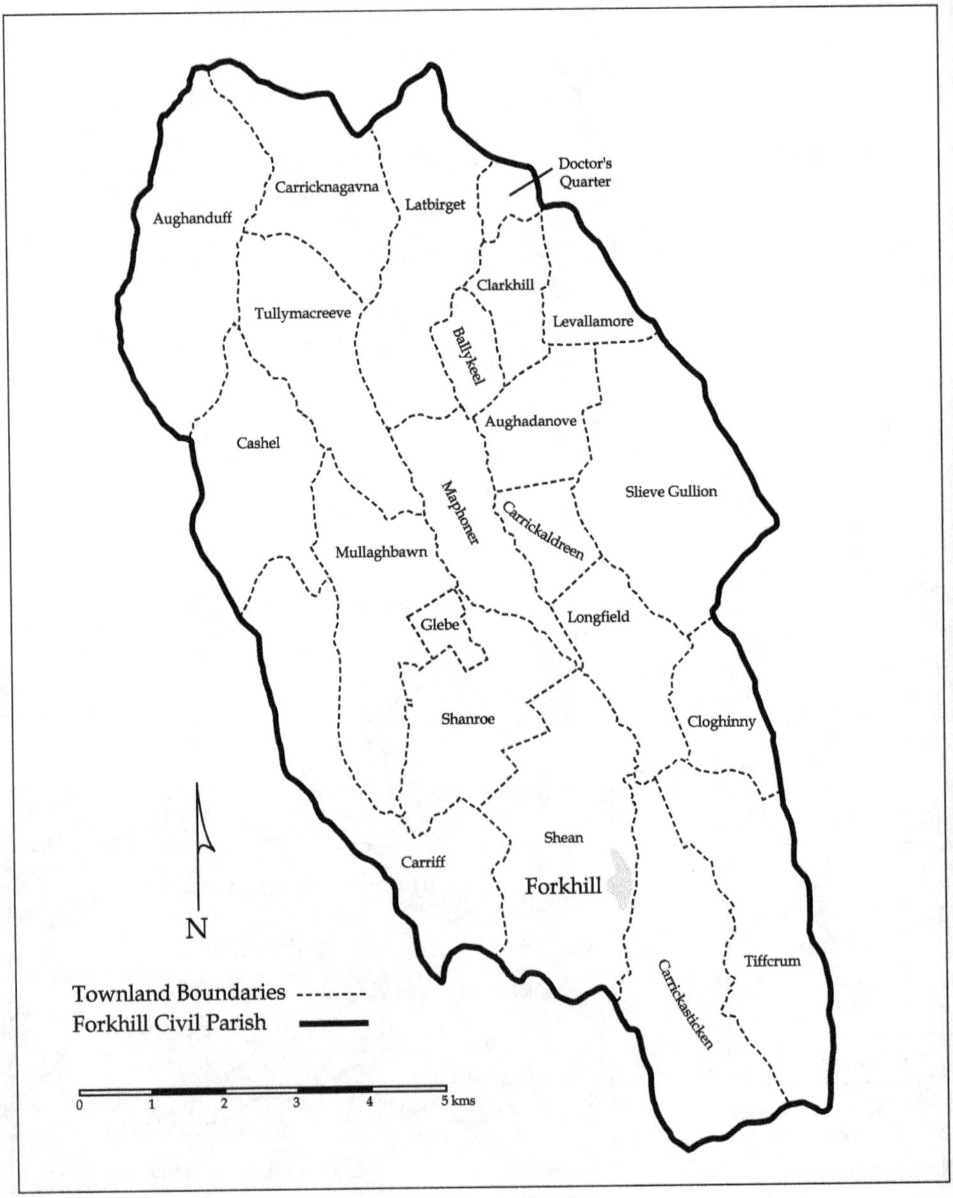

Map 2 The civil parish of Forkhill, showing townland boundaries

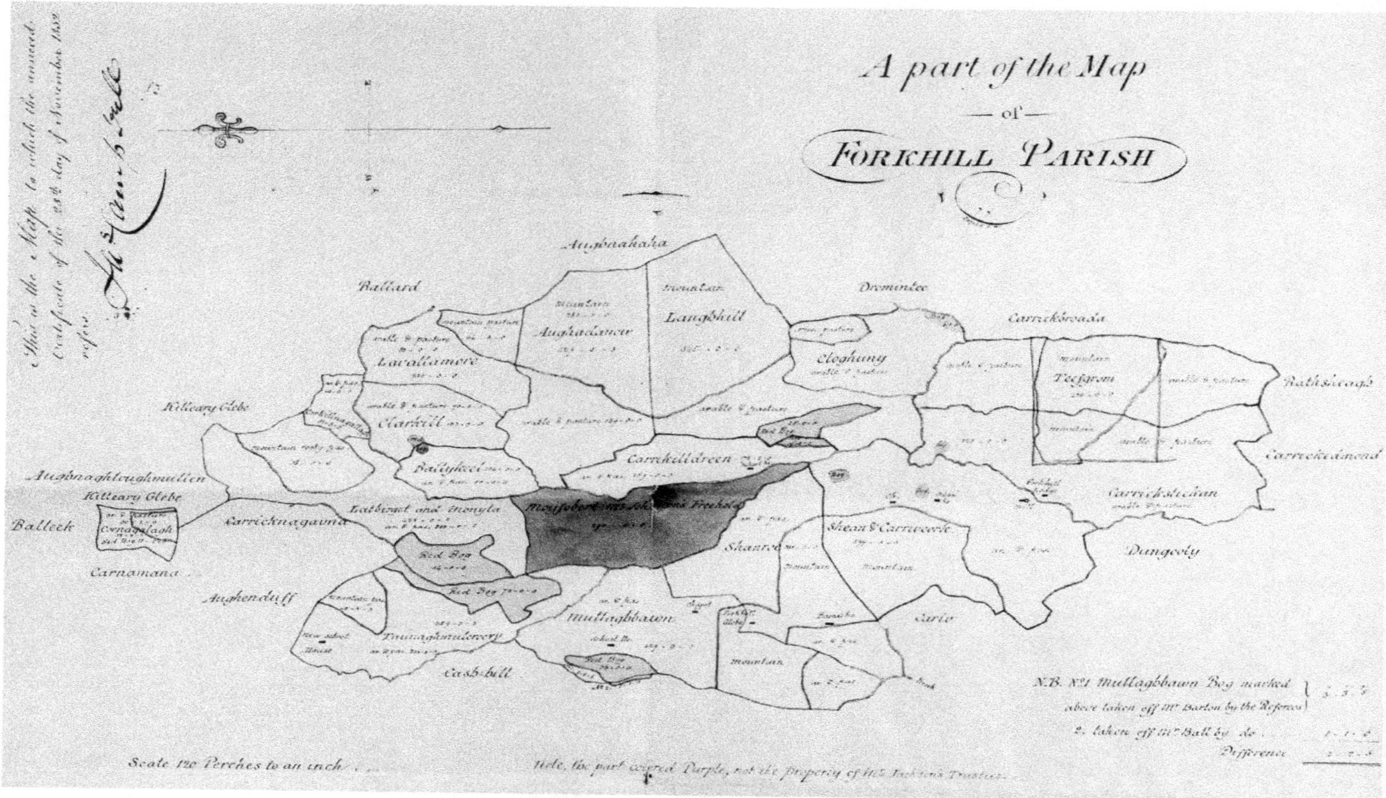

Map 3 The Forkhill estate in 1832 (reproduced with the kind permission of the National Archives of Ireland)

FORKHILL PROTESTANTS AND FORKHILL CATHOLICS, 1787–1858

There is more Irish history in the rocks of Ballykeel than ever Belfast … possessed. It was cradled and nursed there and most likely will never waken.

Art Bennett to Robert MacAdam, 3 April 1850

January 29, 1791

My Dear Dobbs,

With trembling hand and a heart bursting with grief and impotent indignation I sit down to give you some account of the dreadful transactions of last night at Forkhil – you know Barkeley who was stabbed by Donnelly – He is one of the schoolmasters of Forkhil and tho' paid by the Trustees for only Sixty Scholars has for six months taught upwards of an hundred without any additional charge – This had made him in all appearance a great Favorite with the people here – However about Seven yesterday evening a person rapped at his door – on his asking who was there, a voice answered – Terence Burn – Knowing Burn's voice he opened the door, when in rushed a Body of Hellhounds – not content with cutting and stabbing him in several places, They drew a cord round his neck till his Tongue was forced out – it they cut off and three fingers of his right hand – They then cut out his wife's tongue and some of the villains held her whilst another with a case knife cut off her thumb and four of her fingers, one after another – They cut and battered her in different places – She I fear cannot recover – There was in the house a Brother of hers about fourteen years old on a visit to his sister – his tongue those merciless villains cut out and cut off the calf of his leg with a sword – They plundered the house and after all this went up the road with lighted torches at that early hour – Terence Burn did not appear so that Barkeley can only swear to his voice – I made this day a fruitless attempt to take him. What can be done – this county every day grows worse – The association gains ground and there is now hardly a man (of a certain description) in a circuit of many miles who is not in it and armed – write me a few lines to Dundalk – it will be some comfort to me to hear from you. God Bless You.

Edward Hudson
Jonesborough

I

The Sectarian Disease

The author of the foregoing lines was the Reverend Edward Hudson, rector of the parish of Forkhill and a friend of the victim, Alexander Berkley.[1] The original letter is part of the bound manuscripts of the correspondence of the Earl of Charlemont, now preserved in the library of the Royal Irish Academy. Between 1787 and 1795, Hudson wrote regularly to Charlemont in long letters describing his struggle to maintain order in an increasingly disaffected part of the country. The rector was a resolute authority figure and the architect of much change in the parish in the 1790s. These features of Hudson's personality are revealed in his handwriting, which was conspicuous for its bold strokes. But the letter he wrote on 29 January 1791 is different: the handwriting is less assured, almost spidery, as if his hand had been shaking. Although Hudson was not a witness to the attack that night, he has provided an electrifying account. His extraordinary letter leads us to the doorstep of Berkley's house and makes us look inside.

Alexander Berkley was a linen weaver and schoolteacher, one of a small community of Protestants who settled in the parish, a Roman Catholic stronghold, between 1787 and 1790. The settlement of the Forkhill estate was intended to turn the impoverished rural outpost into a thriving community. But the leasing of lands did not proceed without controversy, and antagonism between natives and settlers flared into violence on a number of occasions. The trouble in Forkhill coincided with the appearance of the Defenders in south Armagh in the late 1780s. This exclusively Catholic secret society had originated as a defensive league against Protestant gangs in north Armagh several years earlier and had since moved slowly south. Hudson was convinced that the Defenders were behind the disturbances on the Forkhill estate, but he could not understand why they had inflicted such a brutal attack on Alexander Berkley and his family. Berkley was a popular schoolteacher,

Hudson wrote, and "a great Favorite with the people here." So why was he a target?

Within a few days, Hudson, along with his fellow trustees of the Forkhill estate, provided a chilling answer. In a letter to the bishop of Dromore on 3 February, they claimed that in the midst of the attack Berkley had asked the mob "what he had done to offend them." The men replied that he had done them no wrong but that this was "the beginning of what he and those like him should suffer."[2] The trustees interpreted this as a reference to the Protestant settlers in Forkhill and beyond, who had reason to fear a massacre reminiscent of that of 1641. "There is every reason to dread the most alarming consequences from the effects of this transaction," Hudson wrote. "The protestants are everywhere in the greatest terror; and unless government affords them assistance, must leave the country; as this recent instance of inhumanity, and the threatenings thrown out against them, leave no doubt upon their minds of what the intentions must be against them."[3]

The interpretation of the phrase "those like him" as a reference to Protestants sent a shock wave through Ulster, and reports of the atrocity raced through the countryside. Thomas Prentice wrote that the Forkhill victims had been "sacrificed to the Bigotry & Barbarity of their neighbourhood" in an incident that "would disgrace the wilds of Africa or America."[4] Richard Musgrave, a writer and member of parliament, seized on the attack as confirmation that "the extirpation of protestants of every denomination was the main design of the defenders."[5] Dr William Drennan, who helped found the Society of United Irishmen later that year, wrote in frustration to his brother-in-law, Samuel McTier: "All the world talks of that horrid affair, near Dundalk, and Lord Charlemont, Brownlow, with all the gentlemen of that country had a meeting. They may now ask, 'Why should we tolerate, why should we commit arms and rights to such savages as these Catholics,' and the only answer is 'Why did you make them and keep them savages, for that they are such is without question.' All this will put off the day of general freedom."[6]

The consequences extended even further. More than forty years later, in evidence presented before the Select Committee on Orange Lodges in 1835, Lieutenant Colonel William Verner drew a direct link between the Berkley attack and the escalation of sectarian hostilities in Armagh: "I think the first occasion upon which the opinion became general that there existed a decided hostility upon the part of the Roman Catholics towards the Protestants of the country was a circumstance which occurred at a place called Fork Hill."[7] Virtually all histories of the Orange Order record the Forkhill outrage as the single most brutal attack on Protestants during the Armagh Disturbances.[8] One claimed that the attack left "a deeper impression than any other event of the period on the Protestants of County Armagh."[9] Since then, the attack has assumed mythic proportions in the sectarian imagination of Ulster unionists. A resident of south Armagh reported reading a 1970s newspaper interview with the Reverend Ian R.K. Paisley, a staunch Protestant and leader of the Democratic Unionist Party. When the reporter suggested that Paisley perhaps exaggerated the depth of sectarian feeling in nationalist enclaves such as south Armagh, Paisley replied that he did not, and he referred explicitly to the attack on the Protestant schoolmaster in Forkhill in 1791.[10]

The assumption that "those like him" was a sweeping reference to Protestants everywhere has never been seriously questioned. The fact that the attack involved the Defenders and occurred at the height of the Armagh Disturbances reinforced the view that Forkhill had become yet another zone of conflict in the developing sectarian war; the location of the parish in the middle of south Armagh compounded the evidence. South Armagh is historically charged. It has long been depicted as a theatre of conflict between the majority Catholic population and the smaller Protestant communities that crossed its frontier in the wake of the Ulster Plantation. Its hills ring with the memory of dispossession, of priest hunting, and poverty, and of Catholics ground under the heel of Protestant privilege. The region figures large in the imagination of nationalists owing to its perceived tradition of resistance to outside authority, to English invaders, and to Protestantism. The historian A.T.Q. Stewart has observed the connection between south Armagh's historic resistance to intervention and its deadly serious modern republicanism: "Why should Armagh, the most populous and prosperous of the Ulster counties, be notorious for ambush and outrage since the late eighteenth century, and why should judges in the nineteenth century find the Crossmaglen area especially notorious for murder and outrage? And why should certain border villages, such as Rosslea or Garrison or Forkhill have been the scene of frequent confrontation and incidents long before there was any border?"[11]

This quotation is taken from *The Narrow Ground*, in which Stewart traces the patterns of confrontation in the frontier zones of Ulster to the sectarian alignments created by the seventeenth-century Plantation. From the outset, he writes, "religion provide[d] the vital distinction" between the communities in Ulster.[12] It is difficult to argue with Stewart. Sectarianism, if it wasn't the full answer, was usually part of the answer. Throughout Irish history, Catholics and Protestants have clashed in violent and often predictable sectarian encounters. The segregation of communities, most obviously in terms of religion – but also as a result of geography, schooling, social interaction, cultural expression, and political behaviour – is real. These invisible walls have given historians a licence to consider the two communities separately, observing their interaction primarily during periods of conflict.

The result is that much of Irish historical writing rests on an assumed foundation of conflict between Catholics and Protestants, a conflict it regards as constant and essentially unchanging. In the context of Irish history, sectarianism approaches the status of a historiographical method, characterized by the separation of Irish people into two warring camps, and a historical narrative dedicated to exploring their patterns of confrontation. The concept of sectarianism no longer requires justification or explanation, and it conditions our understanding of the relationship between the two communities to a surprisingly high degree – so much so that we have ceased to be aware of it. Consider the following remarks in a recent study of sectarianism in Ulster:

> Although scholars have begun to explore important aspects of sectarianism in nineteenth-century Ulster, there has been no attempt to provide an in-depth and contextual analysis of this "tradition" of sectarian violence. Despite all of the good work done, a widespread misconception remains within Irish historical studies: sectarian violence in the north of Ireland is almost entirely atavistic and therefore does not merit sophisticated analysis. This assumption can still be found in some of the best works in the field. For most scholars the sectarian violence of nineteenth-century Ulster remains a simple tale of tribal hatred. Why waste precious time and resources on such a depressing and simple story? Why indeed? Simply because tribalism and atavism rest at the heart of the modern Ulster experience. Riots between Catholics and Protestants (and, more importantly, the attitudes that gave rise to such violence) framed the creation of northern society.[13]

This passage calls historians to account for their assumptions about sectarianism, but nowhere is the assumption *of* sectarianism questioned. Nowhere is the concept defined or explained, perhaps because it would seem redundant to do so. To be fair, that particular book focuses on how sectarian violence laid the tracks for Ulster's denominational political culture, which is a compelling evolutionary argument. But beneath it is the assumption that patterns of conflict in Ulster are ultimately traceable to sectarian causes and that alternative explanations need not be sought. Sectarianism has become a rule; it is never entirely out of the frame and has almost become a byword for the social and political history of Ulster in the nineteenth century.[14]

Reducing the last four hundred years of Ulster history to a sideshow of massacre and rebellion, party fights and parades, in a society racked by sectarian disease is not history but caricature. Missing from this narrative is the complexity of the relationship between Catholics and Protestants in Ulster, particularly in its mixed communities.[15] Historian Raymond Gillespie has put the matter this way: "We know very little about what each side of the confessional divide thought of the other side and how those opinions were formed. It seems clear that various confessional groups in Ireland were not, except in times of severe political or economic crisis, totally polarised."[16] This should not qualify as an observation of great insight, but in the context of Irish historiography it does. The comment is contained in a short essay on the practice of local history, which Gillespie suggests might be the most promising forum for this research.

The principle of local history is that when the historian's focus is trained on a single community, it becomes possible to study the area and its people at a microscopic level. This might involve charting the growth or decline of the population, measuring agricultural productivity and industrial capacity, observing the local impact of reforms in health or education, or watching a community cope with disaster or respond to prosperity. The academic justification for local history is that "phenomena that were previously considered understood assume new dimensions when the scale of observation is reduced" and can "call into question conventional long-term views of historical development."[17] In lay terms, it means the breaking down of history into smaller, more knowable bits. On these grounds, Gillespie was optimistic that local historians might be the best equipped to investigate how Protestants and Catholics might have cooperated in the past "and when and why they were unable to do so."[18]

Forkhill was an ideal laboratory for such an inquiry. The rural parish, a Catholic stronghold, was transformed by the introduction of a stream of Protestant settlers in the late 1780s and early 1790s. Most of these Protestants were members of the established church, but their number included a small group of Presbyterians.[19] The census of 1821 returned a Methodist chapel in the townland of Shean, which Samuel Lewis identified as a Wesleyan-Methodist meeting house when he toured the area in 1836.[20] The Protestant community was always a small minority in the parish: at the time of the first religious enumeration in 1834, there were 479 Protestants living among 6,562 Catholics in Forkhill.[21] But although they never constituted more than 10 per cent of the local population, they were a highly significant group. In the spheres of local industry, landholding, education, health and welfare, and law and order, they had a lasting influence on the development of the parish in the crucial half-century before the famine, and they achieved a level of integration with the Catholic community that is often unacknowledged. In this local context, the image of Ulster as an incessantly violent society feeding on a culture of chronic sectarianism is misleading. The degree of exchange between the two communities in Forkhill was too developed to be represented by such a one-dimensional model.

This is not to deny the existence of sectarianism in the parish. Sectarian awareness was ever-present in Ulster's mixed communities; it was part of the atmosphere and had a constant regulatory effect. During times of crisis, whether local or national, the spectre of sectarianism was inevitably revived, and the communities closed their ranks. Religion was the primary badge of identification in Ulster, and that distinction gathered significance throughout the nineteenth century. But the sectarian impulse was not the only impulse regulating social behaviour. For most of the people most of the time, differences of religion between neighbours did not interfere with how one led one's life. Resurrecting these other dimensions of life experience will, I hope, allow a more open-minded study of Protestants and Catholics in Forkhill and a reappraisal of their relationship.

As a social construct, the civil parish has certain limitations: it was primarily an administrative unit, delineated for the purposes of taxation and census taking and for keeping records of births, marriages, and deaths. The boundaries of the parish did not affect the daily lives of the people, and I suspect that in the early nineteenth century few would have been able to describe them with accuracy. The social unit of importance was the townland, the immediate neighbourhood where one was born and reared and where one often stayed to rear a family of one's own. The townland is the smallest administrative division of land in Ireland that remains in use; the average townland covered an area of several hundred acres, though there were many variations of size and shape.[22] The civil parish of Forkhill had twenty-two townlands during this period, and sixteen of them were part of the Jackson Estate.[23] The surviving estate documents – letters, rent books, lease books, and minute books – pertained to an area extending over most of the parish, and for this reason I settled on the parish as my geographical unit of study. Most of my sources (including the results of the poor law inquiry, the board of education files, the papers of the famine relief commission, outrage reports, a manuscript copy of the 1821 census, and records of births and marriages, as well as diverse correspondence, both official and personal) encompass the entire parish in one way or another.

In the following chapters I consider seven historical moments that transpired in the parish between 1787 and 1858. They range across the spectrum of life experience in nineteenth-century Ireland: from settlement and landholding to agrarian protest and rural conspiracy;

from education, economy, and industry to famine devastation and religious controversy. Each one provides a slightly different viewing angle on the relationship between the communities of Catholics and Protestants in Forkhill over the course of seventy years. Some of these moments intersect with national events (the Rebellion of 1798 and the famine of the 1840s), but most of them were parochial and of local consequence only. Some of them were violent (the resistance of the 1790s and the outrage of the 1830s), though life in the parish was mostly peaceable. The resurrection of these moments does not constitute a complete history of the parish; too many secrets are buried for that to be possible. But assembled together, they are a powerful reminder of the complexity – and often the inconsistency – of its history. And the significance of this is not entirely local.

These seven historical moments are microcosms of the themes that run through modern Irish history: the frustrated expectations of the 1790s, tensions over land, rural outrage, education, famine, and religious controversy. If prevailing assumptions about these issues do not always apply at the parish level, perhaps they should be more cautiously applied on a larger scale. This is especially true with respect to sectarianism, which runs like a red thread through them all. Assumptions about the sectarian patterns of Irish history infect a good deal of Irish historiography and proceed from a frame of mind that is difficult to dismantle. L.M. Cullen wrestled with the problem in his study of the 1798 rebellion in Wexford and the forces behind the creation and fracture of political alliances in Ireland in the 1790s. "Sectarianism," he wrote, "is a difficult subject to study." It offers a comprehensible explanation, it has a long pedigree, and there was always a measure of sectarianism in operation. Accepting a sectarian explanation is hazardous, he continued, because it "makes it unnecessary for the historian to interrogate events more closely, and thus the sheer complexity of events and of interpretation alike is not confronted."[24] But it is precisely here, in this web of complexity and contradiction, that the past lies. Revealing it demands more from us than assumptions and casual expectations; it requires a skeptical eye, an open mind, and, above all, a vigilant awareness that the past *lies*.

2

Settlement and Resistance, 1787–1792

The parish of Forkhill lies in the southern bounds of County Armagh, in the ancient barony of Upper Orior.[1] In 1571 Elizabeth I awarded the lands within the barony of Orior to Captain Thomas Chatterton, but when he failed to fulfill the first condition of ownership, that he establish an English settlement, his grant was revoked. In 1612 James II awarded the same lands to Lord Audley under the title of the "manor of Stonebridge," but Audley also failed to settle the property with English or Scottish tenants. Even then the region had a reputation for lawlessness and disorder, and the mainly Roman Catholic and Irish-speaking population was regarded as inhospitable to newcomers. The landscape of heath, rock, and boggy soil was described as "savage," "miserable," and "uncivilised," and its inhabitants "savage," "uncivilized," and "wild."[2] A chaplain and soldier who was encamped in south Armagh in 1690 described the countryside as "one of the *wildest* places of all Ireland."[3]

Despite the best intentions of the Crown, the seventeenth-century scheme of Ulster plantation failed to penetrate much of south Armagh, beyond the establishment of a Presbyterian settlement in the parish of Creggan in the 1730s.[4] A hearth return conducted in 1659 reported only 193 English and Scottish settlers in the barony of Orior among the nearly 700 native Irish.[5] Many of the townlands that later formed part of the parish of Forkhill, such as Carrickasticken, Shean, Shanroe, Mullaghbawn, and Clarkhill, listed only Irish inhabitants.[6] In 1703 the land was reclaimed by the Crown, which finally gave up trying to settle it with loyal subjects and instead sold the manor as a forfeited estate. The lands changed hands several times during the first half of the eighteenth century, and by the time the estate was purchased by Richard Jackson in September 1750 its name had changed from Stonebridge to Forkhill. It was known locally thereafter as the Jackson Estate.[7]

Portrait of Richard Jackson, Esq., the boardroom, Forkhill, County Armagh (photograph by J.E. Madden)

Richard Jackson (1722–87) was connected to the prominent Jackson family of Coleraine.[8] He owned property in the city of Dublin and in County Cavan, as well as in Armagh. He married Nicola Ann Cecil in 1750, but it was a childless marriage. When Jackson purchased the Forkhill estate as a young man, he inherited a rural wilderness and an impoverished tenantry. By some accounts (although the opinion was not universal), Jackson was an improving landlord who attempted to establish a prosperous settlement in Forkhill by attracting industry to the area. In 1762 he took out a patent for a weekly market and two annual fairs.[9] In 1764 and 1765 he placed notices in the *Belfast News-letter* seeking a "Company of rich Linen Drapers" to relocate to the area, offering the local mills and bleach greens under lease "forever."[10] Linen had been a major export from Ireland since the 1730s, and the industry had been concentrated in Ulster from the middle of the eighteenth century. Jackson recognized its potential and hoped to attract drapers and weavers to settle in Forkhill, bringing capital to the district and providing a trade for the tenantry. But when he died in 1787, the estate was far from a thriving concern. A few years later, in 1792, a fellow countryman described the miserable condition of the people: "The inhabitants of Forkhill and its adjacent neighbours are very illiterate, from their mountainous situation, that scarcely affords them potatoes and goat's milk, of course the English language in many families, is scarcely known."[11]

What Jackson had not been able to achieve in his lifetime, he sought to achieve in posterity. He left an extraordinary will that required an act of Parliament to clarify its intent and a board of trustees to supervise its execution.[12] At the time of his death, Jackson was the owner of extensive property in Dublin as well as in the country. He bequeathed his Cavan estate to his wife Nicola Ann, his Dublin property to his widowed sister Susanna Barton, and his Forkhill estate in trust to nine Church of Ireland bishops and rectors, who were charged with the responsibility of managing its affairs. When all his outstanding debts and legacies had been paid, half of the annual interest in his Forkhill estate was to be reserved to Susanna and her daughter Julia Eliza, and upon their death to the propagation of the gospel in the Far East through the work of Protestant missionaries. The balance of the interest was to be devoted in perpetuity to charitable concerns on the estate itself in the spheres of education, health, and welfare. Mindful of his "poor fellow-creatures, who [were] destroyed by the advice of quack doctors," Jackson awarded £100 to the infirmary in the nearby town of Dundalk, in addition to a small annual allowance. He set aside £100 to buy looms for his poorest tenants on both the Forkhill and Cavan estates, and left one hundred greatcoats to be distributed among one hundred of his oldest tenants. Even after these charitable endowments, a very substantial portion of the estate remained, which Jackson set aside for the controversial purpose of "clothing and educating as many, as the fund will allow, children of the church of Ireland, and in giving, at the age of twenty-five years, to each five pounds and a loom, and a small holding in preference to other tenants who may offer."[13]

Under Jackson's proposed scheme, these charitable obligations were to be financed by rental income from the Forkhill estate. But the property was not generating a sufficient income in 1787, apparently as a result of its chronic mismanagement by the late landlord. The Reverend Edward Hudson had a caustic opinion of Jackson's handling of the estate, disparaging him as an improvident and careless landlord who had failed to collect a regular rent and had left most of the property as a "wasteland."[14] Beginning in 1787, the system of the commons and the laxity of rental collection disappeared as the trustees of Jackson's charity attempted to tighten up settlement on the estate.

In October 1787 the trustees placed a notice in the *Belfast Newsletter* advertising the lease of ten of the parish's townlands, consisting of "good Arable Meadow, Pasture and Mountain," and being especially suitable for linen manufacturers.[15] The trustees placed a second advertisement the following year, again appealing to linen weavers, and offering to build houses for prospective linen leaseholders as an incentive to settlement.[16] Their initiative met with good results. Nearly one hundred leases were arranged on the estate between 1788 and 1791. Some of these leases were agreed with local tenants and may have been extensions of earlier agreements, but a large number were new and were awarded to settlers from outside the parish.

The resettlement of the estate proceeded against the will of the people and caused a tremendous upheaval among a population unaccustomed to outside interference. Rumours circulated that the Catholic tenants had been "banished" from their lands to make way for a colony of Protestants.[17] Hudson, in a letter to the Earl of Charlemont in December 1789, defended the actions of the trustees and the integrity of the settlement. His remarks are worth quoting at length, for they constitute the unedited impressions of a Protestant gentleman living among the mainly Catholic poor, and they capture the uneasy coexistence of the two cultures in Forkhill around 1790:

> Your Lordship will hardly believe how little appearances of civilization there are here tho' so little removed from the best parts of the Kingdom – Many traces of savage life still remain amongst us – the same laziness and improvidence – the same love of intoxication, the same hereditary enmities handed down from generation to generation – add to this that they are all related to each other and I believe there are not at this moment Ten Families in this Parish which are not related to almost every other in it. To give efficacy to these evils it unfortunately happens that this place was for 35 years possessed by the most indolent man on Earth. He kept more than half of it waste during that time on which they in fact subsisted – The idea of its being let therefore set them mad – [A rumour] has been industriously spread by the Friends of the party that several of the old Tenants had been dispossessed and that this gave rise to the combination here, now I do most solemnly assure your Lordship that in no instance has even one acre been taken from any man ... They were not only

continued in their old possessions with some [word obscured] but an abatement of rent to the amount of £117 was to have been made them at the very time they broke out and some hundreds of arrear were actually forgiven.[18]

Although Hudson's claim that no land was seized may have been technically correct, he did not acknowledge that people had been living on these lands and had been cleared off their ground to accommodate the creation of new holdings. Instead he played up the sectarian dimension of the local response:

They found some Protestants had taken land whom they determined to drive out. They therefore assembled the Defenders from all parts of the Country and struck such Terror that none of those Protestant but Half a Dozen ever appeared here afterwards ... Those who wish me best are very urgent with me to take a House in Newry and remove myself and Family from this scene of confusion and (as they think) of danger. In some desponding moments, I incline to their opinion ... On the other hand every atom of Man within me revolts at the Idea of flying from my post on the apprehension of danger, and abandoning the few Protestants who have settled here on my faith.[19]

The question of sectarianism, in the context of the settlement and resistance on the Forkhill estate between 1787 and 1792, has two dimensions. First is the matter of religious discrimination in the settlement itself: Did the trustees prefer Protestant leaseholders and expropriate Catholic tenants in order to consolidate a Protestant settlement? Second, precisely what role did sectarianism play in the Forkhill disturbances, in which a number of settlers were threatened and attacked in a sustained campaign of violence that reached its apex in 1791?

THE BUSINESS OF SETTLEMENT, 1788–1791

From what I can piece together from the fragmentary collection of leases and estate papers, the settlement of the Forkhill estate was conducted in two phases. The first lasted from November 1788 to March 1789 and the second from November 1789 to November 1791. In order to answer the first question and determine whether Protestant leaseholders were in fact preferred over Catholics, we must determine the denomination of each leaseholder. In the absence of a religious enumeration of the population (which was not taken in Ireland until 1834 and was not conducted as part of the decennial census until 1861), the only way of identifying individuals as Catholics or Protestants is on the basis of their surnames. Although this method of identification is not an exact science, the existence of recognizably English and Irish names in eighteenth-century Ulster, and the close correspondence of ethnicity and religion, make it an acceptable litmus test. Arbuthnot, Brown, and Hudson are English names that can readily be distinguished from the native Irish Murphys, McParlans, and O'Neales. In the few instances where surnames did not offer a clue, I used the Christian name of the leaseholder, together with the names of the relations and in-laws who were mentioned in the lease, to determine his probable religious denomination.[20]

During the first period of settlement, from November 1788 to March 1789, thirty-nine leases were granted by Susanna Barton and the trustees for lands on the Forkhill estate. Fully two-thirds of these leases were awarded to Protestant leaseholders, while the rest went to Catholics.[21] In terms of the proportion of land awarded, the Protestant leaseholders fared even better. They controlled 86 per cent of the land leased during this first phase of settlement, and the average Protestant farm amounted to more than ninety acres.[22] During the second phase of settlement, from November 1789 to November 1791, the denominational balance of land tenure shifted considerably. Two-thirds of the leases arranged during this period were granted to Catholic leaseholders, and the average farm sizes of Catholics and Protestants were roughly equal.[23] Of the ninety-four known leases awarded on the estate between 1788 and 1791, 43 per cent were granted to Protestants (who controlled 69 per cent of the land under lease), and 53 per cent went to Catholics (who controlled 29 per cent of the land under lease).[24]

Given that Protestants accounted for less than 10 per cent of the parish's population, the amount of land they were awarded during the settlement was highly disproportionate to their numbers, and the imbalance was especially marked during the first phase of settlement. Was this deliberately engineered? The trustees' preference for Protestant leaseholders may have been part of the answer. Hudson intimated as much to Charlemont in 1789 when he confessed to feeling guilty at the thought of "abandoning the few Protestants who have settled here on my faith."[25] But this was not the full answer; there were more plausible reasons for the disparity.

First, the trustees desperately needed an injection of capital in order to turn the finances of the estate around and to meet the charitable obligations of Jackson's trust. They sought prosperous leaseholders who could bring industry to the area, making "our Savages happy against their wills, by establishing trade and industry among them," as Hudson explained in 1789.[26] Their appeal was manifest in the advertisement in the *News-letter*, which referred to the situation as "excellent for Manufacturers" and was directed specifically at linen weavers and drapers.[27] In eighteenth-century Ulster, Protestants were more likely to fit this qualification than Catholics; Protestants dominated the linen industry and few Catholics were head linen bleachers and drapers. "Almost every shilling [was] in the hands of Protestants," an observer of the industry, Robert Stevenson, remarked in 1795.[28]

Second, if a preference did exist, it originated with the clause in Richard Jackson's will concerning the special treatment of Protestant children, who were to be granted fixed holdings on the estate when they reached the age of twenty-five. Jackson's exclusive reference to "children of the church of Ireland ... in preference to other tenants who may offer" suggests that he was the one who intended to establish a Protestant colony in Forkhill. As the executors of Jackson's estate, the trustees were obliged to interpret the clause this way, but they hoped to avoid the inevitable complications by seeking legal grounds for altering the terms of the will. At a meeting in February 1789, they resolved that the clause "which directs a small holding to be given to each of the poor children ... cannot without great inconsistency with the general intent of the said Testator ... be observed." An act of Parliament altered some of the financial arrangements and freed the trustees from a "literal performance" of the troublesome clause. Instead of receiving £5, a loom, and a guaranteed holding on the estate upon reaching the age of twenty-five, the Protestant children of Forkhill would receive £10 and a loom or another article to the value of a loom.[29]

Third, the continual representation of the Forkhill settlement, and the subsequent resistance, in sectarian terms obscures the fact that any influx of settlers into the parish would have met with hostility, no matter what religion they professed. At the end of the eighteenth century, Armagh was the most populous county in Ireland in relation to its size. Charles Coote observed in 1804 that even the bleak, hilly terrain in the southern and "wildest parts" of Armagh was "thickly inhabited."[30] Nevertheless, the local resistance was not interpreted as hostility to outsiders competing for land but was seen as hostility to Protestants, and this interpretation set the stage for the confrontations that followed.

TROUBLE IN FORKHILL, 1789–1792

In his *Memoirs of the Different Rebellions in Ireland*, published in 1801, Richard Musgrave provided a seething account of the treatment of the Protestant settlers in Forkhill in the 1790s. The "new colonists were hunted like wild beasts, and treated with savage cruelty: their houses were demolished and their property was destroyed," he wrote.[31] Musgrave was paranoid in his loathing of popery, and the *Memoirs* were a virtual bible of anti-Catholicism. But the assize indictments for

Armagh tend to confirm his accusations. Most of the reported outrages in Forkhill appear to have been directed against Protestants on the estate, and against five men in particular: the Reverend Edward Hudson, John Dick, Robert Best, William Duncan, and Alexander Berkley.[32]

Hudson narrowly escaped an attempt on his life in the spring of 1789 when he was fired on while patrolling the countryside with a party of the military. Less than a year later he suffered another murder attempt when "some evil-minded person fired a musket loaded with slugs" at him while he was riding on the main road through Forkhill. Hudson's horse was shot dead beneath him, but he escaped injury.[33] In 1791 a house on his premises was destroyed by fire, and in April 1792 three men were found guilty of conspiracy to commit the murder of Hudson and two other gentlemen.[34] Fearing for his safety, Hudson removed himself and his family from the area after 1792 and resigned as rector of the parish in 1795.

John Dick was a farmer and miller who had leased a twenty-acre farm on the Forkhill estate in 1789. Shortly after settling on the estate, he became locked in a bitter turf war with several local men, including the McElevy brothers, Ferdy and Patrick. In 1789 Dick charged both brothers with assault; he brought additional charges of felony against McElevy, John Hanlon, and others at the assizes later that year. In 1791 Dick's mill was burned to the ground, and he charged a number of men with arson, including Ferdy McElevy and Hanlon, along with others whom the *Belfast News-letter* identified as Defenders. The following year the same crowd was charged with shooting at Dick and setting fire to his house, his corn mill, and his cow shed, as well as setting fire to the home of the local constable, Robert Best.[35] At their trials in March 1792, the "Forkhill Rioters ... were found not guilty, no evidence appearing except that of the approver."[36] After this string of unsuccessful prosecutions, yet another attempt was made on Dick's life, whereupon Ferdy McElevy was arrested and tried as a matter of course, but again there was no conviction.

William Duncan was a Forkhill farmer and linen weaver who had leased a farm of twenty acres on the estate in 1789. He supplemented his income by serving as Hudson's tithe proctor, collecting the rates due to the established church. Shortly after settling on the estate, Duncan was the victim of assault, property damage, felony, and theft of firearms. At the 1789 summer assizes he prosecuted two local men, Michael Donnelly and Laurence Connory, for a string of offences but secured no conviction, and the harassment only intensified in the wake of the prosecution. He claimed that his house had been vandalized and robbed, his brother assaulted, and his daughter attacked. In 1790 Duncan filed a litany of charges against two local men, John Bennet and John Mullan, including assault, felony, breaking and entering, theft, and murder.[37] Bennet was sentenced to death, but at the last moment he was reprieved through the intervention of Lord Gosford, and the sentence was reduced to transportation. The head of the grand jury had urged Gosford to consider John Bennet an object of mercy if he wished to maintain the "peace & security of the County of Armagh."[38]

Throughout this period the same names recur in the pages of the Armagh indictment books: Ferdy McElevy, Patrick McElevy, John Hanlon, John Bennet, Michael Donnelly, Laurence Connory, and others. All these men were charged with violent offences ranging from robbery to murder; all of them were believed to be sworn Defenders. Ferdy McElevy, who was accused of firing at Hudson on a number of occasions and who engaged in a particularly bitter war with John Dick was identified by the *Belfast News-letter* as "one of the persons who had the command of the Defenders."[39] Throughout the 1790s, McElevy was Forkhill's most high-profile troublemaker and a notorious recidivist. Between 1788 and 1798 he appeared before grand juries in Armagh, Louth, and possibly Monaghan at least ten times to face charges of assault, felony, robbery, shooting, mill burning, and "having arms & being a papist." According to the *Freeman's Journal*, "Ferdinand McAlevy ... [was] one of the desperate gang called 'defenders, or tongue cutters.'"[40]

The Defenders' origins can be traced back to 1784, when Protestant gangs in north Armagh attacked and ransacked Catholic homes for weapons in a transparent effort to enforce the surviving penal law that forbade Catholics from bearing arms. The raids and robberies of the Protestant Peep O'Day Boys inspired the lower orders of Catholics to form their own organizations for the purpose of self-defence.[41] This period of outrage, which spilled over into the southern reaches of the county, persisted for nearly ten years and was widely known as the Armagh Disturbances.

The history of the Armagh Disturbances has been thoroughly scrutinized in recent years, particularly in the work of David Miller and L.M. Cullen.[42] Both have resisted the trap of a simple sectarian explanation and have offered more sophisticated and locally based explanations for the conflict. Neither Cullen nor Miller denies the influence of sectarian tension, particularly as an aggravating factor, but both have looked elsewhere for the genesis of the disturbances. Cullen challenges the argument of nineteenth-century historian W.E.H. Lecky that the disturbances in Armagh were rooted in land hunger. The Armagh economy was becoming increasingly protoindustrial as a result of the linen industry, and this transformation had actually reduced competition for land among Catholics and Protestants. Cullen argues that the root cause of the disturbances lay in the political fragmentation among the gentry of Armagh over the issues of parliamentary reform, volunteering, and Catholic rights, which created tensions at the local level, which in turn fostered the spread of Defenderism and eventually led to the foundation of the Orange Order. Miller prefers a socio-economic explanation for the disturbances, arguing that the growth of the linen industry in the county transformed the attitudes of a generation of young linen weavers, who no longer relied on the land to earn their living. Once the land had lost its economic significance, a generation of landlords lost their influence over thousands of mobile and prosperous weavers. According to one estimate, there were between 16,000 and 20,000 weavers in Armagh in the 1780s.[43] These farmer-weavers, both Catholic and Protestant, wanted to be treated according to their rising social status and demanded the right to bear arms. Conflict over this issue, followed by panicked efforts to contain local disturbances, created conditions that encouraged the spread of Defenderism (and later Orangeism). Within a few years of their origin, the Defenders had spread to the southern reaches of the county, and their presence was felt in south Armagh early in 1789.

The emergence of the Defenders in south Armagh has presented historians with a quandary. The factors that caused the political anxiety and breakdown of social control in central Armagh did not apply equally to the southern parts of the county, which remained overwhelmingly Catholic, mainly Irish-speaking, and poor. Despite the efforts of Richard Jackson, the linen industry in Forkhill was undeveloped in the 1790s and had not transformed landholding relationships among farmers and tenants. The population of the parish still consisted of chronically poor undertenants, who depended on the indulgence of their landlords while scrabbling an existence in a "mountainous situation."[44] The equation between Defenderism and rising affluence among the lower orders of Catholics, and the prospect of their bearing arms and becoming a viable political threat, did not apply to Forkhill. Cullen has acknowledged that the conditions in south Armagh were different from those elsewhere in the county, and he recognizes that the outrages on the Forkhill estate must be examined in the light of local circumstances.[45]

In April 1789 Hudson arrested a suspected Defender near Jonesborough, a village four miles from Forkhill. Hudson had been touring the neighbourhood with a military party in his capacity as a local magistrate and chaplain to the Volunteers, a largely Protestant part-time militia. A set of papers was seized from the suspect (who was known as Sharkey), including the rules of the association and a copy of the Defenders' oath.[46] The papers revealed little about the nature and purpose of the organization beyond its secrecy, exclusivity, and anticipation of violence. The rules prohibited rowdy behaviour, drunkenness at meetings, and disclosure of the society's secret passwords. Rule 4 declared that no person who had formerly belonged to another organization would be accepted into the Defenders without a written recommendation. Rule 9 required members to arm themselves with a gun and bayonet. The structure of the Defenders appeared to have been modelled on the society of Freemasons: the association was headed by a grand master, and local lodges were headed by deputies and committee members. Soon after, Hudson learned that the Creggan association held monthly meetings and was formally organized with a proper "cabinet," headed by a man known as the Deep Fellow. The movement had organized court martials for trying local delinquents and could assemble its associates almost instantly using a system of whistles.[47]

The Defenders had evolved in the tradition of the Whiteboys, Oakboys, and other rural protest societies that had conducted sporadic campaigns of intimidation against perceived oppressors in the 1760s and 1770s. The Whiteboys, named for the white shirts they wore over their clothes, had emerged in County Tipperary in 1761 and spread to a number of southern counties in the 1760s and 1770s. Their grievances were broadly agrarian. They objected to the enclosure of local commons by landlords who were anxious to let the land for profit; they attempted to regulate rates for conacre, or potato ground, by publicly declaring "fair rents" and punishing tenants who agreed to pay more; and they attacked middlemen who collected tithes for a fee on behalf of the local clergymen.[48] The Whiteboys assumed the mantle of local law enforcers, redressing grievances, rooting out perceived injustices, and challenging the regular forces of authority when they dared to intervene. Failure to obey the directives of the Whiteboys was punishable by destruction of property, injury to livestock, arson, assault, and even murder.

In a landmark study of rural disturbances published in Ireland in 1836, George Cornewall Lewis described the offenders who committed these acts of revenge and intimidation as "administrators of a law of opinion." In this character, "they look, not merely to particular, but also general results; not merely to the present, but also to the future; not merely to themselves, but also to those with whom they are leagued, and with whom they have an identity of interests."[49] Eric Hobsbawm has defined the phenomenon of social banditry in similar terms.[50] Bandits, he wrote, "right wrongs, they correct and avenge cases of injustice, and in doing so apply a more general criterion of just and fair relations between men in general."[51] Epidemics of banditry typically broke out during periods of social upheaval, he said, when a community or society was confronted with outside forces that threatened to dissolve the traditional order. In response, bandits engaged in campaigns of terror and intimidation, dispensing their own brand of justice according to a highly particular and widely understood code of behaviour.[52]

The emergence of the Defenders around Forkhill in the early 1790s suggests close parallels with banditry. The parish was located in a remote and mountainous region of south Armagh, only occasionally patrolled by parties of the Volunteers. There was no permanent law enforcement presence in the area until 1795, when a military barracks was established. The people were desperately poor, their economy was one of subsistence and survival, and the parish had a large pool of restless and landless young men, and no industry. Until the death of Richard Jackson in 1787, the people of Forkhill appear to have been relatively undisturbed by outsiders. Hudson's comment about the late landlord's indolence suggests that he was not unduly interfering. The settlement of the unleased lands on the estate upset the existing social order; local people were displaced, a "foreign" population was introduced, and a tighter measure of outside authority was imposed. In anger, the people allegedly "assembled the Defenders from all parts of the Country and struck such Terror that none of those Protestants but Half a Dozen ever appeared here afterwards."[53]

In the opinion of Hudson, Musgrave, and other pillars of the eighteenth-century establishment, the Protestant settlers in Forkhill were attacked on account of their religion: Protestantism was their only offence, and the actions against them were therefore sectarian. This explanation is insufficient and, in a strict sense, untrue; the situation was much more complicated. The Defenders' campaign of intimidation and punishment against a handful of Protestant settlers was ruthless, but it was not primarily sectarian. The four main targets – Hudson, Best, Duncan, and Dick – had been singled out as enemies of the community on account of their actions over the course of several years. The attacks on them by parties of the Defenders were systematic, typical, and predictable.

The Reverend Edward Hudson was the sworn enemy of the Defenders. As the trustee who had superintended settlement on the Forkhill estate, he was deeply implicated in the introduction of a foreign population and the displacement of local tenants. As a magistrate and as chaplain to the Volunteers, he was vigorous in his pursuit of local Defenders and had personally arrested Ferdy McElevy and the Forkhill Rioters. The extent to which Hudson bore the weight of responsibility for the campaign against the Defenders is underscored by a note in the minute books of the Forkhill trustees in August 1789, recording (somewhat prematurely) their "thanks ... to the Reverend Mr Hudson for his exertions as a magistrate in putting an end to some mischievous disturbances on this estate."[54]

Robert Best was the head constable for the barony of Upper Orior, and he too was active against the Defenders. During the 1789–92 period he had arrested a number of people who had refused to pay the cess, a local tax levied for road building and other improvements. This tax was regarded as excessive (it was known in Armagh as the "cut") and was a key grievance of the Oakboys and other protesters in the last quarter of the eighteenth century.[55]

For several decades the Oakboys, Steelboys, Whiteboys, Rightboys, and other agrarian protesters had attacked the tithe proctors and the collectors of the cess and had destroyed mills and storing sheds in order to obstruct the export of corn and grain from hungry areas.[56] The rash of mill burnings and the burning of haystacks and cowsheds in Forkhill in 1792 suggest a similar pattern of resistance. And, indeed, the other two principal targets of the Defenders – John Dick and William Duncan – were tax collectors. Dick was the miller on the Forkhill estate, entitled to receive one-sixteenth of the grain he milled as a standard toll; Duncan was the local tithe proctor, who worked for Hudson. The tithe proctor often evaluated and ultimately collected the tithe for the landowner or tithe owner, for which he received a commission or fee, which ranged from one shilling to two and sixpence in the pound. This system gave the tithe proctor "a vested interest in over-valuing the tithe, particularly where the assessment was based on the growing crop."[57] Tithe collectors were universally despised and were targeted by agrarian protesters much more frequently and violently than clergymen of the established church.[58] Writing in 1836, George Cornewall Lewis observed that "the class of persons called tithe-proctors [were] particularly obnoxious."[59] W.H. Lecky agreed, stating that "the tithe farmer ... was much more hated than the clergyman."[60]

There was a definite economic strain to this type of protest. The various taxes exacted from the people (toll, tithe, and cess) were paid in cash or in kind – in portions of corn or potatoes that were based on the acreage of each tenant and were often regarded as excessive.[61] On another level, taxation was a powerful symbol of the authority of both church and state. Attacking tax collectors or refusing to pay taxes was an expression of resistance to the cardinal administrative apparatus in the country and an explicit challenge to the authority of the state.

There is a final element to the Defenders' persecution of these Forkhill settlers – revenge. Hudson, Duncan, Dick, and Best each took the fatal step of prosecuting his attackers, a classic form of antisocial behaviour. In this society, handing over local men (however guilty) to the law, providing information about their doings, or testifying against them were acts of the deepest betrayal. Informers were universally reviled, and Hudson, Dick, and Duncan all suffered attempts on their lives after they had prosecuted local men for criminal offenses.

Thus, the Forkhill disturbances and the character of Defenderism in south Armagh were far more complicated than most accounts of the period suggest, and they cannot be dismissed as random acts of terrorization driven by sectarian hatred. Although sectarian tension aggravated the disturbances, the conditions for social protest already existed outside this historic arena of conflict. With this in mind, we will turn to the most notorious outrage of the period – the attack on Alexander Berkley and his family in 1791.[62]

THE BERKLEY OUTRAGE

On 28 January 1791, Alexander Berkley was at home with his wife and her young brother in Mullaghbawn, in the north end of the parish. Around seven o'clock in the evening, there was a knock on the door, and the familiar voice of a neighbour called to the family. When Berkley opened the door, a crowd of men rushed in and overpowered him. They tied a cord round his neck, forced out his tongue, and then cut it off. They severed the fingers and thumb from his right hand with a case knife and committed the same abuses on his wife. They cut out the tongue of her brother and sliced the calf of his leg with a sword. When their business was done, the men paraded up the road with torches, defiant. Both the schoolmaster and the boy survived the attack, but Berkley's wife died of her injuries in the Dundalk infirmary several days later.[63]

The attack on the Berkley family was immediately labelled a sectarian outrage. As mentioned in chapter 1, the trustees provided their proof for this charge in the letter they wrote to the bishop of Dromore, telling of their interview with the shattered Alexander Berkley, who described how he had asked his attackers whether he had ever offended them. "They said not; but that this was the beginning of what he and those like him should suffer." The trustees interpreted this reply as a threat to the Protestant settlers of Forkhill who, they said, were now living in terror, "as this recent instance of inhumanity ... leave[s] no doubt upon their minds of what the intentions must be against them."[64] Musgrave was even more explicit than the trustees, claiming that the "barbarous treatment of this colony by the Romanists ... [confirmed] that the extirpation of protestants of every denomination was the main design of the defenders."[65]

A different version of the circumstances behind the attack was published in 1792 in a pamphlet by "J. Byrne" entitled "An Impartial

Account of the Late Disturbances in the County of Armagh." Byrne traced the origins of the attack on Berkley to the upheaval of settlement on the estate and the displacement of Catholics by incoming Protestant settlers: "By the will of the late Mr. J—n, it seems that whenever a Papist's lease was expired, that they should be banished their rocky habitations, and Protestants reinstated into the land of their fathers." Berkley was singled out for attack because of the controversy surrounding his appointment as schoolmaster at Mullaghbawn in preference to another young teacher. This young teacher, "Mr K—e," had won favour with the people because he had promised to teach the children their prayers in Irish, while Berkley, it was rumoured, would not teach the children "any thing but the Protestant prayers."[66] According to Byrne, William Duncan and a fellow conspirator named Mr H—e had played a cruel trick on the young teacher who was competing with Berkley for the teaching post at Mullaghbawn. "They took an opportunity to intoxicate Mr. K—e, and in that state brought him to the Rev. Mr. H–d–n [Hudson], when at dinner: and it is said, that when they entered the room, that Mr. H—e pushed K—e against a side-board, and overturned all that were on it." After witnessing this drunken display, Hudson dismissed the young teacher from his promised employment, offering the post to Berkley instead. In a footnote, Byrne stated that he had interviewed Berkley several months after the attack, and Berkley had confided that it was his firm opinion that the dispute over the teaching post was the reason behind his cruel treatment. "But," said Berkley, "I did not merit it, as I engaged an usher that was master of the Irish language, and taught 40 poor children, free of any cost to their parents: but on Saturdays, said he, I learned them prayers in English."[67]

Byrne's version of the events in Forkhill must be received with caution. First, there are several key details missing from his account, including the turf war between Berkley and Michael Donnelly, and Berkley's apparent intention to bring further charges against local men at the spring assizes in 1791. Second, Cullen has suggested that the pamphlet was intended to counteract loyalist propaganda that was exploiting the Berkley mutilation to discourage further political concessions to Catholics; and thus that Byrne, in depicting the attack as a purely local vendetta, had a political motive.[68] This argument forms part of Cullen's striking theory that the name J. Byrne was a pseudonym and that the real author of the 1792 pamphlet was the infamous United Irishman and Armagh priest, Father James Coigly.[69]

The attack on the Berkley family was the work of the local Defenders. Both the nature of the crime and the identity of the men involved place this point beyond dispute. It was a surprise attack, carried out under cover of darkness by a mob who were determined to inflict brutal injuries on their victims and perhaps end their lives. The only man ever convicted of the attack was a ringleader of the Defenders, known as "Captain" Peter Murphy, who was arrested along with his brother and father in February 1791. Thomas, Laurence, and Peter Murphy stood trial at the Armagh assizes in April 1791 charged with twelve counts of maiming. Peter Murphy was found guilty and ordered to be hanged at the bridge of Forkhill on 3 May and then gibbeted. Thomas and Laurence Murphy were charged with the murder of Berkley's wife but were eventually freed for lack of evidence.[70]

Berkley's trouble with the Defenders had begun soon after he settled on the Forkhill estate in 1789. That summer he charged two local men, Michael Donnelly and Laurence Connory, with assault, robbery, and theft of firearms. Shortly after these prosecutions, Berkley had a further altercation with Donnelly; in the assize book, the charge is recorded as "Cut & Stab." The case was heard at the spring assizes in 1790, and Berkley was assisted in the prosecution by his brother-in-law William Duncan. This time Donnelly was sentenced to death and "took it to death with him, that Mr D—n swore his life away." Duncan fled the parish shortly afterwards. Berkley, who remained behind, assumed the responsibility of answering for the execution.[71] Donnelly had been arrested for firearms offences on at least two previous occasions, which suggests that he was closely involved with the Defenders, and his execution would have provided clear grounds for revenge by his associates. That is why Alexander Berkley was attacked in January 1791. His attackers told him so. Their threat to do similar harm to "those like him" referred to traitors like him who passed information to the police and prosecuted their neighbours. Informing was the ultimate act of betrayal in this rural society and was punished with a severity that surpassed any other act of discipline by the "midnight legislators."

Threats, attacks, and mutilations of suspected informers or trial witnesses were far from uncommon. In 1791 Prudence McLaughlin of Killibegs had her ears cut off when she gave evidence against a suspected Defender.[72] In July 1796 Terence Woods was attacked by a gang of armed men who broke into his home in the middle of the night. He suffered two deep cuts to his tongue, one of his ears was cut off, and his other ear was left mangled. There were "strong grounds to believe that the said outrage was committed … because he had prosecuted two persons to conviction at the last Assizes in Omagh."[73] In his classic study of rural disturbances, Lewis reviewed extensive testimony on the brutal punishments that were executed on anyone who dared to inform on a member of "the system." The severest sanctions, in the form of vicious beatings, bodily mutilations, and murder, were

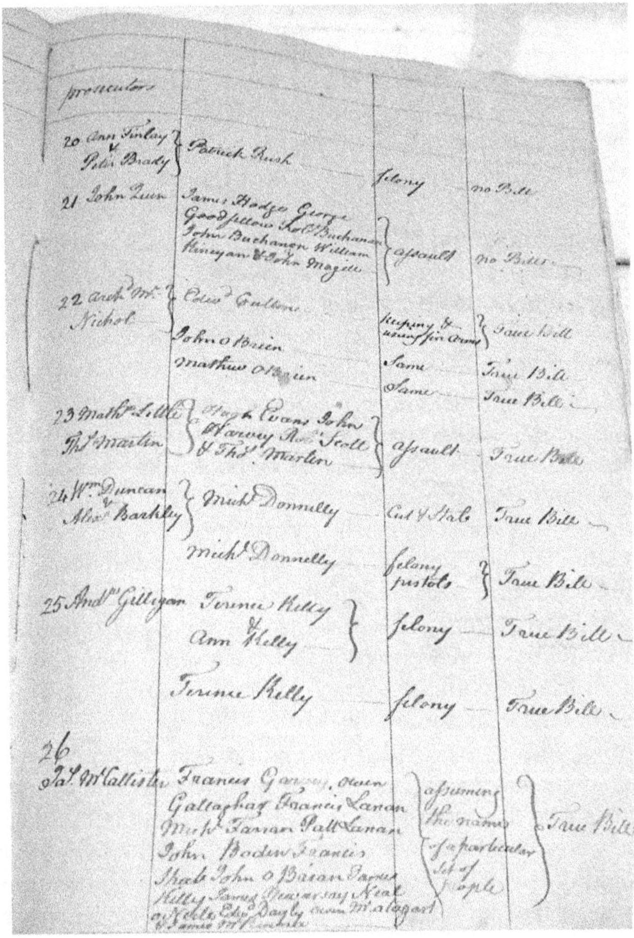

The indictment book for County Armagh, showing the prosecution of Michael Donnelly by Alexander Berkley and William Duncan at the spring assizes in 1790 (Armagh Public Library, photograph by J.E. Madden)

reserved for prosecutors, witnesses, and informers.[74] According to Lewis, "there is no name of more ominous sound in Ireland than that of informer. A man who has given information or evidence against a Whiteboy is doomed to certain death. If he attempted to return from the assizes to his house, he would be hunted through the country like a mad dog; every hand would be raised against him."[75]

Shortly after the outrage, the *Hibernian Journal* reported that the attack had been an attempt to silence Berkley, who planned to testify against other local Defenders at the Armagh assizes that spring.[76]

Cutting off a person's ears may have been an allusion to the fact that the victim had overheard information or gossip and passed it to the authorities.[77] Similarly, Berkley's tongue was likely cut out to discourage in the strongest terms – symbolically and actually – his inclination to testify against Defenders at their trial. After the attackers carved out his tongue, they cut off the four fingers and thumb of his right hand and did the same to his wife, "which operation took them above ten minutes." This was a cruelly deliberate mutilation that was intended to leave Berkley, who earned most of his income as a linen weaver, without the use of his hands. Although the circumstances surrounding the establishment of the linen industry in the parish are not well known, when Berkley's attackers severed every finger from his right hand, they ensured that he would never again work at a loom. In their letter to the bishop on 3 February 1791, the trustees claimed that the victims were likely to die "as, if they live, they are incapable of earning their subsistence."[78]

The trials of Peter, Thomas, and Laurence Murphy were held in April 1791. The Reverend Edward Hudson attended the proceedings and was sitting in the gallery on the day that Berkley appeared to give his testimony about what had happened on the night of 28 January.[79] "He described his own sufferings briefly," recorded Hudson, "and went on with firmness till he came to mention his wife – Here he was quite overcome and there was a Dead Pause in the Court for some minutes."[80]

There is no question that Alexander Berkley had been singled out for horrific abuse (no other attack of this period was so violent), and the Defenders did intend to make an example of him. But in sending their message to "those like him," they were referring to their enemies in the community – magistrates, policemen, tax collectors, and especially informers. They did not mean Protestants in general. And in this they were fatally misunderstood.

3

Rebellion, 1795–1798

Ireland in the 1790s was a laboratory of tension, with disruptive elements at work at every level. As individual events, the rise of the Volunteers, the foundation of the Society of United Irishmen, the ripple effects of the French Revolution, and the outbreak of disturbances in Armagh might not have disrupted the social order. But as coincidental events, the result was cataclysmic. The Rebellion of 1798, which lasted from May until September, claimed at least thirty thousand lives, a death toll exceeding that of France's three-year Reign of Terror.[1] For the United Irishmen, the tragic and ironic consequence was Ireland's loss of legislative independence and its incorporation into a United Kingdom in 1801 through the Act of Union.[2]

The Rebellion of 1798 is usually presented as a play in three acts: the outbreak of the rebellion in Wexford and Wicklow in May, its eruption in Ulster in June, and the invasion and capture of French forces at Kinsale in September. In Ulster, it amounted to a handful of ill-fated risings in Antrim and Down, which were soon crushed by the military, the leaders later being executed. Most of the accounts of the rebellion in the north focus on these standoffs at Saintfield and Ballynahinch in June 1798. The Presbyterian heartland of Antrim and Down was the birthplace of the movement, and 1798 was the year that mattered. Often eclipsed in these accounts is the spread of the revolutionary movement elsewhere in Ulster, particularly to the southern reaches of the province. Beginning in the mid-1790s, the United Irishmen worked hard to sow the seeds of insurrection in the borderlands, especially in the Defender strongholds of south Ulster. Their efforts were repaid. This chapter tells the story of the United Irishmen of south Armagh, who were drilled and prepared for an uprising in the spring of 1797.

THE UNITED IRISHMEN

The rise of the United Irishmen must be considered against the background of radical politics in Britain, America, and France during the last quarter of the eighteenth century. The classical republicanism that inspired the dissent behind the American Revolution and the French Revolution spilled over into Ireland, where it increased the political expectations of the middle classes and stirred agitation for parliamentary reform. Ulster Presbyterians were particularly receptive to the ideas of Thomas Paine and the French revolutionaries, and the first Society of United Irishmen was founded in Belfast in October 1791. The founders of the society included William Drennan, a doctor and radical thinker from Newry. Writing in May 1791, he envisioned a society devoted to "the Rights of Men ... its general end Real Independence to Ireland, and Republicanism its particular purpose."[3] The founding members of the society were committed to parliamentary reform and equitable representation. In addition, many were persuaded that Catholics should be admitted to the civil rights that were denied them under the surviving penal laws, including the right to enter parliament, belong to corporations, and hold high civic and military office. This commitment to political equality was instrumental to the platform of the United Irishmen and paved the way for cooperation between the society and various Catholic organizations, including the Catholic Committee and, later, the Defenders.[4]

The Catholic Committee was a conservative body that had been established in 1773 to lobby for removal of the penal laws. The members of the committee enjoyed a cosy relationship with the Protestant Ascendancy – the powerful Anglo-Irish elite – and they preferred a policy of supplication on the question of political reform. In 1791 the leadership of the Catholic Committee was taken over by a group of Dublin businessmen and professionals, who adopted a more strident approach to the reform question. In July 1792, the Dublin barrister Theobald Wolfe Tone, a founding member of the United Irishmen, was hired as the committee's secretary. Tone's massively popular *Argument on Behalf of the Catholics of Ireland*, which argued a persuasive case for the political expediency of Protestant support for Catholic emancipation, had been published the year before.

In December 1792 the Catholic Committee organized a convention in Dublin in order to demonstrate publicly its determination to secure full political rights. The convention was a great feat of democratic representation; every county in Ireland was represented by between one and four delegates who had been elected by a system of nominations and elections held at the parish level in the summer and fall of 1792.[5] The grassroots involvement in the selection of delegates had "encouraged the extension of the Catholic question deep into the Irish countryside" and had an enormous politicizing effect.[6] Just as important, the convention brought together the leaders of various radical societies. Of the 231 delegates elected to the convention in 1792, forty-eight were members of the Dublin Society of United Irishmen, and a number of others were leading Defenders or radical sympathizers.[7] At this stage, the Catholic Committee preferred not to draw attention to its alliance of interests with the United Irishmen, though the government's continued refusal to grant full emancipation to Catholics laid the groundwork for future cooperation.[8]

The United Irishmen worked to mobilize popular opinion on various fronts in the early 1790s. They established the *Northern Star*, a daring radical newspaper that endorsed the cause of parliamentary reform and legislative independence; they revived old companies of the Irish Volunteers and established new ones, including a short-lived National Guard, which was based on the French example and committed to republican principles. Their agenda was taken up by numerous Presbyterian congregations in Ulster during the winter of 1792–93, and calls for parliamentary reform and Catholic emancipation were formally endorsed at the annual meeting of the Synod of Ulster.[9] The government regarded these initiatives as subversive, and as the popular movement for reform gathered momentum, it attempted to shut down the Society of United Irishmen and other radical groups.

In 1793 the Irish parliament passed legislation restricting public assemblies and prosecuted several United Irishmen for printing and distributing libellous material. The following May, the society itself was suppressed by proclamation and forced underground. During the next two years, the outlawed society set out to create a revolutionary organization that reached into every corner of the country. One of its early initiatives was the agreement of a pact with the rural Defenders in 1795–96. The precise circumstances of this event are unclear, but the alliance involved some of the well-known Ulster families who had provided the leadership of the Defenders several years earlier. The new friendship allowed the United Irishmen to tap into the Defender networks that criss-crossed south Ulster, and thus reach tens of thousands of potential rebels. The Defenders had already infiltrated the largely Catholic Irish militia, which had been established in 1793 as an auxiliary defence force in response to the outbreak of war between England and France.

The Defenders were drawn into an alliance with the United Irishmen for several reasons. First, certain elements within Defenderism were receptive to the ideas of the French Revolution. References to the "tree of liberty" and the prospect of the liberation of Ireland by the French army had crept into the passwords and oaths of the association by 1795. The early relationship between the United Irishmen and the French military (contacts had been made by 1794) no doubt appealed to the Defenders. Second, a revolutionary impulse was shared by both movements. A set of Defender documents seized in 1795 contained a handbill posted by the Sligo Defenders. "Our forced vengeance is entirely and solely against the oppressors of the poor," they had written.[10] They planned to abolish the tithe and cess, to fix the wages of labourers and the prices of goods, and to regulate the price of land. Any landlord who demanded a higher rent would be punished; any tenant who agreed privately to pay a higher rent than allowed would be punished. These demands were not new, but their fusion with the language of the French Revolution and with universal expressions of liberty and equality may have created the impression of common ground with the United Irishmen. In fact, the social radicalism of the Defenders was nowhere articulated in the political program of the United Irish society, and this would eventually prove to be a fault line.

A more pressing reason for cooperation was the revival of conflict in Armagh in 1795. In late September, a violent clash took place between gangs of Peep O'Day Boys and Defenders at the Diamond, near Loughgall in north Armagh. In the wake of the fight, the Peep O'Day boys and other elements in the Protestant community established a formal protective league against the Defenders: the Loyal Orange Order.[11] The order was an explicitly sectarian organization (its secret articles declared that no Catholic could be made an Orangeman "on any account"), but its manifesto declared that no man would be persecuted for his religious opinion, and the association claimed no responsibility for the sectarian outrages that followed on the heels of its formation. During the autumn of 1795, hundreds of Catholic families were forced from their homes in a campaign of persecution referred to as the Armagh Outrages.[12] Although it cannot be established that Orangemen organized these raids on Armagh Catholics, historians agree that there was probably a high level of Orange participation in an unofficial capacity.[13]

The Armagh raids aroused alarm among the Catholic population and increased their receptivity to the message of the United Irishmen at a crucial moment. The United Irishmen seized that moment. As the United Irishman Thomas Addis Emmet explained, they were able to convince the Defenders that "the *something* which the Defenders vaguely conceived *ought to be done for Ireland* was by separating it from England to establish its real as well as nominal independence;

and they urged the necessity of combining into one body all who were actuated with the same view ... The Defenders, by specific votes in their own societies, agreed to be sworn United Irishmen and incorporated into the nation."[14]

SPREADING THE WORD

In a skeletal form, these were the circumstances that helped shape the alliance between the United Irishmen and the Defenders in 1795–96. The consolidation of contacts at the leadership level was followed by several years of "revolutionary evangelism," marked by the employment of emissaries of the society, who travelled up and down the countryside, and a massive propaganda effort using the popular press.[15] Throughout the 1790s, many Irish newspapers were bought by Dublin Castle and dared not endorse radical political views in print. To counter the muzzling of free speech, the United Irishmen had founded the *Northern Star* in 1792. The *Star* reported extensively on the progress of the revolution in France and the evolution of democracy in the American colonies, contrasting the corruption and tyranny of the Irish government with the embrace of liberalism overseas.[16] The *Star* faced several financially crippling prosecutions for printing treasonable material, and in 1797 it was suppressed by troops under General Lake, who had requested permission to "seize and burn the whole apparatus."[17] Before its suppression, the *Star* had been widely circulated in Antrim and Down and was especially popular in regions where the rebellion broke out. Access to the newspaper in south Armagh is more difficult to determine. Father James Coigly, a leading figure in the United Irish movement in Ulster, had expressed frustration at the irregularity of the paper's delivery: "I have written once more about the *Star* ... Be convinced that the negligence of the proprietors as to that Point has done a Vast deal of Harm to the Cause."[18]

The reported circulation of the *Star* is not necessarily an indication of its readership, since after the paper had been read it was often passed on to others. Writing from Jonesborough, near Forkhill, in August 1794, Hudson expressed amazement at the political interest of the people. "The change in the Natives here is truly astonishing – Formerly a Newspaper would have been a phenomenon amongst them – at Present they may vie with the Northerns in thirst after Politicks – he who can read has generally a large audience about the door of his cabin whilst he is endeavouring to enlighten his countrymen."[19] Just a few months before, in early March, Hudson had reported to Charlemont that the people of Forkhill had "given up all thoughts of Politics" and appeared "sullen and despondent."[20] This shift in temper indicates how quickly the political interest of the people could be engaged through the medium of the press. Along with the *Northern Star*, countless penny pamphlets flooded the countryside in the 1790s, condemning the corruption of government and encouraging Irishmen to unite in the face of despotism. In July 1794 Hudson had intercepted a handbill that was circulating in Armagh, Down, and Louth – one that he had condemned as "the wickedest of all I have seen." The handbill, addressed to "Friends and Fellow-Countrymen," was directed at the masses of rural poor, whose labour was exploited by the powerful elite.

> Who makes the rich? The answer is obvious – it is the industrious poor. What makes the shuttle fly, and the plough cleave the furrow? – the industrious poor. In whose hands are all the useful arts, the very arts, the improvement to which, enable the rich to make their money, and to display their pride and wickedness? Are they in the hands of the rich? – No! – They must then be in the hands of the industrious poor ... Think of politics ... think of your rulers; think of republics ... think of the money they are robbing you of to keep you in slavery and ignorance ... and you may be convinced that the day of emancipation is not far distant; and if you are men, if you are Christians, be united, be prepared, and be determined to do yourselves justice.

The pamphlet was signed "One of the People."[21]

The author of this handbill is unknown, and it may not have originated with the Society of United Irishmen. Yet the connection it draws between the oppression of the poor and the deficiencies of a corrupt political system echo the arguments later made by one of Ireland's earliest socialists, James Hope. Hope was a Templepatrick weaver of humble circumstances who had been a member of the Irish Volunteers before joining the United Irish movement in 1795. He was active during the Rebellion of 1798 and was interviewed in the 1840s by R.R. Madden, one of the first historians of the United Irishmen. Hope regarded parliamentary reform and the extension of political rights to Catholics as the only way to overcome the "aristocratic monetary influence" that kept the working classes of Ulster in chains. Between 1796 and 1798 he served as "an emissary, going from place to place throughout the country, organizing the people."[22] In 1796 he established a branch of the society at Newtownhamilton in south Armagh. The village, which was the site of a Presbyterian settlement in the 1730s, subsequently became a major centre of the United Irishmen in south Ulster.[23] Another leading United Irishman, Charles Teeling, worked to unite the Peep O'Day Boys and Defenders in the smaller towns of Ulster. According to Hope, "even [they] were made friends, and joining in sworn brotherhood, became United Irishmen."[24]

The lower orders of the Catholic clergy were another set of revolutionary agents. In the summer of 1792, parish priests had been instrumental in organizing elections at the parish level for delegates to the landmark Catholic Convention, an event that is considered an early stage in rural politicization.[25] Despite the Catholic hierarchy's condemnation of both Defenders and United Irishmen, a number of priests were involved in these movements throughout the 1790s. The most infamous priest to be implicated in the rebellion was James Coigly, whose role in the insurrection has yet to be fully determined.[26] Coigly had been educated in Paris but fled the city in the early days of the revolution and returned to Ireland in late 1789. He soon became involved with the Belfast Society of United Irishmen and had close links with the Defenders; his cousin, Valentine Derry was a leading Defender and United Irishman in County Louth.[27] Operating out of Dundalk throughout the 1790s, Coigly was politically active in the rural regions of Armagh, Down, and Louth, and was well known to Colonel John Ogle, head of the Forkhill yeomanry.[28] Shortly after Coigly's arrest early in 1798, Ogle wrote to Edward Cooke inquiring "if one person's evidence respecting Quigleys signature will be sufficient – As I had a correspondence with him some time ago."[29]

Two other Catholic clergymen from south Armagh were accused of political sedition during the same period. In May 1798 the dean of Loughgilly recommended the arrest of two priests of "infamous character" who lived in the mountains of south Armagh: Father William Cullen and Father McKoin (also written Keown and Quinn).[30] Cullen was the parish priest at Forkhill and had been awarded a lease on the estate at the time of the settlement in 1788. According to Warburton, this "Priest of Forkhill ... was supposed to be concerned in cutting out the Tongue of the Protestant Schoolmaster there about 7 years ago."[31] In the nearby parish of Creggan, Father Paul MacDonagh was suspected of close involvement with the United Irishmen. More mysteriously, he was reputed to possess miraculous powers which he directed against his enemies and the "oppressors of his people." In 1798 word of this man reached Hudson, who informed Charlemont that a priest with supposed healing powers had converted several Protestants to Catholicism.[32] Father MacDonagh was arrested on suspicion of membership in the United Irish movement in 1799 and sentenced to transportation, but he managed to escape and returned to his former parish, where he was causing further trouble by 1803.[33]

Several other priests from south Armagh were named among the subscribers to a book of patriotic poetry printed in Newry in 1797, entitled *Odes and Elegies Descriptive & Sentimental with The Patriot: A Poem*.[34] A list in the preface, which identifies nearly five hundred subscribers to the book, is a rare index to local centres of radicalism on the eve of the rebellion. L.M. Cullen has called the list a "who's who" of the United Irish movement in Armagh and Down. It included such well-known United Irishmen as William Steele Dixon, William Drennan, Henry Joy McCracken, Lord Edward Fitzgerald, and Thomas Russell. Particularly intriguing was the number of clergymen, both Protestant and Catholic, who were listed among the subscribers, including the Reverends Andrew Levins of Kilcurry, Joseph Jackson of Newtownhamilton, James Coigly of Dundalk, and three Catholic priests from Newtownhamilton. Nearly fifty of the subscribers (or roughly 10 per cent) lived around south Armagh or in border areas touching the county. None of them was from Forkhill – though one, a postmaster named Nicholas Gaussan, lived in nearby Jonesborough (he was arrested in 1797 for treasonable practices but never convicted).[35] The ecumenical readership of *The Patriot* does not prove that Protestants and Catholics cooperated in the United Irish movement in south Armagh, but as L.M. Cullen suggests, it is an indication that certain political opinions were shared across the spectrum.[36]

Alongside church, chapel, or meeting house, another potential site of subversion was the schoolhouse. In Nancy Curtin's occupational breakdown of 1,004 known United Irishmen in Ulster between 1795 and 1798, thirty-one were revealed to be schoolmasters (3.1 per cent). It is interesting to note that two Forkhill schoolmasters, Samuel Dickson and John Burgess, were turned out of their schools in the latter half of 1797. Unfortunately, no explanation was recorded, though earlier that year Dickson had been censured by the trustees for unspecified "misconduct."[37]

The massive effort that the United Irish movement had undertaken to spread the revolutionary message throughout rural Ulster was well repaid. By the spring of 1797, the society claimed to have more than 117,000 sworn members in the nine provinces of Ulster.[38] The returns for Armagh indicate that membership had increased exponentially between October 1796, when just 1,000 United Irishmen were counted, and May 1797, when a membership of 17,000 was returned.[39] Although these figures were inflated, it is clear that membership in the society was growing steadily, particularly after the attempted invasion by France in late 1796.

THE RISING OF 1797

In December 1796 a large French invasion fleet carrying 15,000 soldiers and a determined Wolfe Tone attempted a surprise landing at Bantry Bay, off the coast of Cork. Bad weather prevented the French troops from reaching the shore, and although they lingered off the coast for several days, their presence was discovered and they were forced back to France. This failure did not deter the Ulster rebels, who believed that the French would return and that rebellion was imminent. In County Armagh, a series of pitched battles between rebels and yeomanry kept the countryside in upheaval throughout the first half of 1797.

In January James Dawson of Forkhill reported to Dublin Castle that the Newry yeomanry was full of United Irishmen and that the countryside around Jonesborough barracks was particularly badly affected.[40] The gravity of the situation became clear in February, when a man who had been arrested in Newry offered to inform against a band of United Irishmen in south Armagh. This intelligence led to the arrest of twelve men near the village of Cullaville one evening near the end of the month. As the military party led the prisoners away, "signals were given from all the hills, and in the middle of the day they were pursued by between 3 and 4 hundred Men; about an hundred and fifty were armed with Musquets and marched in ranks like Soldiers, the remainder were armed with pikes [and] bayonets."[41] The armed mob pursued the military party and the twelve prisoners all day and into the night. As they travelled, they alerted the countryside by sounding horns and lighting fires on hilltops. Throughout the night, the number of rebels swelled, and several witnesses reported that the mob numbered no less than three thousand, including "a vast number of women who appeared to be more violent than the men."[42] Several militia parties and yeomanry corps were called out to quell the disturbance, including the recently organized Forkhill yeomanry under the command of Colonel John Ogle. These troops were fired upon several times during the night but escaped injury. Two local clergymen intervened the next morning and managed to disperse the mob.[43] Local magistrates and officers identified the rebels as a crowd of United Irishmen and expressed alarm at the level of disaffection in the countryside. From his home in Loughgilly, Dean Warburton claimed that the whole country was "*sworn* and *united*," and Walter Synnot despaired of the countryside, where "almost every man is a United Irish man."[44]

On 13 March 1797, in an effort to circumvent rebellion, the commanding officer of the northern district issued a proclamation ordering the people of Ulster to surrender their arms.[45] The disarming of Ulster had begun. Meanwhile, to suppress rebellion in Armagh, Generals Lake and Knox launched a campaign of terror in the disaffected parts of the county. The *Northern Star* reported in April that a party of militia marching from Monaghan to Armagh had been instructed to "load with ball cartridge for they were now in a country of rebels, and if they saw FIVE of them together they were to fire at them."[46] From the perspective of government, an insurrection in Ulster was a real threat in the spring of 1797; the number of United Irishmen in the province reportedly doubled between January and April.[47] Knox reported that the countryside around Armagh had grown progressively worse, and a rising appeared imminent. "There is but one Report thro' the Country which is that whether the French come or not (and they are soon expected) the United Irishmen are to rise as soon as the ploughing season is over."[48] In a diary entry on 12 April 1797, Alexander Hamilton, a United Irishman from Newtownhamilton, wrote that several prisoners charged with administering the United Irishmen's oath had been acquitted that day, and "bonfires were lighted on ye Tops of all the hills round Armagh."[49] On the same day, a correspondent based in Newry reported to Dublin Castle that another leading United Irishman, Sam Turner, had "been in the mountains and the people are expected to rise on Friday."[50]

There were stirrings in Forkhill as well, despite the presence of the militia and the recently established yeomanry corps under Colonel Ogle. Local legends abound about Ogle, who was known as a ruthless and brutal authority figure. An English soldier, he had married Julia Eliza Barton, the only daughter of Susanna Barton and niece of the late Richard Jackson, in 1790 or 1791. It was likely under his influence that a military barracks was established in the parish in 1795, near the site where Alexander Berkley had been attacked four years earlier. Ogle was not satisfied that this measure was sufficient to curb the spread of revolutionary sentiment in the parish, and in 1796 he had requested and received permission to form the Forkhill Yeomanry. His request was backed by a petition "expressing the Sentiments of 88 of the principal inhabitants of the parish of Forkhill."[51]

Ogle's anxieties were not unfounded. The United Irish movement had made inroads into the parish by early 1797, and throughout the spring he sent letters to Dublin Castle describing his crusade against local rebels. Although Ogle may have exaggerated the effect of his role as a magistrate (and was always pressing the administration for additional money and resources), he was a target of the United Irishmen and genuinely feared for his life. "I have quieted Forkhil and neighbourhood, I've been three different times shot at when in the execution of my duty as a magistrate, I am now seriously threatened and in danger of assassination by the United Irishmen," he wrote in March.[52] In early May he wrote again to Dublin Castle, providing more information about the activities of the United Irishmen around Forkhill:

> On Monday a person in this neighbourhood is to administer the United Irishman's oath to one of our Tenants, at the same time is to shew him some papers in which are their system ... when I mean to apprehend and commit him ... This immediate neighbourhood has so far been tranquil ... but it now seems

to be severely infected with the traitors who surround it. Twelve of them conspired against and attacked me on Monday night, I luckily had my pistols and to them I owe my existence – this is the second attack in less than two months. I cannot sufficiently describe to you the villainous disposition of the Northern inhabitants (and who were until of late respectable people) to all who are inimical to their traitorous cause.[53]

Ogle also described the recent surge in tree cutting in the parish; one night he had seen the "rebels" loading twenty carts with trees. Tree cutting was another indication that the people were preparing for rebellion because the wood was used to make pike handles. According to local tradition, the rebels cut the trees on a windy night, lapping the point of the saw with a woollen thread to deaden the sound.[54] A well-known local ballad, "The Carrive Blacksmith," was written in memory of Thomas Lappin, a blacksmith and United Irishman from Forkhill who was arrested by the yeomanry for fashioning pikestaffs for the rebels. According to local tradition, Lappin refused to reveal any information about the activities of his associates, despite a flogging by the yeomen at Belmont Barracks that continued for several days.[55]

One week after Ogle had alerted Dublin Castle about the activities of the local United Irishmen, a violent confrontation took place near Forkhill between a mob of several hundred rebels and a regiment of the Ancient British Fencibles. Although the Forkhill rebels far outnumbered the forty soldiers, they were badly beaten in the ambush on 13 May 1797. Between ten and twenty-five of the rebels were killed, and many more were taken prisoner. The precise circumstances of the attack remain unclear, but a report in *Faulkner's Journal* claimed that a party of the Fencibles in Dundalk marched to Forkhill to confront a mob of United Irishmen. Outside the village, the soldiers surprised a crowd of "several hundred Defenders, or United Irishmen (the terms are synonymous) collected close to a bog." The commanding officer of the militia ordered the party to fall back, but the crowd advanced on the soldiers. "He then ordered his men to charge, and in less than half an hour the banditti were completely put to flight. Thirteen of them were killed upon the spot, and eighteen so severely wounded, that it is supposed not one of them can recover; many who escaped were also desperately wounded."[56] General Lake privately expressed regret about the incident the following day and hinted that the military had exceeded its mandate: "You will of course of [sic] heard of the behaviour of the ancient British at Forkhill ... I feel quite wretched but hope I get out of the scrape and never be in such another."[57] That night, a reported mob of two thousand rebels attacked the home of

Ogle's mother-in-law, Susanna Barton, tore part of it down, and set fire to the premises.[58]

The government declared martial law several days later, and throughout the month of June the military exercised brutal force in an effort to stamp out disaffection in south Armagh. Nakedly partisan accounts of the disarming of Ulster make it difficult to estimate how much of the military force was necessary and how much was recreational violence, but even some loyalists began to express unease about the level of brutality. A yeoman named John Giffard condemned a search for arms in the mountains outside Newry conducted by the Ancient British Fencibles which turned into a bloody rampage. He described a clearing in the woods that was littered with "the dead bodies of boys and old men – slain by the Britons though no opposition whatever had been given by them and as I shall answer to almighty God, I believe a single Gun was not fired but by the Britons or Yeomanry."[59] However, the orders of General Knox held firm: "By Terror only they are to be disarmed."[60]

The policy of military terror in Ulster achieved its intended result. The United Irish network was smashed and the province was almost totally disarmed.[61] On 14 June Ogle reported that the countryside around south Armagh had been quiet since the capture of several ringleaders in the middle of May, and he was confident that "the business of the United Irishmen [was] quite at an end."[62] Ogle's self-congratulation was slightly premature, but ultimately he was right: the rebellion in south Armagh was over. The rebels arrested for firing on the military and attacking the home of Susanna Barton were tried at the Armagh assizes in September 1797. Sixteen men were convicted and eight of them were sentenced to death. Attorney General Arthur Wolfe informed the Chief Secretary's Office that the other rebels would be kept as hostages, and if there were any further outrages in the area, "those convicts shall, from time to time, as occasion may require, be executed."[63] After the September executions of eight local men, and with the noose around the necks of eight others, the revolutionary movement in south Armagh virtually collapsed. By mid-1797, many of the leading United Irishmen in Armagh, Louth, and south Down had been arrested, and the rebels who managed to evade capture (such as Samuel Turner and Father James Coigly) had fled the country. Turner switched his allegiance in late 1797 and informed against his former associates.[64] Coigly was arrested in England early in 1798, convicted of treason, and hanged at Maidstone Gaol.[65]

At an executive meeting of the United Irish society on 10 May 1798, where county leaders had gathered to finalize plans for the insurrection, it was clear that the organization was in a shambles. William Donaldson, a leading United Irishman from Newtownhamilton who was once described by Lord Blayney as "the most leading man in this Kingdom," appeared "timid about Armagh."[66] John Conellan, a Dundalk apothecary who represented Louth at the meeting, supplied a return of supporters that was "so inconsiderable" that the secretary refused to write it down.[67] It was decided that Counties Antrim and Down were to rise first, seizing Blaris Camp and Belfast, and the other counties were "not to stir" until they heard news of the insurrection. However, General Nugent had deployed soldiers to stop all communication between Down and Armagh, and no message was able to get through.[68] A Forkhill ballad called "The Market Stone" recounts the disappointment of the local people at their paralysis in 1798:

We had caves upon Slieve Gullion
We had hideouts on Slieve Mor
Slieve Brea and Carna Gamna
As in '41 before

But no man came from Sheelagh
Tho' we did get news from Down
Brought by a linen weaver
From Carrickfergus town

And the news was bad I tell you
And left us very low
The traitors they were busy
As in the long ago

So still in Carna Ghishen
The ashen handles lie
While from the forge in Quilly
No more bright sparks shall fly

McSherry's Glen no more shall hear
The tramp of marching men,
We might have done a little
Had we got the message then.[69]

Still, history has strange footnotes. The correspondence of Lord Downshire contains two tantalizingly brief references to a small rising in south Armagh near the end of June 1798. One of these is in a letter written on 26 June and says, "They are up in numbers in the Fews mountains and over Dundalk and Forkhill." Several days later another correspondent informed Downshire, "There was a rising a few nights ago at Dundalk. The intention was to drive all the gentry into the town, and then massacre them. It was discovered in time, and the rebels driven towards Forkhill."[70] Two men from Dundalk, John Hoey and Anthony Marmion, were executed for their part in the rising on 25 July, but there were no other known local martyrs in 1798.[71]

Most accounts explain the failure of the 1798 rebellion in Ulster in a context that includes the United Irishmen's dependence on reinforcements from France, the penetration of the United Irish leadership at the highest level by government informers, the extermination of the rebels by General Lake's military machine in the spring of 1797, and the distraction of conflict between Defenders and Orangemen in Armagh. It was speculated that the escalation of sectarian hostilities in Ulster was encouraged by the government as a useful "counterrevolutionary strategy of tension," and the government helped matters along by recruiting members of the Orange Order into additional yeomanry forces in the spring of 1797.[72] The government was keenly aware of popular opinion about the Orangemen. General Knox admitted that the Orangemen were "bigots" who would resist Catholic emancipation, but he insisted that the Orange Order formed the government's only barrier against the United Irishmen.[73]

By mid-1797, the Orange Order had succeeded in breaking up the alliance of Presbyterians and Catholics in Ulster and constituted a formidable barrier between the Defender strongholds of south Ulster and the United Irish heartland of Antrim and Down. In his autobiography, published posthumously in 1798, Father James Coigly accused the government of provoking sectarian conflict by enlisting Orangemen into the yeomanry corps. He wrote that several leading gentleman in Armagh had told him that it was "of great utility" to the government that religious disputes should exist between Catholics and Presbyterians.[74] One of these gentlemen may well have been the Reverend Edward Hudson, who reported meeting the "Popish Priest from Louth" in May 1797.[75] For his part, Hudson had predicted the dissolution of the alliance as early as 1794. "The two Poles will never meet to crush the Equator between them," he wrote, referring to the alliance of Presbyterians and Catholics in Armagh.[76]

Modern historiography tends to support the view that the rebellion in Ulster was defeated primarily by the sectarianism that tore apart the brotherhood of United Irishmen, and blame is placed squarely on the shoulders of the Defenders.[77] But the image of the Defenders as a unilaterally sectarian body sometimes approaches a caricature, seizing on the ugliest feature of the Defenders and exaggerating it, so that other features recede into the background. Although the Armagh Defenders had begun life as a defensive association of Catholics who were victimized by the Peep O'Day Boys, by the early 1790s they had developed a fairly sophisticated organization, with a diverse membership and a middle-class Catholic leadership.[78] In some places, such as the Forkhill estate, they appeared to serve as a subversive force policing the community, punishing informers, attacking the constabulary and magistracy, and harassing tax collectors. In other places, their concern was the correction of grievances connected with land tenure, wages, and taxation. The spread of the United Irish gospel apparently persuaded a number of them that the route to redressing these grievances lay in the fundamental restructuring of Ireland's political apparatus, which would have to be accomplished by force. This is the call that the Forkhill rebels, sitting at the market stone, claimed that they were waiting for in 1798. Admittedly, it is not known when the "The Market Stone" was written – whether shortly after the events of the late 1790s or in the patriotic fervour that surrounded the commemorative celebrations at the rebellion's centenary.

It also is difficult to know what heights the sectarian temperature reached in Forkhill in 1797. The existence of the local yeomanry corps from late 1796 probably fanned the flames of religious division in the region, especially after the brutal crackdown on the Armagh rebels in the spring of 1797 and the savage rout of the mob outside Forkhill in May.[79] Unfortunately, Colonel Ogle provided no information about his yeomanry corps – how widely it was recruited and how active it was. The fact that he was fired upon many times as he patrolled the countryside around Forkhill was likely not because he was a Protestant; it was because he was a yeoman, a hostile magistrate, and, by most accounts, a thug, who at the 1795 spring assizes faced charges of assaulting two local men.[80] It is worth noting that when, in the spring of 1797, Ogle reported to Dublin Castle on the level of disturbance in south Armagh, he described the disaffected as "offenders," "rebels," "rascals," "traitors," and "United Irishmen" – but never as "Catholics." And although a number of churches in Armagh were burned and attacked by angry mobs in the late 1790s, the Protestant church in Forkhill was unscathed. (A 1798 return of the establishment churches in the rural deanery of Creggan reported that the Forkhill church, the most prominent symbol of Protestantism in the parish, was "in perfect repair" both inside and out.)[81]

But there is no question that times had changed. Jim Smyth has remarked upon the collapse of "gentry hegemony" in Ireland in the 1790s and the sudden vulnerability of the Big House.[82] The torching of Forkhill Lodge in 1797 was a dramatic local example of this fall from grace. Just two years earlier, Susanna Barton had been the recipient of a petition from the inhabitants of Forkhill in recognition of her patronage in financing the construction of the new militia quarters, Belmont Barracks. Her admirers thanked her for her kindness and many indulgences, noting that trade in the parish had been much improved under the "genial rays of [her] fostering attention."[83] It is not known how many tenants signed this petition, and it would be unwise to assume that the sentiments they expressed were entirely representative. But her late brother, the former landlord of the estate Richard Jackson, had been warmly regarded by the local people, Catholics and Protestants alike.

There is an extraordinary story about Richard Jackson holding a meeting with the Oakboys at Forkhill Lodge during the disturbances in the summer of 1763. The Oakboys, or Hearts of Oak, consisted mainly of Ulster Presbyterians who were agitating for reductions in both the county cess and the tithe. An estimated twenty thousand Oakboys were active in Armagh that summer, and an observer who saw them parading along the road to Markethill said that they "fill'd at least two miles of the road."[84] He noted that they marched in companies, and he counted thirty of them on the road, each with its own drums, horns, fiddles, and bagpipes. On 5 July an armed party of several thousand Oakboys marched to Forkhill, where the group descended on the house of Richard Jackson, who was then a justice for Armagh. "Having notice of their visit some days before [Jackson] ordered his house to be kept open for as many as it could contain, and offered to regale the rest with several barrels of ale. A park was opened for their horses, all of which their chiefs politely refused. Whereupon Mr J[ackso]n road [sic] in company with six of these persons whom he knew, into Newry." Once there, he "signed some papers drawn up by the rioters [and] with much difficulty got out of their hands."[85] The civility and respect which Jackson paid to the protesters was uncommon and contributed to his reputation locally as a good-hearted landlord.

This sentiment was echoed in a well-known Irish ballad, "The Boys of Mullaghbawn," which laments the fate of several men from Forkhill who were "charged with combination" and transported from Ireland. Local tradition traces the song to the disturbances of the 1790s, when men were allegedly transported for involvement in the Defender disturbances and for membership in the United Irish movement. The song implies that the men had been betrayed by a member of the community, an informer, whose low character is contrasted with the integrity of the former landlord. "Squire Jackson was unequalled, for honour or for reason / He never turned a traitor, nor betrayed the rights of man."[86] On Jackson's death in 1787, the *Belfast News-letter* reported that his body was attended to the grave by a great number of his tenants and labourers, and "the distress manifested by these poor people was truly affecting." The stone slab that marks Jackson's grave in the old Protestant churchyard in Forkhill declares that he was a "firm friend to the religious and civil constitution of his country, he exerted his most strenuous endeavour for its improvement by an almost constant residence on his estate ... [and] by a lenient indulgence to his poorer tenants."[87]

It appears that a system of patronage had existed between Jackson and his tenants, and the lax management of the estate that Hudson complained about in 1789 represented a measure of generosity on Jackson's part, rather than negligence. This understanding between landlord and tenants was disrupted by Jackson's death in 1787, when supervision of the estate was taken over by business-minded trustees, who were determined to strike at the root of the inefficiency and introduce "improvements" on a grand scale. Nevertheless, Jackson's patronage of his tenants continued because of his charitable bequests in the spheres of education, medical assistance, and charity for the old and infirm. Indeed, his influence continued to be felt for at least the next sixty years.

4

Land and People, 1821

Historical sources are often generated by an event, such as the 1791 attack in Forkhill, which elicited widespread alarm, or the 1798 rebellion, which generated extensive correspondence between Dublin Castle and local authorities. But sometimes sources capture a historian's attention because of what they are and because they are worthy of examination as artifacts themselves. Several years ago I had the extraordinary luck to find a manuscript-bound copy of the 1821 census for Forkhill – extraordinary because most copies of the census for every parish in Ireland were destroyed in the fires that swept through Dublin's Four Courts in 1922. Scraps of local censuses for several counties are preserved in the Public Record Office, but only a few complete volumes of the original manuscripts for the Ulster counties are known to have survived, and these relate only to County Fermanagh. The Forkhill census was buried midway in a stack of old folios that were stored in the study of the current Church of Ireland rector of south Armagh. The books, which include the minutes of Richard Jackson's trust dating back to 1789, the account ledgers for the charity, and the 1829 tithe applotment book for the parish, had been passed down through the hands of successive Church of Ireland rectors for close to two hundred years. They had long since outlived their usefulness for the clergymen and had been left to gather dust.

The 1821 census was the first general enumeration of Ireland carried to completion and the first tentatively reliable estimate of the population. Although a statutory census of Ireland had been undertaken between 1813 and 1815, it was plagued by administrative difficulties and its results are generally considered unreliable.[1] The enumeration had been carried out by constables, who were generally disliked and distrusted, and supervision of the work was entrusted to inexperienced grand juries. The fact that the census was held during a period of unrest in many parts of the country further handicapped the enterprise. By 1814, only ten districts in Ireland had furnished complete returns, and twenty-six districts had provided defective returns.[2]

Learning from this experience, the government passed legislation in 1815 which sought to improve the uniformity of the next enumeration, scheduled for 1821. Under the new law, enumerators were carefully selected, screened, and instructed in their duties. Preference of appointment was given to tax collectors, because they were familiar with their districts and had some practice in keeping records. In order to determine whether or not the appointees were qualified, they were required to make preliminary test returns specifying the names and number of the townlands in the parish to which they had been assigned, the names and addresses of all resident clergymen, and the names and addresses of schoolmasters and their schools. Once the Chief Secretary's Office had approved the test returns, each enumerator received a set of instructions describing in detail how he should undertake the business of enumeration. The instructions were framed on the principle that nothing should be required from the enumerator "but matter of fact, excluding anything depending solely on opinion or deduction." Enumerators were instructed to execute their duty "in the mildest and most inoffensive manner," and the spirit of this instruction was manifest throughout the guidelines.[3] Conflict between officials and local people during the collection of hearth returns had arisen in the past, whether out of ignorance, suspicion, or resentment at the presence of government officials in the countryside, and the government was prepared for hostility to the enumeration. In advance of the census, the Dublin administration sent a letter to all resident clergymen in the country, requesting their help in explaining to their parishioners the purpose of the census. This measure seemed to have a good effect, and few disruptions to the enumeration were reported.[4]

To encourage uniformity among the returns, the enumerators were issued with a specific set of definitions for each category of inquiry and were equipped with a sufficient number of notebooks, in ruled columns, for filling in the required information.[5] The manuscript book of the Forkhill census was organized and completed in accordance with these instructions. The twenty-two townlands were arranged alphabetically, from Aughadanove to Tullymacreeve, and each household was assigned a number within the townland.[6] The enumerator for Forkhill was Robert Balmer, a substantial Protestant farmer who was constable for the barony of Upper Orior and lived in the townland of Tiffcrum.[7] Balmer was instructed to begin work on the morning of 28 May 1821, going from house to house every day except Sunday until the census was complete. He was required to report his progress to the Chief Secretary's Office every two weeks.

As a resident of Forkhill and as a local constable, Balmer was in a better position to provide an accurate return than enumerators who were strangers to their districts. Indeed, although the nationwide results of the 1821 census proved much more comprehensive than earlier attempts, they were admittedly imperfect.[8] It is believed that the national population return of 6,801,826 was an underestimate, owing to undercounting, boundary confusion, and the absence of seasonal labourers during the enumeration months of June and July.[9] Because of Balmer's familiarity with the parish and the people, the results for Forkhill were probably better than the average.

The census of 1821 collected information under six headings: the names of all members of the household, their relationship to the head of the household, their ages, their occupations (where relevant), and the size of their homestead.[10] A final column, headed Observations, was appended for comments on miscellaneous items, such as cases of illegitimacy and physical disabilities. The government did not inquire into religious affiliation in Ireland until 1834 and did not include a question on religion in the decennial census until 1861.[11] However, some unknown hand has gone over the Forkhill census with a pencil, marking 106 households as Protestant. It is difficult to determine when these notes were added, but the style of the handwriting suggests that they are from the nineteenth century. It appears that the unknown writer also neglected to label six households that were almost certainly Protestant on the basis of their distinct surnames. In all, 112 Protestant households could be identified with reasonable certainty. The identification of these Protestant households presented the opportunity of asking a question that had not been asked and of attempting to construct a religious enumeration of the parish around 1821.

Using the identification of the 106 Protestant families marked in the manuscript, I created two banks of surnames: one of Protestant names and one of Catholic.[12] I assumed that every dependent member of a household who was related to the head of the household by blood or marriage shared the religious affiliation of the household head, and I assigned their denominations on this basis. For the unrelated members of the household, such as lodgers, apprentices, and servants, I used the name bank, checking their surnames against the list of verifiably Protestant and Catholic surnames. In the few cases in which a surname did not match a name in either list and could not be otherwise determined, I considered the Christian name of the individual, for the census revealed some evidence of religiously conscious naming practices.

Using this method, I was able to ascribe a religious affiliation to every individual who was named in the 1821 census: 5,791 Catholics and 537 Protestants (33 others were identified only as "inhabitants" and were not enumerated individually).[13] Given the degree of estimation involved, the results are not equivalent to an actual religious census and are probably imperfect. However, they do correspond to other religious returns for the parish during the mid-nineteenth century. According to the transcribed returns of the religious census of 1834, there were 6,562 Catholics and 479 Protestants in Forkhill, while a diocesan return commissioned in 1836 identified 6,582 Catholics and 481 Protestants living in the parish.[14] Allowing for the passage of more than a decade, the figures for 1821 appear to be tentatively reliable estimates.

The census data collected on age, gender, family relationships, land occupation, and employment could form the basis of endless inquiries into the system of land tenure, economic status, patterns of marriage, the constitution of families, and modes of employment. For the historian of nineteenth-century Ireland, accustomed to the scarcity of records on the structure of rural life, the 1821 census is an invaluable resource. I cannot do justice to the information it contains and have chosen to narrow my focus to three categories of inquiry: the constitution of households and families; the occupation of land; and the distribution of labour. Inquiry into these particular aspects of life will permit us to construct a social profile of Forkhill in the early 1820s and also to compare the communities of Catholics and Protestants within each category. The second part of the inquiry is instrumental to the argument of this book – namely, that our assumptions about the behaviour and characteristics of Catholics and Protestants in Ireland condition our understanding of the past, sometimes to the point of distortion. The seeds of sectarianism are sown in the assumption that Catholics and Protestants are fundamentally different. But were they really so different?

HOUSEHOLDS AND FAMILIES

In 1810 an Englishman named John Gamble made a tour of Dublin and the north of Ireland, recording his observations in a volume of *Sketches*. In a memorable passage, he described the difference between Catholics and Protestants, and their families: "The Protestant ... is often thirty before he marries. At thirty the passions cool, and he seldom has a very numerous offspring. The Catholic, more thoughtless, more improvident, more amorous perhaps, takes a wife when he is yet a lad, piles up a heap of sods into a cabin, eats potatoes, and gets children like a patriarch of old. It is no unusual thing for his wife to bear ten or twelve, or even more, children ... These poor, naked, ill-fed, neglected children grow up hardy, stout and vigorous men ...What a contrast to the sickly and delicate sons of fashion, who are nursed, and pampered, and dandled into effeminancy!"[15]

Gamble was not alone in his assumptions about families in Ireland, although the lack of reliable data on pre-famine Irish family size has made it difficult to contest generalizations.[16] The 1821 census will allow us to test such assumptions, especially those about the difference between Catholic and Protestant family sizes. But before doing so, it will be useful to have some idea of the organization of family groups in the parish. Using the system of classification devised by the anthropologists Eugene Hammel and Peter Laslett, I sorted 1,188 of the 1,197 households in the parish into one of five categories: solitary households (head of the household living alone); non-related households (two or more people unrelated by blood or marriage); simple family households (a married couple or a widow/er living with one or more children, i.e., the biological family); extended family households (the biological family and one or more persons related by blood or marriage to a member of the conjugal family unit); and finally, multiple family households (two married couples of different generations living under the same roof).[17]

Within both communities, the simple family household was by far the most common. Close to three-quarters of all households consisted of biological families rather than extended or multiple family groups. This indicates that the people observed a particular pattern of land inheritance (subdivision), in which the farm was carved into portions and divided among the male heirs, rather than being passed intact to the eldest son. Over the course of two or three generations, the practice of subdivision reduced the size of farms very considerably, making it more difficult to provide sustainable homesteads for the next generation and prolonging the time before adult males came into their inheritance. In some parts of Ireland, it was not unusual for a young man to marry and bring his wife into his parents' household, thereby creating a multiple family household. Often this was not a desirable situation: the young man remained under the thumb of his father, who was still the head of the household, and there was frequently tension in households that contained two generations of married people. But multiple families account for only 4 per cent of the households in Forkhill, suggesting that the preferred cultural route within both communities was for young couples to set up independent homesteads upon marriage.[18]

As a consequence, the establishment of independent households in Forkhill occurred quite late. In 1821 less than 10 per cent of all heads

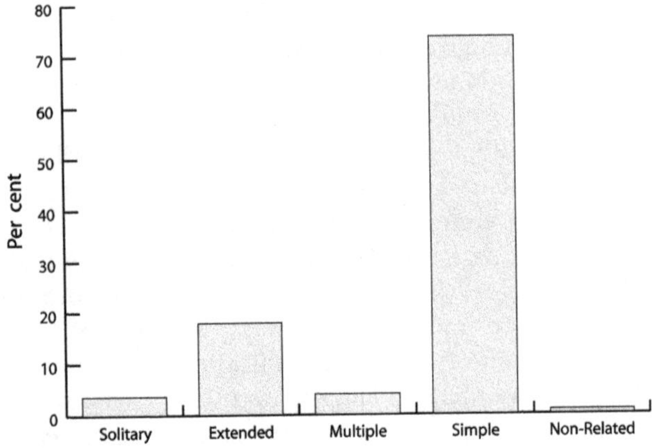

Figure 1 Types of household, 1821

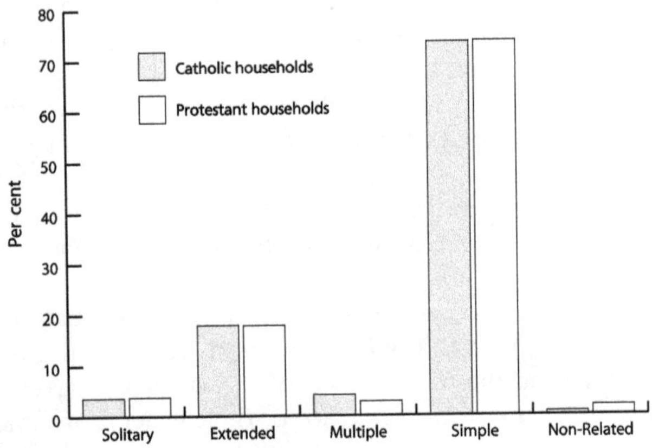

Figure 2 Types of household by denomination, 1821

of households were under the age of thirty, and fully two-thirds were over forty years.[19] This is despite the fact that the population itself was decidedly young: 68 per cent were under the age of thirty. It can be argued that the scarcity of land prevented the early establishment of households and perhaps also affected patterns of marriage and childbirth. If land had been readily available, there probably would have been a greater number of independent households in 1821. Indeed, the pattern of inheritance in the Protestant community, which controlled a greater proportion of land, suggests that this observation is true. Among the 112 Protestant households, nearly 20 per cent of household heads were under the age of thirty. In the Catholic community, which was not as land-rich, the figure was less than 8 per cent. The discrepancy is an indication that the early establishment of independent households was desirable where possible – but often was not possible.

Apart from this distinction, there was considerable similarity of household organization between Catholics and Protestants (see figure 2). Both groups contained a majority of simple family households and a large number of extended family units, and both had far fewer households of single individuals, multiple families, and unrelated groups.[20] The similar pattern of household composition suggests that at the most basic level of human organization (the family unit), the behaviour of Catholics and Protestants was virtually identical.

The size of the households and families within both communities was also similar. The enumerator was instructed to include all persons residing in the house on the day of the census as members of the "household," including servants, lodgers, visitors, and orphans. According to this definition, the average household in Forkhill in 1821 consisted of 5.3 persons – which was comparable to available figures for other parts of the country. F.J. Carney has conducted an analysis of pre-famine Irish household size and composition based on a one-in-six random sample of the surviving manuscript returns for the 1821 census: a total of 2,663 households in Cavan, Meath, Fermanagh, King's, and Galway.[21] Among these five counties, the mean household size ranged from 5.45 to 5.86 persons, which was actually higher than the reported average for Forkhill.[22]

A denominational breakdown reveals a slight discrepancy between the communities. The average size of Catholic households in the parish was 5.3 persons. Protestant households were marginally larger, with an average of 5.5 persons. This does not mean that Protestant families were larger, however.[23] Rather, the discrepancy appears to involve the number of individuals who were attached to Protestant households as domestic workers: more Protestant than Catholic households had servants, and Protestants typically employed more servants per household than Catholics.[24] This tendency resulted in a slightly inflated mean household size for Protestants in Forkhill.

More interesting is the size of the simple or biological family, though this is a difficult figure to calculate with certainty. The average biological family in Forkhill (based on the 872 households that were strictly simple family units), was 5.06 persons.[25] This is probably an undercount, though by what margin it is impossible to know. The reconstruction of biological families from census data does not account for the invisible cases of miscarriage, abortion, infant mortality, child mortality, fosterage, seasonal migration, and emigration that divested families of their kin. If we can accept that the two communities were affected in similar ways by these unknowns variables, however, then a comparison between the family size of Catholics and Protestants is a valid exercise. The result of this comparison is striking. The average Catholic family consisted of 5.06 persons, and the average Protestant family consisted of 5.05 persons, making the size of biological families within the two communities virtually identical. The image of Catholic families as larger than average and spilling over with children (as per John Gamble's description) is misleading. In this context, the problem of land scarcity appears to be less a consequence of population pressure than of a system of land tenure and inheritance that was unsustainable over the long term. The occupancy of land in Forkhill appears to have followed this pattern.

THE OCCUPATION OF LAND

The occupation of land in the parish is important for two reasons. First, within a decade of the enumeration, south Armagh became a cockpit of outrage, beginning with the tithe agitation of the early 1830s. As we shall see in chapter 7, agrarian outrage was a feature of the land system and the scarcity of ground, and the increasing inability of the land to support the population. Analysis of the size and distribution of farms in Forkhill in 1821 will give us some idea of the situation the people faced twenty years later, on the eve of the famine. Second, farm size can be a rough index of socio-economic status, though this correlation must be handled carefully. According to the rules governing the census question on land, the enumerator was obliged to fill in the number of acres occupied by each household. The return was thus an indication of property occupation rather than of individual property holdings.[26] For example, if a landholder leased land to another small farmer or labourer, this portion was not included in his own census return; it was in the return of the undertenant.[27] A comparison of land returns in the census with those in the tithe applotment book for 1828 suggests that this often occurred.

The size distribution of the 1,197 farms is displayed in figure 3 and is broken down according to denomination in figure 4. The census reveals that the farms in Forkhill were very small indeed, the average size being only 4.3 acres; 21 per cent of all farms in the parish were under 1 acre, and 63 per cent were less than 5 acres.[28]

In the Catholic community, farms were concentrated in the 1–4 acre and 5–9 acre range; the average Catholic homestead was 4.1 acres. The vast majority of these households were farming households that derived their sustenance and principal income from working the land. The pressure of supporting a family on a farm of this size must have been tremendous. Not only did these few acres have to yield enough

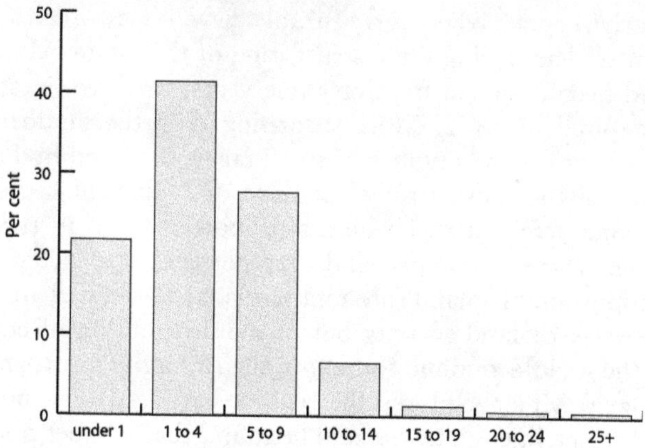

Figure 3 Size distribution of farms, 1821

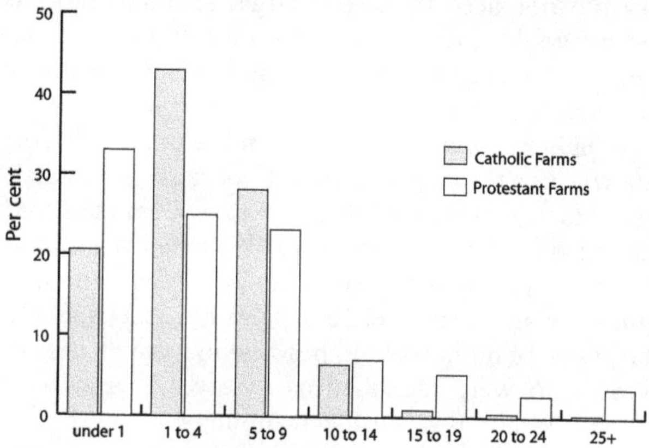

Figure 4 Size distribution of farms by denomination, 1821

to feed a family of five (on average), but they had to be superabundant, yielding crops that could be sold for cash at market in order to pay the rent, which was due twice a year. A system of crop rotation, which was favoured by agriculturalists as a way of enriching the soil by allowing it to lie fallow every few years, was out of the question. More worrying was the prospect of providing for the next generation; when divided among sons, a farm of four acres was a meagre inheritance.

The profile of farms in the Protestant community was rather different. Proportionately, there were more substantial Protestant farmers than Catholic farmers. Nearly 12 per cent of Protestant farms were larger than fifteen acres; among Catholics, the figure was less than 2 per cent. As I explained in chapter 2, this pattern is traceable to the settlement of the early 1790s, when forty sizable new leases were granted to Protestant settlers during the restructuring of the estate. Most of these leases had been assigned for thirty-one years, or three lives, and had not yet expired in 1821. More surprising than the number of large Protestant farms is the number of small farms occupied by Protestants at the time of the census; fully one-third of Protestant farms were of less than one acre – a much higher proportion than in the Catholic population, where it was just under 21 per cent.[29]

The proportion of small Protestant farms, however, was an indication not of poverty or land scarcity but of the distribution of labour. In a study of the socio-economic context of the Armagh Disturbances in the 1780s, David Miller explored the relationship between land and participation in the linen industry, and he found that competition for land among weavers was less intense in the parts of Armagh where the linen industry prospered. Since weavers earned their primary income at the loom, they did not need to keep a large farm and required only as much land as would hold a cabin and a small garden.[30] This feature of the linen economy explains how Armagh, which was one of the most prosperous counties in Ireland because of the linen trade, could also support the highest population density in the country.[31] Although the linen trade was not thriving in Forkhill, more than one-quarter of the labouring population were identified as weavers, spinners, or flax dressers, indicating that the industry was still carried on to some degree. Thus we might expect to see a correlation between participation in the weaving industry and farm size. To test this hypothesis, I calculated the average farm size of all household heads who were identified as "farmers" and all who were identified as "weavers," and compared the results.[32] The correlation was evident. Among farmers the average farm size in the parish was 5.7 acres, while among weavers it was 2.5 acres – less than half. Significantly, the average size of Protestant farmers' farms was 10.0 acres, compared with an average of 5.5 acres for Catholic farmers' farms.[33] Again, this disparity is probably a consequence of the land settlement of the 1790s and the early pattern of land distribution among Protestant and Catholic leaseholders.

In the Protestant community, the relationship between farm size and employment extended beyond the weaving trade. Of the 112 Protestant households in the parish, 37 were situated on less than one acre of land. The majority of these households derived their principal income from the skilled trades or professions: six heads of household were engaged in skilled trades, five were professionals (four teachers and the resident surgeon), nineteen were employed in the linen industry as weavers or spinners, two were servants, and two were pensioners. Only three heads of household were labourers; in other words, only 8 per

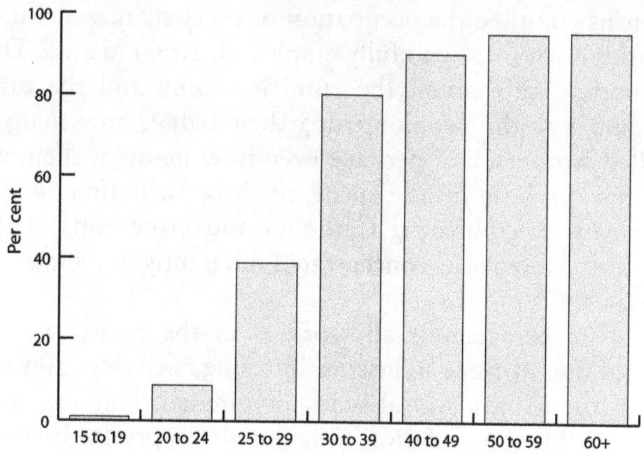

Figure 5 Proportion of males in each age group who were heads of independent households, 1821

cent of Protestant households situated on less than one acre derived their principal income from labouring or from working the land. The profile of land occupation and labour in the Catholic community was rather different. Among the Catholic households situated on less than one acre, 34 per cent of the household heads were designated as "labourers," indicating that they had no other trade and derived their principal income from labouring on neighbouring farms.

THE LANDSCAPE OF LABOUR

The census of 1821 revealed that the population of the parish was decidedly young. More than 40 per cent were under the age of fifteen and close to 70 per cent were under the age of thirty. The age structure of the parish matches the model for preindustrial populations in which the high survival rate of women of childbearing age had lowered the death rate, while the birth rate remained at a relatively high level.[34] This demographic profile had significant social and economic implications for families. In young populations, the relatively large number of children in the household placed heavier burdens on the family by increasing the number of mouths to be fed without necessarily widening the family's income base. Although the families in Forkhill were not large by European standards, their farms were very small, and this stretched their resources considerably. The possibility of putting children to work on the land became more remote as the subdivision of land steadily reduced the size of the farms.[35] The occupation profile for the parish reveals that families employed several strategies to cope with the situation, which we will discuss below.[36]

The census recorded the occupation of every man, woman, boy, and girl in Forkhill who was gainfully employed, 2,799 in all.[37] This profile can tell us not only about the rural economy and the diversity of industry but how the people earned their living, how many of them were skilled workers, and perhaps even how many of them were educated. It tells us how people spent much of their time, and it offers another means of comparing Catholics and Protestants in the parish to see whether labour was concentrated differently in their communities and, if so, why.[38]

Close to 95 per cent of all workers in the parish were engaged primarily in one of three industries: farming, weaving, and household service. Of these, agricultural work dominated. Fully 74 per cent of the male working population was involved primarily in farming, whether as "farmers," "labourers," or "farmer/labourers." The difference between farmers and labourers in the census was based on the amount of land they occupied rather than on how they divided their labour, though contemporary accounts suggest that this distinction was often artificial. Enumerators were instructed to record every person who held two or more acres of land as a farmer; if he also worked as a day labourer, his occupation was to be recorded as "farmer and labourer." However, many men who were technically labourers also held small portions of land, calling themselves farmers "in the common language of the country." Despite this minor confusion, the census returns clearly demonstrate that the vast majority of people, and the majority of households, supported themselves by working the land.

When we examine the occupational profiles of Catholics and Protestants, some meaningful distinctions emerge. First, proportionately more Catholics than Protestants were employed as farmers and/or labourers. More than three-quarters of the Catholic male working population were farmers or farm workers, and 78 per cent of Catholic heads of households earned their living by working the land. In contrast, Protestants were much less likely to be engaged in agricultural work. Less than half of Protestant male workers were farmers or labourers, and only 40 per cent of Protestant household heads derived their income primarily from the land. As I suggested in the section on farm size, Protestant households were less dependent on farming and on the land because of their greater participation in the skilled trades, especially the weaving industry. Fully 28 per cent of Protestant working men were weavers or flax dressers, a degree of representation more than three times higher than among Catholic working men. This trend can be traced to the initiatives undertaken to settle the parish with weavers in the late 1780s and to the provisions for young weaving apprentices made in Richard Jackson's bequest.[39] For this reason, I hesitate to

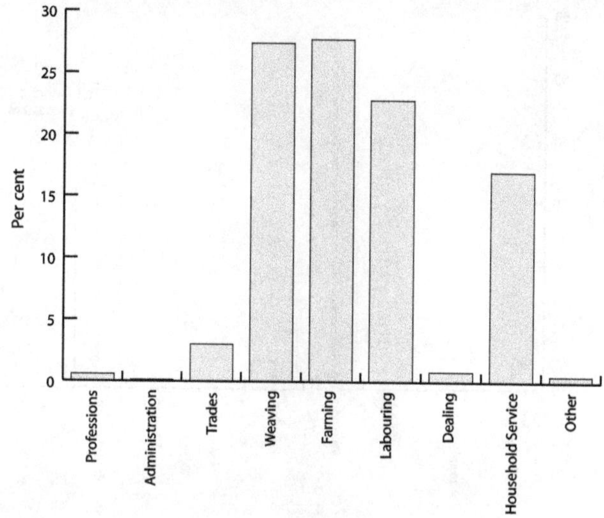

Figure 6 Occupations of males and females, 1821

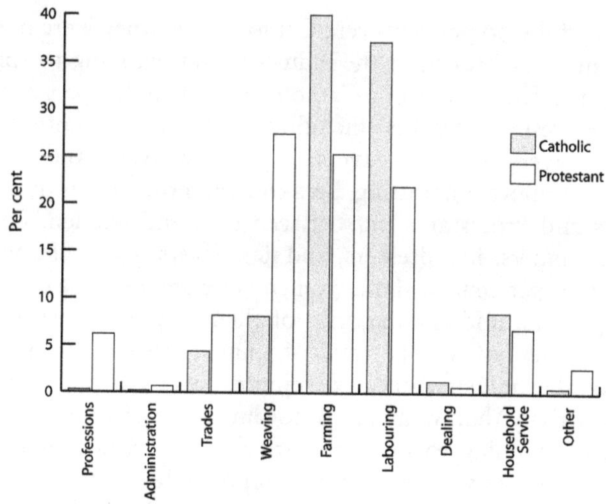

Figure 7 Occupations of males by denomination, 1821

attribute the varying distribution of occupations in the denominations to cultural differences; opportunity was a more important factor.

Although proportionally the representation of Protestants in the linen industry was greater than that of Catholics, there were in fact many more Catholics engaged in the industry. Of the 770 workers in the parish who were identified as weavers, spinners, flax dressers, or

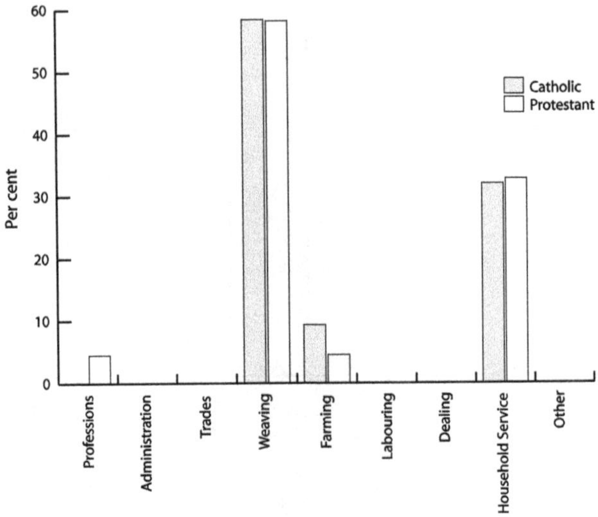

Figure 8 Occupations of females by denomination, 1821

flax dryers, fully 90 per cent were Catholics, and they were numerically superior in every branch of the industry, from weaving to spinning to flax dressing. There were 115 Catholic weavers in the parish compared with 40 Protestant weavers (including linen weavers, cotton weavers, woollen weavers, farmer/weavers, labourer/weavers, and journeymen weavers). A more interesting breakdown, however, is not between Catholics and Protestants but between men and women. Of the 770 weavers, spinners, flax dressers, and flax dryers, 597 were women (78 per cent); 99 per cent of these women were spinners, flax spinners, or farmer/spinners, and the majority of them (63 per cent) were under the age of twenty-five. The ratio of spinners to weavers was characteristic of the industry, because spinning was a much more labour-intensive activity than weaving. According to an 1812 estimate, it took six days of spinning to produce yarn for one day's weaving, and at least four spinners were required to supply one full-time weaver with yarn.[40] The ratio of spinners to weavers in Forkhill in 1821 was roughly 6:1.

The 1821 census is one of the rare occasions in the history of this parish when the role of women was recorded. Virtually every eyewitness whose testimony I have drawn upon to write this history has been a man, preoccupied for the most part with the doings of other men. Reading through the 1821 census – which lists the names and ages and family bonds of every daughter, sister, mother, and grandmother – is an almost startling reminder of women's presence in the parish. But here, too, their roles are strictly supporting. Women were identified on the basis of their relationship to the head of the household, who in nearly all cases was a man. The enumerators assumed that married women were housekeepers, and wives were assigned no separate occupation. Women who never married (spinsters) remained at home or lived with married siblings, or they might serve as a housekeeper in the home of an unmarried or widowed man. Most female children lived with their parents and started work at the age of fifteen, either within the household as spinners or outside the home as servants or housekeepers. In households where the father had been widowed, the eldest daughter usually assumed the role of housekeeper. Widowed women were identified as "widows," though if title to the land had passed to them, the enumerators were instructed to record them as "farmers."

A sizable proportion of households in the parish (17 per cent) were headed by women, most of them widows. Two of these households had rather unusual constellations. The forty-eight-year-old widow of Henry McClore lived on a three-acre farm in Carriff with her son Patrick Murphy and her two daughters, Margaret Louther and Mary Murphy. Margaret, twenty-one years of age, was identified in the census as an illegitimate child, and the others may have been born outside wedlock as well. Two other women, Jane Gass and Catherine Burns, were lodgers in the house, along with an infant girl, Margaret McConly, who was labelled "illegitimate." The other household was in the townland of Shean, where Sarah Cooley, aged seventy years, lived next door to the Methodist chapel with her illegitimate daughter, Isabella McNeill, and her five illegitimate granddaughters: Julia Colethorpe, Eleanor Begley, Mary Dougall, Elizabeth Dawson, and Mary Magill, whose ages ranged from one to sixteen years. These households, which were conspicuous in the parish, raise an interesting question about the extent of illegitimacy in the region in the pre-famine period. The enumerator, Robert Balmer, recorded twenty-eight cases of illegitimacy (entered in the column of "Observations"), but it is unlikely that this figure represents its full extent.[41] Bearing children out of wedlock was a cultural taboo, and people would not willingly have been forthcoming about cases of illegitimacy in their household.[42] Balmer probably recorded the cases of which he had personal knowledge, and the pattern of identification supports this theory. All of the recorded instances in the census involve individuals twenty-five years old and younger, and sixteen of them were under the age of ten – which suggests that public memory of illegitimate births faded as the years passed.

The third major occupational sector in the parish was household service, which accounted for 17 per cent of all occupations. Here, too, women were heavily represented, accounting for 69 per cent of those employed in this service, most of them being recorded as "servants."[43] This figure does not include the 830 women who were identified as "wives" and for whom no other occupation was recorded. Interestingly, among the population of Catholics and Protestants, the proportion of household workers was very close, particularly among working women: 32 per cent of female Catholic workers and 33 per cent of female Protestant workers were attached to households as servants or housekeepers. Among Catholic and Protestant men, the gap was slightly larger: 8.5 per cent of male Catholic workers and 7 per cent of male Protestant workers were employed in a domestic setting.

The age profile of these household workers is revealing. The vast majority of servants (81 per cent) were under the age of twenty-five, and only 6 per cent were over the age of forty – a sign that household service was a temporary occupation rather than a vocation.[44] Like the work of spinners and labourers, domestic service was a transitional phase between adolescent usefulness and adult independence. Household service fulfilled a further function: it seems to have served as a means of regulating household size by allowing large families to farm out their children to households that could afford to keep them; 30 per cent of the servants in Forkhill were under the age of fifteen, and a handful were under ten. The youngest, Edward Murray, was only seven years old. The system of fosterage provided a means for families to relieve economic pressure by sending one or two children to work in other households and earn their keep.

The long-standing practice of migrant labour served a similar purpose. Many young men, once they reached the age of fifteen, regularly left the parish to work the harvest in England or elsewhere in Ireland. A look at the gender balance in the parish shows a higher proportion of males to females under the age of fifteen years, which is common in most populations.[45] But after age fifteen, the ratio is reversed, which indicates the prevalence of migrant labour in the parish rather than a sudden change in the birth ratio. The stabilization of the gender ratio after the age of thirty suggests that migrant labour was the pursuit of young landless men who eventually settled down as small farmers.

The remaining occupations (the professions, administrative posts, trades, merchant business, and dealing), account for only a fraction of the population (5 per cent), but they were a significant group. Forkhill was a remote parish, situated in the mountains more than five miles from the nearest town, and the day-to-day operations of the community depended almost entirely on the natural and human resources within its bounds. The trades were well represented in the parish and included a basket maker, a cooper, a carter, a thatcher, blacksmiths, carpenters, kilnmen, millers, stonemasons, slaters, and wheelwrights. A religious breakdown of the trades reveals that there were carpenters, blacksmiths, millers, wheelwrights, and tailors of both denominations; there were two shoemakers (both Protestant) and three brogue makers (all Catholic). But I suspect that, given the relative isolation of the parish, there was a regular exchange of services and that the trades were an important arena of social interaction.[46] Catholics were the sole providers of a number of services in the parish (basket weaving, stonemasonry and barrel making appear to have been their preserve), and most Protestants probably took advantage of the convenience of dealing with local tradesmen. In terms of merchants and dealers, Protestants had little option but to deal locally with Catholics, including the butcher, the baker, the local grocer, and both of the shop assistants.[47]

Protestants evened the exchange with the provision of services in health and education. The only "surgeon" in the parish, Dr Leslie, was a Protestant – and he was a busy man. According to the dispensary registry, 6,664 people were treated in the Forkhill dispensary between 1832 and 1835.[48] As we shall see in chapter 5, the system of education also was administered by the Protestant community. By 1821, there were eight schools in the parish, all of them funded by Richard Jackson's charity and each under the supervision of a Protestant schoolmaster or schoolmistress.[49] The resident magistrate and justice of the peace was a Protestant, Mr James Dawson.[50]

Finally, there were two households of clergymen in the parish, one on each side of the river. The Reverend Doctor James Campbell was the Church of Ireland rector of Forkhill from 1817 to 1858.[51] He lived in the Shanroe Glebe, not far from the church, on a farm of eighty-two acres, and his household staff included a butler, a groom, a cook, a housemaid, and two carpenters. The local Catholic priests lived in humbler circumstances in the townland of Longfield on a farm of fifteen acres. The parish priest was the Reverend Nicholas McIvor, then seventy-one years of age, who was recorded as a "farmer & priest." Living with Father McIvor were a curate, a visiting priest, and McIvor's nephew, Patrick Mulligan, who was training for the priesthood. A housekeeper, Bridget Hughes, her two young children, and three servants completed the household.[52]

A SUMMARY REPORT

This chapter has been rather dense. What can we distill from all these numbers and comparisons? At the outset, I stated two objectives: to construct a social profile of Forkhill in 1821 and to compare, within these categories, the communities of Catholics and Protestants in the parish. An analysis of the age structure of the parish revealed that the population in 1821 was young, conspicuously so, and increasing at a rapid rate. Typically, families were not unusually large and even fell below the mean family size reported in other parts of the country. But the farms in Forkhill were small – too small to support many of the families that were dependent on agriculture as their sole source of income. The relationship between shrinking farm size and an increasing population was to reach crisis proportions within twenty years, and there is evidence that the people were already feeling the pressure in 1821. This can be seen in the high proportion of labourers and spinners between the ages of fifteen and nineteen, the number of young men absent from the parish during the enumeration, and the number of children who were farmed out to other households to work as servants.

At first glance, the distribution of occupations shows a healthy proportion of the population engaged in the weaving industry – an auspicious sign in a community where land was scarce. But closer analysis of the industry suggests that weaving was on the decline. There were relatively few full-time weavers in the parish in 1821, and they were a clear minority compared with the small army of local farmers and labourers who were competing for land and work.[53] The social profile of Forkhill in 1821 was characterized by an increasing population, dwindling resources, and the homogenization of the rural economy. Already, a process had been set in train that would make the poverty, unrest, and famine of the next thirty years difficult to avoid.

In terms of our comparison between Catholics and Protestants, I am left with the feeling that there was not much difference between them. Both had the same type of household and family. Their families were remarkably close in size; they employed servants in roughly equal proportions; and they were situated, for the most part, on small farms. Certainly, there was a coterie of Protestants who were wealthy and had more land and employed more servants than others, and it had no equivalent in the Catholic community; but this small elite amounted to a handful of households and was not typical of the Protestant population in general.

One important difference was the extensive engagement of Protestants in the weaving industry and their greater representation in the trades. They could afford to live on smaller farms because they earned their income through trade and industry and thus had a security which many Catholic farmers lacked. But because this security and prosperity was situated in such small farms, these Protestants did not represent a threat to the land-hungry Catholic population, nor would they have been an obvious source of resentment. Even though they were prosperous, they did not necessarily seem to be so. If Protestants had been big farmers, in Big Houses, coming and going in horse-drawn carriages, the chasm between the communities would have been more painfully clear and might have inspired more hostility than it did. But the reasons for the scarcity of land and the sources of resentment had roots within the Catholic community, and over the course of the next twenty-five years these disputes would be resolved internally – and often violently. We shall examine this dynamic more closely in chapter 6, but will turn next to the history of education in the parish from 1790 onward.

5

Education, 1790–1861

In 1834 Father Daniel O'Rafferty, the parish priest of Forkhill, completed an application for a grant-in-aid from the national board of education. The board had been created in 1831 and had only lately begun processing applications, but O'Rafferty wasted no time. He objected vigorously to the existing network of schools in the parish, which were endowed by Richard Jackson's charity and had provided the Catholic children of Forkhill with a Protestant education for almost fifty years. According to O'Rafferty, the "seduction" of Catholic pupils by the trustees of the charity and the sly proselytism of the curriculum in their schools was "the grand source of obloquy, dissension and strife" in the parish. He was sure that the establishment of a non-denominational national school, in which literary education and religious education were carefully separated, would "soon dry up this fountain of anarchy and discontent."[1]

The relationship between religion and education in Ireland had been cultivated since the mid-sixteenth century, when Henry VIII had attempted to establish a system of Protestant schools in every parish in the country. In his view, nothing kept his Irish subjects so "savage" and "wild" as their persistence in a different language, and a 1537 statute establishing free schools in Ireland was explicit about its purpose: "That every person … inhabiting this land of Ireland … shall use and speake commonly the English tongue and language."[2] Other initiatives followed, including the ordinance under Elizabeth I to establish free schools in every diocese in Ireland and the establishment of charter schools in the 1730s. All of these schools shared a distinct political purpose: the civilization of the Catholic population through education in the English language, instruction in English manners, and subscription to Protestantism. Until the nineteenth century, all state-sponsored schools in Ireland were primarily instruments of religious conversion.

None of these schools enjoyed any measure of lasting success, however, and, although they persisted into the nineteenth century, they never enrolled more than a small fraction of the student population.

This contemporary view of the relationship between religion and education inspired the most controversial of the eighteenth-century penal laws in the wake of the Williamite wars (1689–91). These discriminatory measures directed against the Catholic Church and Catholic laity were intended to shore up the Protestant interest in Ireland, and they included the infamous 1695 statute banning education under Catholic schoolteachers. This "Act to restrain foreign education in Ireland" forbade any papist from teaching school in Ireland under threat of fine, imprisonment, and transportation. The several statutes passed between 1695 and 1709 restricting Catholic education were intended to limit the opportunities for the education of Catholic priests and to direct children into the Protestant schools – not to reduce the population to a state of ignorance and subjugation.[3] But they failed in their purpose. The early eighteenth century witnessed the beginning of what P.J. Dowling has called a "guerrilla war in education" as Catholics resorted to clandestine measures to educate themselves. An underground system of hedge schools emerged in the countryside.[4] These makeshift classrooms were held outdoors and out of sight, often on the sunny side of a hedge. Because the schools were most often headed by Catholic schoolmasters and were therefore illegal, the students took turns acting as lookouts, ready to warn the schoolmaster if any suspicious person approached, giving the class time to disperse. The schoolmasters were often itinerant, and they relied on the hospitality of the students and their families for an income and lodging. Householders who harboured a hedge school were liable to be fined, and "popish" schoolmasters were hunted by the authorities at a reward of £10.[5]

This misunderstood feature of the statute spawned one of the best-known stories of the penal days in south Armagh. Peadar O'Doirnin was a well-known poet and scholar, born in north Louth to a Catholic father and a Protestant mother in 1704. He received his elementary education at a hedge school and spent several years travelling throughout the west of Ireland, visiting the best-known schools and studying with celebrated bards. He applied himself to all branches of mathematics, history, music, and poetry and was reportedly fluent in "all the living languages of Europe" as well as in Latin, Greek, and Hebrew.[6] When O'Doirnin returned to Armagh, he set up a hedge school in a chapel on the Louth border, sometime in the 1730s or 1740s. Soon afterwards, the school came under the scrutiny of an unpopular landlord, Johnston of the Fews, who determined to capture the poet, cut off his head, and claim the £10 reward. O'Doirnin was forced to abandon his school and go into hiding. According to legend, Johnston was out searching for O'Doirnin one day when he was seized by a party of Whiteboys. The Whiteboys brought Johnston to the poet and asked him to pronounce a sentence on their prisoner. O'Doirnin thought awhile and then told the Whiteboys to release their captive. A humbled Johnston gave the poet his word that he could return to his school in south Armagh and would be protected against his enemies. O'Doirnin started a new hedge school in the Forkhill area where, in the quiet hours, he turned his attention to "the study of Scripture and meditation." On the morning of 3 April 1769 he lay down on a bench near the door of his school and died in his sleep.[7]

This story about O'Doirnin is mostly fable. At no time did the penal laws reward the beheading of Irish schoolmasters, and the improbable trial is better interpreted as a fantasy reversal of authority roles in eighteenth-century Ireland. But the other elements of the story – O'Doirnin's impressive learning, his prolific poetry, his love of the Irish language, and his reputation as a teacher – have been verified. The legend that has grown up around O'Doirnin is a reminder of the depth of regard for learned men in the countryside and the people's keen interest in education at a very early stage.[8]

The worst strictures of the penal code lasted for less than a century and were removed with the passage of relief legislation between 1778 and 1793. Once the ban on Catholic teachers was lifted, the hedge schools flourished. According to an educational census carried out in the 1820s, Ireland had nine thousand hedge schools in 1824,[9] and more than twenty-five Catholic hedge schools, or "pay schools," were in operation in the south Armagh parishes of Creggan and Killeavy.[10] Curiously, there was not a single pay school reported in the parish of Forkhill. For some thirty years, the children of Forkhill were otherwise schooled, and their schooling had a distinctly Protestant cast.[11]

THE FORKHILL CHARITY SCHOOLS, 1790–1834

When Richard Jackson wrote his will in 1776, he reserved a substantial portion of the estate's annual income for a charitable education fund, which was intended to provide free schooling for the poor children of the parish. The concept of free education was not new in Ireland, but the successful implementation of a working system, particularly in an impoverished rural setting, had few precedents. But if Jackson's attitude towards education was enlightened, his religious outlook was resolutely conservative. His will directed the trustees to clothe and educate "as many, as the fund will allow, children of the church of Ireland," giving clear preference to the Protestant children of the parish. The trustees of his estate doubted that these terms could be implemented without resistance, and they bargained a compromise. Shortly after the first school was opened, it was reported that "children of all Religious Denominations on the Estate and surrounding neighbourhoods are freely admitted and partake of the Benefits of said Schools altho' the Religious Education therein is that of the Church of Ireland pursuant to the said testator's will."[12]

The first schoolhouse was opened in 1790 in the townland of Shean, and two more – at Mullaghbawn and Aughadanove – soon followed.[13] The superintendent of the board, the Reverend Edward Hudson, was charged with the selection of sixty children for education in each school, but there is no record of how he made the selection. Samuel Dickson was appointed master of the Aughadanove school and was guaranteed an annual salary of thirteen shillings for each child who enrolled.[14] The schoolmaster of Mullaghbawn was Alexander Berkley, the Protestant linen weaver who had settled on the estate in 1788. Less than one year after he took up the post of schoolmaster, Berkley and his family suffered the savage assault described in chapter 2.[15] In the wake of the incident, the Forkhill schools were shut down by the trustees, on the grounds that they were ill equipped "to protect Protestant schoolmasters in the execution of their duty."[16] The trustees' policy remained in effect until August 1791, when they decided that it was safe to reopen the schools.

In an account of the Armagh Disturbances published in 1792, J. Byrne traced the attack on Berkley to the controversy surrounding his appointment as schoolmaster in preference to another young teacher, who was more popular with the people. As I explained in chapter 2, Byrne's version of the disturbances of the 1790s must be received with caution, for a number of important details are missing from his account. Nevertheless, Byrne's mention of this episode is another indication of the lively interest in local schooling, and the fact that Berkley was teaching more than one hundred students in a schoolhouse built for sixty is further evidence of the early demand for education.[17] In May 1795 the trustees recommended that limits be placed on the number of pupils on the rolls, since the schoolhouses were filled to capacity and the teachers were unable to attend properly to all the students.[18] The strain on resources increased when the schoolmasters fell into the habit of taking paying students from outside the estate as a way of supplementing their incomes. This gave rise to accusations that the schoolmasters devoted most of their attention to the paying pupils and neglected "the 'charity children,' as in derision they called the 'tenants.'"[19] The trustees addressed the problem by setting an annual salary for each of the Forkhill schoolmasters regardless of enrolment in their schools. In 1808 the salary of a Forkhill teacher approximated £40 per annum plus a dwelling house.[20] Despite these salaries, the minute books suggest that the trustees had some trouble finding and retaining suitable schoolmasters. In May 1797 Samuel Dickson was fined forty shillings for unspecified "misconduct" at his school and for failure to attend a meeting of the board. He was turned out of the school later in the year, as was the schoolmaster for Mullaghbawn.[21]

We know little about how the charity schools were run on a daily basis – what subjects formed the curriculum and what school texts were used, apart from certainty that the Bible was always at hand. However, among the church registry papers is a document entitled "Hints of Mrs Barton's relative to Forkil Charities," written sometime between 1791 and 1804, which gives us some insight into the operation of the schools in the early days. Susanna Barton evidently took an active interest in the charity schools, and she made a number of practical suggestions to the trustees, including that they fix an age for admission to school and a leaving age, since the pupils tended to "idle away years in going when they like it." She promoted education for girls in the parish, and under her guidance several sewing schools were established where girls could learn knitting and "plain work," along with instruction in reading and writing.[22] Also under her influence, diligent students were promised assistance in finding trades and apprenticeships once they finished school, though it appears that preference was given to Protestant pupils. Around the same time, there was a request for a clock to be installed to improve the punctuality of the students' attendance.[23] During several seasons of acute poverty, the trustees set aside money for the purchase of clothing, which was distributed among the poorest students. Later, bread was distributed to children in the infant schools.[24] The network of charity schools expanded in the early nineteenth century; in 1807 there were 365 pupils enrolled in five schools – three boys' schools and two sewing schools – and a new schoolhouse was built at Longfield in 1811.[25]

As an aside, I have to state my amazement that children in Forkhill were actually attending school at the turn of the century. The people in this parish were dirt-poor. They lived in thatched cabins with mud walls and earthen floors, and shared the space with pigs and goats. In the winter months, the children in these cabins ate a breakfast of a little oatmeal and milk beside the hearth before putting on shoes (if they had them) and heading across the fields to school. There they entered another world. They sat at desks in ordered rows, with books open before them, fresh sheets of paper, and the strange feeling of a pen in their hands. Numbers and letters were foreign to them, but they learned what each letter of the alphabet meant, how to spell their own names, and how they didn't have to count on their fingers to add numbers together. Having once been students ourselves, we can appreciate how wonderful school was for some of these children and how painful it must have been for many of them. But as people who have grown up in a literate society, in which education is no longer a privilege but an expectation, we cannot imagine how very strange it must have been for all of them.

THE EDUCATION INQUIRIES, 1806–1827

In 1806 the government appointed a commission of inquiry on Irish education. The committee worked for six years and produced fourteen reports during that period, including the findings of an investigation into the origins and operations of English schools of private foundation in Ireland.[26] The 1812 report included the five charity schools in Forkhill, which were then operating on a combined annual budget of £375. The commissioners noted that the Forkhill charity funds were intended for the instruction and clothing of all the poor children in the parish "indiscriminately but under the supervision of Protestant Masters and Mistresses." Many of the students were apprenticed to trades when they left school, principally the weaving trade, and at the expiration of their apprenticeships they received £10 and a loom.

The highlight of the 1812 report is the return of attendance in the schools, which was helpfully broken down according to denomination. According to the report, of the 380 pupils attending the five charity schools in Forkhill, "about fifty" of them were Protestants; the remaining 330 (87 per cent) were Catholics.[27] The fact that so many Catholic children were attending the Forkhill charity schools is significant, for throughout this period (1790–1824) one principle remained constant: the Protestant foundation of the schools. In 1792 the secretary of the board of trustees was directed to become a member of the Society for Promoting Christian Knowledge, a Protestant education society that became active in Ireland that year.[28] In 1794 the board stipulated that every child in the Jackson schools was required to learn and repeat the collect of the day and would receive a halfpenny for doing so.[29] Further, the trustees directed the schoolmasters to ensure that the children of Protestant parents attend a church service every Sunday.[30] Samples of the children's handwriting and needlework were regularly presented to the board; the trustees awarded prizes for the best readings from the New Testament; and clergymen of the established church occasionally visited the schools to inspect the students' progress.[31]

The next major education inquiry came twelve years later, with the appointment of a royal commission in 1824. The commission sat from

June 1824 until June 1827 and produced nine reports based on the testimony of witnesses along with input from the Catholic hierarchy and statistical evidence accumulated during an extensive educational census.[32] As part of the inquiry, the commissioners undertook to visit every school in every parish in the country, gathering a mine of information on teachers, students, the operation of the schools, and the condition of the schoolhouses.

By 1824 five more schools had been established in the parish of Forkhill, bringing the total to ten. Seven of these schools were within the bounds of the estate and were endowed by the Jackson trust, while the three outside the estate were connected with the Kildare Place Society.[33] Unlike most schools in this period, which operated in converted outhouses or abandoned cabins, the Forkhill schoolhouses had been built especially for the purpose and were all in good condition, being valued at from £200 to £300 each. The schoolteachers earned a respectable annual income (which ranged from £20 to £40), as well as being provided with a dwelling house.[34] The uniqueness of the school system in Forkhill becomes clear when we examine the state of education in two adjacent parishes. Close to twenty-five pay schools were scattered throughout the parishes of Creggan and Killeavy, and the schoolhouses were rough and ready – small cabins, outhouses, and cowsheds. One schoolhouse was an impossibly small six feet square. These were the hedge schools of old, and most of them were under the supervision of Catholic teachers, whose income reflected the poverty of their surroundings. The annual salary of a hedge schoolmaster was between £10 and £12, but it could be as little as £5, since the teachers were dependent on the subscriptions of the students. Often this was not a living wage, and the report stated that one of the schoolmasters in Creggan was forced to close his school for a period each year in order to work the harvest in England.[35]

Once again, the commission inquired into the levels of enrolment, and the attendance figures for an average of three months were provided, as well as a breakdown of the denomination and sex of each child.[36] The commissioners also inquired whether or not Scripture was read in the school and which version was used. According to the 1825 attendance returns, between 415 and 460 pupils were enrolled in the ten schools in Forkhill. Using the 1821 census return as an index to the student population, between 25 and 28 per cent of children between the ages of six and fourteen were enrolled in the schools.[37] Girls were well represented, attending both the sewing schools and the regular schools, where they made up between one-quarter and one-third of the student body. A more significant number is the denominational return; a minimum of 68 per cent of the children in these schools were Catholic, and the figure may have been as high as 74 per cent.[38] This is despite the fact that all ten charity schools were headed by Protestant masters and mistresses, and the Authorized Version of the Bible was read daily in each of them. The importance of this denominational imbalance is difficult to overstate, particularly in light of the fallout over the national school system within less than a decade. On the basis of these attendance figures, it seems that many of the people in Forkhill wanted their children to have an education, and they were not sufficiently offended by the Protestantism of the charity schools to neglect the opportunity.

RELIGIOUS TENSIONS IN THE 1820S

The Catholic priests in Forkhill were another matter, and relations between them and the Protestant schools became increasingly strained. In the spring of 1825, the board of trustees recorded that the number of Catholic children attending the schools in Forkhill had declined sharply owing to the interference of the Catholic clergy, who objected to the attendance of their parishioners at the charity schools.[39] The timing of the clerical intervention is significant, for the Forkhill schools had been in operation for more than thirty years. Why in 1825 was the prospect of interdenominational education suddenly intolerable?

The immediate catalyst was the controversy over the Kildare Place Society. This organization, also known as the Society for Promoting the Education of the Poor of Ireland, had been founded in Dublin in 1811 with a mandate to provide free elementary education for poor children. Unlike most privately run educational initiatives, which were funded by evangelical societies, the "leading principle" of the Kildare Place Society was "to afford the same facilities for education to all classes of professing christians without any attempt to interfere with the peculiar religious opinions of any."[40] Although the Bible was read daily in these schools, doctrinal matters were not discussed.

In 1812 the Kildare Place Society was endorsed by the Irish education commission as a possible model for a system of universal elementary education. During their tour of the countryside, the commissioners had been appalled by the state of education in the hedge schools, which they branded "ill-taught and ill-regulated," and they made a series of recommendations designed to improve elementary education through the establishment of a national school board. Crucially, they declared that the success of such a system would depend on strict adherence to the principle of non-denominational instruction: "No attempt shall be made to influence or disturb the peculiar religious tenets of any sect or description of Christians." The philosophy of the Kildare Place

Society and the vision of the education commission were an ideal fit. In 1816 the society applied for its first parliamentary grant and was awarded more than £6,000.[41] Within five years, it was operating nearly 400 schools and had enrolled more than 25,000 students. It published the first major series of progressive textbooks in the British Isles and established model schools for training teachers. Although the hierarchy of the Catholic Church remained uneasy about the Protestant majority on the society's board of governors, it accepted the reading of Scripture without comment and gave the society its cautious approval. The Dublin barrister and Catholic agitator Daniel O'Connell served on the board of governors, and members of the Catholic gentry became patrons of individual schools.[42]

Then, with little warning, the friendly relationship began to unravel. In the early 1820s, the Kildare Place Society abandoned its religious neutrality, using part of its income to finance schools run by evangelical societies such as the London Hibernian Society and the Association for Discountenancing Vice. More serious, the society's stricture against Scripture reading in the schools was increasingly ignored. The Catholic clergy's reservations about the lay reading of Scripture was recorded by H.E. Bell, who toured Ulster in 1824 and included his observations on the education controversy in an unpublished memoir.[43] Bell was granted an interview with the Catholic archbishop of Armagh, who outlined in no uncertain terms the Catholic Church's opposition to education in mixed schools. The church objected to every school in which the Authorized Version of the Bible was read, even if it was read by a Roman Catholic teacher, and to every school in which the Douay Version was read by a Protestant teacher.[44] The bishops had lately agreed that the Bible was not to be authorized for instruction in school or for reading by laypersons, except with the help and direction of the Catholic clergy. The new agenda pursued by the Kildare Place Society on the question of Scripture reading prompted O'Connell to resign from the board of governors in 1820, and he subsequently led an agitation against the society with the support of leading Catholic clerics.[45] Complaints against the Kildare Place schools were articulated in a petition presented to the House of Commons by Henry Grattan on behalf of the Irish Catholic bishops in March 1824. The petition enumerated Catholic grievances against education, including the lack of government funding for Catholic schools and the proselytism of the evangelical societies connected with the Kildare Place schools.

The controversy over the Kildare Place Society did not occur in isolation. The conflict had been sparked by the Protestant religious revival in England at the end of the eighteenth century, which soon spread to Ireland. This was the era of the Second Reformation, a half-century of evangelical activity designed to revive the church, to curb ecclesiastical abuses, and to spread the gospel. In Ireland, the Second Reformation refers to the intensive missionary effort to convert Roman Catholics to Protestantism through a proliferation of Bible societies, the distribution of religious tracts, and the influence of evangelical education societies.

The evangelical revival collided with a similar resurgence in Irish Catholicism. The reorganization of the Catholic Church had begun at the end of the eighteenth century with a surge in church building, an increase in the numbers of vocations to the priesthood, renewed interest in devotional practices, and the establishment of Catholic Bible societies.[46] The revitalization of the Catholic Church was a reflection of the changing social and political landscape in Ireland in the early part of the nineteenth century. With the repeal of the most debilitating penal legislation by 1793, the Catholic interest in Ireland had grown more confident, more prosperous, and more politically influential. Its middle-class leadership was frustrated by the continued exclusion of Catholics from full civil rights (in particular, the right to sit in Parliament, to belong to corporations, and to hold high civic and military office). The campaign for Catholic emancipation was taken up in earnest by Daniel O'Connell and a fellow barrister, Richard Lalor Sheil. In 1823 they founded the Catholic Association with the intent of pursuing "all legal and constitutional measures as may be most useful to obtain Catholic emancipation."[47] The association remained the preserve of the middle and upper classes until 1824, when O'Connell introduced a new category of membership, the "associate member," who could join for the sum of only one penny a month, thus giving the poorest Catholics in the country a stake in the association.[48]

Although the Catholic Association did not catch fire in Ulster to the extent that it did elsewhere, the advance of the emancipation cause alarmed northern Protestants.[49] In 1825 the Protestant gentry of Armagh requested a meeting of the county to consider "the dangers which threaten the Protestant religion."[50] A series of Protestant meetings were held in Cavan, Louth, and Armagh in the fall of 1828, and more than two hundred ultraconservative "Brunswick clubs" were established throughout the country by the following year.[51] In January 1829 the Protestant gentlemen of Armagh held a meeting expressly "for the purpose of petitioning against Catholic Emancipation." At the meeting, the county's leading landlords, magistrates, and clergymen declared that the efforts made by the Catholics of Ireland "to obtain an increase in political power" were dangerous: "It is our duty to oppose the encroachments by every lawful and constitutional means ... to withhold any further concessions, and to control their present intemperance."[52] In June 1829 three gentlemen landlords who lived in Louth, near the Armagh border, were attacked one night as they returned home from Dundalk. Their assailants called them "bloody Brunswickers" and beat them to within an inch of their lives.[53]

On 28 December 1831 the leaders of Armagh's Protestant community held a meeting in the courthouse at Armagh and adopted a series of resolutions expressing the "alarm" of Irish Protestants at their treatment by the government in the wake of Catholic emancipation, which had been granted in 1829. They complained that the government continued to fund the Catholic seminary at Maynooth although it had withdrawn support from the Protestant scripture societies; they protested the inadequate level of protection offered to Protestant clergymen during the recent agitation against the tithe; and they said they regarded the government's proposal to change the constituency of Ireland's boroughs as "fatally injurious to the Protestant interest" because it would transfer power vested in Protestant corporations into the hands of Catholics. At the meeting, Hunt Walsh Chambré, a magistrate, Orangeman, and landlord of a large estate in the parish of Killeavy, which bordered Forkhill, declared that the Protestant community possessed "at the lowest estimate, nine-tenths of the property, industry, education and intelligence of Ireland."[54] He did not conceal his disdain for a government that would consider stripping this community of its privilege and influence. To Protestants such as Chambré, the proposed upset to the balance of power was both baffling and alarming.

The pitch of Protestant anxiety during this period expressed itself in language reminiscent of the seventeenth century: "Let the Protestants of Ulster come forward, and lay their grievances at the foot of their King ... If the Ministry tremble before the yelping hounds of Popery, where will they fly from the roar of the lion of the North?" The leading landowners of Armagh implored the government to defeat the constituency bill, which threatened to send sixty Roman Catholic members as their representatives to the "once-Protestant" House of Commons. If the establishment of a government of Roman Catholics was permitted, they warned, the dissolution of the Union would be imminent, and they declared that although "civil war" was a "miserable alternative," they were prepared to consider it.[55] Similar threats were uttered at a meeting of nearly five thousand Protestants at Tandragee in January 1832. There, Lord Mandeville reminded the crowd that although it was their duty to love their brothers, they must not cease their protest against erroneous religion, and they must be ready, if called upon, to seal that protest with their blood. As for the allegiance they owed to the king and to the laws of the country, Mandeville declared that their ultimate duty was to serve the "King of kings." They must be guided by "conscience," he said.[56]

This was the wider context of the dispute over education in Forkhill. The inflammatory language of Protestants such as Mandeville and Chambré, and the animosity that gathered ground throughout the 1820s, escalated tensions at the parish level. Catholic attendance at the charity schools was adversely affected in 1825, almost certainly because of the intervention of the parish priests. In November 1825 the trustees reported that the "improper interference" of the Catholic clergy against their parishioners' participation in the schools appeared to have had little lasting effect and earlier levels of attendance had been restored.[57] Catholic attendance declined in 1831 (again at the behest of the priests) but recovered its former level the following year.[58] This trend did not continue.[59] The outcome of the education inquiry of 1824–27 was a plan for a central board to superintend "schools of general instruction" with a non-denominational curriculum, in which Catholic and Protestant children would be schooled together. This was the blueprint for the national school system, established in 1831, which eventually made Forkhill's charity schools redundant.

Before we address this stage in the evolution of local education, I would like to restate several points about schooling in the parish up to the 1830s. For an extended period, the charity schools had replaced the hedge schools, supplanting a widespread and popular system of Catholic education. From 1790 to 1836, many Catholics in Forkhill willingly attended Protestant schools. These were not non-denominational schools; they were determinedly Protestant, in accordance with the terms of Richard Jackson's will. Pupils listened to Protestant teachers, read the Protestant version of the Bible, and encountered Protestant clergymen throughout the school day. Resistance to the charity schools came from the Catholic clergy who, from time to time, demanded that Catholics withdraw their children. The priests exercised a good measure of control over their parishioners, but their discipline was hard to sustain over a long period, and attendance at the schools rose again whenever a storm had passed. This pattern changed in the 1830s with the emergence of a viable alternative to the charity schools in the form of the national school board.

THE NATIONAL SCHOOLS, 1834–1861

In July 1834 Father Daniel O'Rafferty wrote to the Reverend Dr James Campbell, rector of Forkhill, on the subject of the national schools.[60] According to O'Rafferty, the unwillingness of the Forkhill charity schools to adopt the "liberal" (non-denominational) system of education recommended by the board of education could no longer be tolerated. He asked Campbell to support an application for aid to build a national schoolhouse in the parish, adding, "If the System of

Education recommended by that Board had been adopted in all the Schools in this parish, this application would not be necessary. But you know that is not the case, and that the Catholics cannot in conscience send their children to them."[61]

O'Rafferty was goading the rector. He knew perfectly well what Campbell's reply would be, and his decision to write the letter on 12 July was deliberately provocative. Campbell replied sharply in a letter to the priest, whom he addressed somewhat disrespectfully as "Sir." "I cannot for an instant acquiesce in your views or lend any cooperation whatever for the attainment of the purposes which you have mentioned," he wrote.[62] O'Rafferty proceeded anyway, and the application sent to the board of education was supported by fourteen men in the parish. All were Catholics save one, Arthur Johnston, a Protestant landlord who donated the site for the school in the townland of Maphoner – a townland that sat in the middle of the parish but was not part of the Forkhill estate. In his application, O'Rafferty described the long-standing conflict over education in the parish. The system of education in the charity schools was most avowedly not nondenominational, he explained, and it bordered on proselytism. Religious tracts and Protestant Scriptures were used as schoolbooks and read daily, which "is what the Catholics chiefly object to."[63] The Forkhill trustees "seduced" the pupils, he said, by giving a penny a week to every child who attended their schools, a sum that was increased to two shillings at their quarterly examinations. In addition, premiums of food and clothing were promised to the poor scholars. O'Rafferty was blunt: "Avarice and Poverty ... induce some people to send at the expense of conscience their children to these schools. Hence the grand source of obloquy, dissension and strife in this parish. But the intended school house would ... soon dry up this fountain of anarchy and discontent."[64]

Persuaded by the application, the board granted £81 towards the building of a schoolhouse in Maphoner in August 1834. The Forkhill committee raised an additional £47 in local contributions, and the first national schoolhouse in the parish opened its doors on 18 August 1836.[65] The schoolhouse measured seventy-two by eighteen feet, with a rough earthen floor. It had no proper ceiling, and therefore was very cold in winter.[66] The first schoolmaster was a local man, Felix Hanratty, who had been educated at a national school in Newry. He earned £8 a year from the board, in addition to a small gratuity from the children. Boys and girls attended the school five days each week, from ten o'clock in the morning until three in the afternoon. Religious instruction was offered on Saturday mornings. At these sessions, the children repeated part of the catechism, read from Scripture, and listened to an explanatory lesson from the clergyman. Parents were not obliged to send their children for religious instruction "beyond their own free will and consent."[67]

Attendance at the Maphoner national school grew steadily, from an initial roll of 86 (56 boys and 30 girls) in 1836 to 237 pupils by 1842. According to the Church of Ireland cleric, between 40 and 88 children read extracts from Scripture in 1839, although he did not state if these were Protestant or Catholic pupils.[68] In 1838 the privately endowed school at Aughanduff, which had been under the auspices of the Kildare Place Society (and was not financed by the Jackson trust) was taken into the national school system.[69] A female teacher, Margaret Trodden, was appointed to this school in 1842, principally to instruct the girls in needlework; but her literary qualifications were "not of a high order," and O'Rafferty concluded that a separate girls' school was needed. Between 1842 and 1847, the national board received applications for grants-in-aid for at least six new schools in south Armagh. The applicants were nearly always Catholic clergymen, although landlords also applied for funds on behalf of their tenants. No Church of Ireland clergymen supported the applications.

Support for the national school system took an inevitable toll on attendance at the Forkhill charity schools. The "Protestant poor schools" soon lost a significant number of pupils to the new national board, though they fought redundancy.[70] The trustees opened an infants' school in 1836 and expanded the Mullaghbawn schools in 1838. Significantly, they also employed an Irish-language teacher named Patrick Groogan; in August 1836 the trustees observed that the "number attending his school and deriving advantages from his teaching in the native tongue are considerable – being 46 scholars."[71]

After several years of decline, attendance at the charity schools increased in 1840 and again in 1842, when 791 students were reported on the rolls.[72] There are two reasons for this. First, the population of Forkhill increased by 16 per cent between 1831 and 1841 and the national schools at Maphoner and Aughanduff could not accommodate the growing number of children seeking places; but there was plenty of space in the charity schools. Second, although the national schools charged their students a penny a week, the charity schools remained free and even rewarded students for attendance. According to O'Rafferty, children at the Protestant schools were given a penny a week, and some received as much as two shillings and six pence at the quarterly examinations. The premiums of money, clothing, and food that were distributed to the charity school pupils were tempting for families who were living from hand to mouth on the eve of the famine.

Despite this, the Catholic clergy persisted in their attacks on the charity schools well into the 1850s. In 1853 the Reverend James Campbell informed J.G. Beresford, the Anglican archbishop of Armagh, that a "great failure" had recently occurred with respect to the Forkhill schools because of the "unwarrantable interference and denunciations of the Roman Catholic priesthood."[73] Attendance had dropped, then partly recovered, but the trustees were fighting a losing battle. When Father Hugh Mulligan applied to the national school board in 1855 requesting aid for a "badly needed" third school in the parish, he explained that the children of Forkhill had been prevented from attending the endowed schools "by order of the most Reverend Dr Dixon, as their creed would therein be tampered with."[74] This was despite the fact that the endowed schools were – in Mulligan's own words – "excellent schools" with "ample endowments." The commissioners agreed to take a third parish school into the national system in 1856, provided that its name was changed from the proposed St Patrick's to Forkhill National School. The new schoolhouse was in the townland of Shean. Slated with earthen floors, it was equipped with four desks for thirty students.

The national school system was supposed to remove the walls between denominational groups in Ireland, but in many places it had precisely the opposite effect. Although the new national school at Shean was open to children of all religious denominations (as were all the national schools), Father Mulligan predicted that the outcry caused by parties interested in maintaining attendance at the charity schools would likely prevent the Protestant community from taking advantage of this opportunity.[75] The personal intervention of the Roman Catholic archbishop of Armagh in the dispute over the Forkhill schools underscores the seriousness with which the church viewed the situation and emphasizes its resolve to prevent Catholic children from attending the endowed schools, regardless of their quality. The outright clerical ban on attendance at the charity schools had a crippling effect. By 1857 there was talk of turning the Mullaghbawn charity school into a boarding school, the intent being to bring in Protestant students from outside the parish.[76] In May 1858, at a special meeting of the board of trustees, it was decided that the regular schools and sewing schools at Tullymacreeve and Aughadanove would be discontinued.[77]

LANGUAGE AND LITERACY IN THE NINETEENTH CENTURY

To this point, we have considered the charity schools and the national schools in terms of the levels of enrolment between 1790 and the

1850s. The results they achieved in terms of quality of education are more difficult to measure, though literacy levels provide a useful starting point.[78] The first national inquiry into literacy in Ireland was the census of 1841, held ten years after the establishment of the national school system.[79] The difficulty with the census data is that they reported the results of a subjective inquiry (the "declared ability to read or write") rather than of an objective test. Determining one's own ability to read and write allowed wide scope for misrepresentation, and some historians of literacy argue that the results of self-evaluation often overestimate ability.[80] However, a study of literacy in nineteenth-century Ireland has found a strong correspondence between literacy evidence in marriage registers and the reported ability to read as declared in the census of 1871.[81]

When the first literacy figures for the parish were collected, the charity schools had been in operation for fifty years.[82] Despite this, the literacy results as reported in 1841 were not impressive: only 28 per cent of males in the parish were able to read, and only 16 per cent could both read and write.[83] Among females, the results were poorer still: only 16 per cent of females in Forkhill were able to read, and even fewer could read and write.[84] Thus, despite the fairly high levels of participation of Catholic children in the charity schools, it appears that many of them did not leave school with basic literacy skills. As we know, the attendance of Catholic children was interrupted throughout the 1820s and 1830s by the local clergy, who ordered parents to remove their children from the charity schools. It would be interesting to know whether the levels of literacy of those who had attended the charity schools between 1790 and 1820 were any different. But the breakdown of literacy levels according to age was not available until 1861.

The establishment of the national schools accelerated the trend towards literacy throughout Ireland, and Forkhill was no exception. In 1861, 44 per cent of males and 30 per cent of females could read, a fact that reinforces the connection between improved levels of literacy and the adoption of a third national school in Forkhill in 1856.[85] The generational divide was apparent. Among men aged forty years and over in 1861, 37 per cent were able to read, while the figure for males of between five and thirty-nine years was 48 per cent. Among women aged forty years and over, only 20 per cent were able to read, while the figure for those between five and thirty-nine years was 36 per cent.[86]

The 1861 census also marked the first correlation between literacy figures and denomination, revealing a striking disparity between the communities in Forkhill. In 1861, 90 per cent of Protestant males in Forkhill were able to read, compared with 42 per cent of Catholic males. Likewise, 75 per cent of Protestant females could read, compared with 29 per cent of Catholic females.[87] The reasons for this disparity are difficult to determine, though tradition, expectation, and opportunity all probably played a role. Of these, tradition may have been the most influential. There was a long history of literacy in the Protestant communities of Ulster because of the emphasis that the Protestant churches placed on reading the Word. It was the duty of every Christian to be able to read the Bible. In the Catholic Church, Bible reading by lay people was strongly discouraged. The controversy over Scripture reading in the Kildare Place schools and the archbishop's directive against the attendance of Catholic children at the Forkhill schools are two examples of this. But as we have seen, the universality of education after 1831 removed this barrier by providing secular instruction in reading and writing. Between 1861 and 1901, the gap between the literacy levels of Catholics and Protestants, and between those of men and women, narrowed significantly.[88]

Through their focus on reading, writing, and speaking English, the national schools influenced another nineteenth-century trend: the decline of the Irish language. In certain quarters of Irish nationalism, the national schools were later singled out for attack, charged with destroying the native language because of their insistence on proficiency in English.[89] In fact, the available figures for language usage in the nineteenth century indicate that this trend had begun well before 1831. The Reverend Henry Stewart reported on the waning of the Irish language in the parish of Creggan in south Armagh in 1814. The people all spoke Irish, he wrote, and some spoke nothing else. However, "the English language is gaining ground upon the other," and only in a very few cases did he need to solicit the services of an interpreter.[90] He remarked as well that the people were "most anxious" to give their children schooling and children attended school regularly for half the year.[91] In a survey of the parish of Tullaroan in Kilkenny in 1819, William Shaw Mason attributed the decline of the Irish language to the hedge schools, "where English alone is taught." Increasingly, the Catholic Church also played a role by conducting mass and other services in both English and Irish as early as 1796.[92]

The erosion of the Irish language remarked upon by contemporaries was confirmed by the 1851 census, which was the first to inquire into the knowledge and usage of Irish among the population. The census returns enumerated individuals who claimed to speak Irish only, as well as those who spoke both Irish and English. The results were broken down by age and were recorded for every barony in Ireland. Some 29 per cent of the people living in the barony of Upper Orior in 1851 claimed a knowledge of both Irish and English; one-quarter were between the ages of ten and twenty, which suggests that the Irish language was being passed down in some families.[93] However, only 148 people in the entire county of Armagh claimed no knowledge of English; all of these people lived in south Armagh, and most of them were women between the ages of forty and seventy-nine.[94] This figure represents less than one per cent of the population of the barony of Upper Orior, meaning that 99 per cent of the population had some knowledge of English. The results of the 1851 census reveal the presence of the English language – even among remote and isolated rural communities – before the famine and before the establishment of the national schools.

The history of schooling in Forkhill from 1790 to 1861, like so much else in the history of this parish, resists sweeping generalizations. It was pockmarked and inconsistent – occasionally a metaphor for harmony and cooperation, at other times a reflection of tension and acrimony between the rival denominations. The attendance figures for 1812 and 1825 tell us that a considerable number of Catholic children went to the charity schools, but they do not tell us why this was so or how the parents of these children regarded the schools and their Protestant teachers. The attendance records unfortunately do not capture the undercurrent in the schoolroom. Perhaps inevitably, owing to the sectarian geography of the population in Ireland, the national school system soon became, in practice, a network of denominational schools. Less inevitable though more unfortunate was the fact that the conflict surrounding the establishment of the national schools reinforced existing prejudices and rekindled animosities between the religious communities.

Nevertheless, Catholic attendance at the charity schools does challenge the belief that the denominations in Forkhill were divided into two armed camps over the issue of education. There was more fluidity than either side would later be willing to admit. It also shows the degree to which rival clergymen inflamed the situation. From the office of the archbishop down to the parish priest, the Catholic clergy were resolutely opposed to the charity schools, and their will prevailed. The clash over the Forkhill national schools application in the 1830s was not a purely local conflict, however; the inflammatory gestures on both sides were provoked by events at the national level. One of the most divisive issues was the tithe agitation of the early 1830s and the ensuing disturbances in the decade before the famine. We examine the impact of these events in the next chapter.

6

Outrage, 1832–1852

In early 1807 it was reported that "disaffection [was] very apparent amongst the lower ranks in the neighbourhood of Forkhill."[1] In August a Killeavy landlord, Jonathan Seaver, confided his fears of a resurgent conspiracy among a band of men calling themselves Regenerated Defenders.[2] These men had recently held a meeting at Derrynoose, and similar incidents were reported from Newtownhamilton and Balleek. These meetings were held under the cover of supper parties at private homes, "a custom entirely novel and totally beyond the limits of the incomes of such individuals."[3] The magistrates suspected that "a very strong and busy system of Defenderism" existed in south Armagh and that the large dances taking place throughout the country on Sundays were held for the purpose of advancing the organization.[4]

At a dance held on the outskirts of Newry in December 1811, the country people were addressed by strangers, who had come from a distance "to make Proselites and instruct the people in mischief and wickedness."[5] In January 1812 James Dawson, the assistant barrister for Armagh, who lived on a large estate in Forkhill, learned that the Threshers were holding meetings in the countryside southwest of Newry.[6] The Threshers were members of a secret oath-bound society that had emerged in Connacht in 1806–7, fuelled by grievances against tithes, priests' fees, labourers' wages, and the price of land. Close to seventy young men were reported to have attended a funeral near Newry in early 1812, wearing matching handkerchiefs around their necks. Later they convened in a nearby field, where they formed ranks and marched.[7] By June 1814, the clandestine meetings in Armagh had become "frequent," and there appeared to be a "general inclination to riot ... among the lower class of Roman Catholics whenever they think their party strong enough to beat those whom they consider inimical to their interest."[8]

During the fall of 1814, scarcely a week passed without some attack on property in the vicinity of south Armagh.[9] The rector of Newtownhamilton, William Barker, complained of a litany of outrages against himself, his tithe proctor, and his labourers. Hay ricks were scattered and burned, corn sheaves set alight, flax destroyed, trees cut down, and farm equipment vandalized.[10] Barker was a deeply unpopular magistrate as well as a cleric, and these deeds were almost certainly part of a campaign of harassment reminiscent of the Defender outrages of the 1790s. Yet a fellow clergyman, William Richardson, reacted with disbelief to the suggestion that the disturbances proceeded from the "exorbitant rents" exacted by the magistrate, confiding to the Earl of Gosford, "Barker is the last man I should suspect to be guilty of extortion."[11]

Richardson, along with most Protestant gentry in the countryside, had no doubt that the outrages in Armagh were sectarian. The rector of Creggan described the Threshers as a "popish Banditti who have leagued themselves against the few Protestants among us."[12] When a clash between a crowd of country people and police at Glassdrummond in June 1816 left three men dead, Dawson called for the baronies of Upper Fews and Upper Orior to be disarmed, claiming that the Catholics had five hundred stand of arms (all unlicensed and illegal), while all "but an handful" of the Protestants had been disarmed.[13] Throughout this period, Dawson kept a close eye on the sectarian temperature in the countryside. In 1816 he wrote to Dublin Castle concerning a memorial that had been submitted to the government requesting a stay of execution for a Protestant man from Armagh who had been convicted of an agrarian outrage. At the same time, two Catholics from Creggan were awaiting execution in Armagh jail, both convicted of involvement in similar agrarian outrages.[14] Dawson suggested that treating the two cases differently might be imprudent in the current climate: "I fear it would not tend to tranquillize the barony ... to execute the two Papists and to reprieve the Protestant."[15] Like the Reverend Edward Hudson before him, Dawson viewed the disturbances primarily along sectarian lines, and he took matters personally: "I have been so goaded by the R.C[atholics] thro' the last years," he complained.[16] So it was with puzzlement that he reported to Dublin Castle in July 1816 that the attacks that kept the countryside in an uproar were confined to the houses of Catholics. "Most extraordinary," he wrote.[17]

The history of outrage in nineteenth-century Armagh should be written around this observation, for Dawson accidentally got it right: most of the outrage in south Armagh was committed within the Catholic community. This observation was rarely made, however. Instead, the filing drawers of Dublin Castle were full of letters from alarmed

Protestant landowners who, like James Dawson, Jonathan Seaver, and William Richardson, warned of conspiracies stirring among the "popish banditti."[18] This fear mongering trickled down to the smaller Protestant farmers and their tenants, including those in Forkhill, who petitioned the government for protection in June 1832, in the early days of the tithe agitation.

On 22 June three Protestant farmers from Forkhill – William Freeland, Thomas Smith, and Matthew Jeffers – swore an affidavit on behalf of the Protestant inhabitants of the parish:

> That from the present demoralized state of the country and particularly of the Roman Catholic part of the population who appear determined to resist and set the laws of the land at defiance, the Deponents Individually and collectively are in dread and fear that the lives and properties of themselves, their Protestant brethren and neighbours are daily in danger of being destroyed unless strongly protected by being supplied with arms for their defence. That on the night of Wednesday the 13th of June inst. the neighbourhood was most dreadfully alarmed by the whole Roman Catholic population flying through the country, calling at every house and giving what deponents conceive to be a watchword and from which they apprehend some serious consequence may arise, that Deponents have heard and have some very good reason for believing that large numbers of armed bands were seen parading and patrolling several parts of the country to the terror of the peaceable and well-disposed inhabitants on that night. That deponents with about thirty or forty others are willing to come forward and act as Special Constables for the preservation of the peace if supplied with arms for their defence by the Executive Government of this country and that we tender our services either as yeomanry or in any other way in which the Government may think our Services would be best employed. That deponents do further swear that they are not Bigotted nor do they feel any animosity towards their Roman Catholic brethren, but merely the preservation of their lives and properties, and the peace, harmony and good feeling of the country.[19]

In an accompanying letter to the chief secretary, the magistrate Hunt Walsh Chambré provided the context of their alarm:

> In this season of the year it is the custom of the lower orders of Roman Catholics in this vicinity viz. on Midsummers Eve ... to assemble and parade thro' the country by night with garlands and lighted torches and upon those nights to light fires in many places on the roads, but I have remarked last year they kept up a constant firing of shots at those processions particularly firing when they passed the residence of a Protestant Inhabitant which has caused much discontent and alarm. There is a large number of persons also in the

habit of collecting at the Killeavy pattern in Co Armagh ... which is held on the 6 July each year – at the last that was held large bodies of Ribbonmen paraded at it, with scarfs and sashes accompanied by music and from which I have myself heard much firing ... From the very agitated and disorganized state of this part of the Co Armagh the few Protestant Inhabitants who reside in it are under the greatest alarm at this time for their safety.[20]

The response from Dublin Castle was less than encouraging. The authorities replied that they could not be seen to make a distinction between the parties by arming such a "Protestant Defence Association." Besides, if they did issue firearms, and "the arms were not kept in a depot, they would probably be taken possession of by the disaffected."[21]

These first-hand accounts of the situation in Forkhill in 1832 introduce two themes that are central to any discussion of outrage in nineteenth-century Ireland. The first is sectarianism. In the politically overheated atmosphere of the 1820s and 1830s, collective action by Catholics was nearly always perceived as a threat to the Protestant landed interest, and this anxiety is manifest in the language of the petitioners. Also inseparable from this discussion is the spectre of ribbonism, which is alluded to in the farmers' petition and is addressed explicitly in Chambré's letter. There were fears that the ribbon "system" had gained a foothold in the parish. These suspicions proved to be correct, though many of the attendant assumptions were not.

On 14 January 1837 two brothers, Hugh and Peter McGill, from the townland of Tiffcrum appeared before a Forkhill magistrate and declared that "they did belong to a society called Ribbon Men."[22] Hugh claimed that he had been a member for eight years, and Peter for three years.[23] The pair volunteered to provide the authorities with information on the ribbon system in Forkhill, under the condition of strict confidence. Although the authorities in Dublin Castle were keen to learn as much as possible about the extent of the ribbon system in the countryside, their experience of informers during the 1790s had made them skeptical of voluntary confessors. Consequently, the Forkhill head constable was directed to inquire into the characters of Hugh and Peter McGill, their trade and means of support, and whether they were "needy" men: "It would be very desirable to ascertain ... whether [their confession] was done from any personal motive, such as that of revenge, or with a view of getting a reward."[24] Unfortunately, there is no record of any further communication on this subject. However, the McGill brothers did provide a good deal of information about the local society, and we shall draw on their testimony in an exploration of the ribbon system and its operations in south Armagh between 1832 and 1852.

Historically, the term "ribbonism" has been used to describe a clandestine network of rural conspirators who were dedicated to a program of agrarian agitation and sectarian harassment while nurturing the dream of overthrowing English rule in Ireland. Although the movement was organized in at least fourteen counties by 1822, attempts to analyse ribbonism on a nationwide scale have proved unsatisfactory, and there is much debate about the connectedness of the movement at the national level.[25] In Ulster it was perceived as a sectarian society against the Orange Order; in Munster it began as a league against tithe proctors; in Connacht, it combated rack-renting and evictions; and in Dublin it was associated with trade unionism.[26] From its early stages, ribbonism also served as a friendly society under various guises, including the St Patrick's Association and the Hibernian Benevolent Society, with networks in Liverpool and Manchester, and later in America.[27]

Contemporaries viewed ribbonism as an outgrowth of the eighteenth-century Defenders and primarily as a defensive league against the Orange Order. According to a police informer, the name "ribbonmen" had come about by chance in a fight between Catholics and Orangemen at Derry in 1810 or 1811, when the Catholics had worn small red ribbons around their wrists as a way of identifying one another.[28] But from an early stage, there were fears that ribbonism was an insurrectionary society constructed along the lines of the United Irishmen, and the earliest use of the term that Tom Garvin has found is in a letter from Belfast dated 1811: "Ribbonmen, a new term for U. Irishmen."[29]

Within a few years, the ribbon system had gathered ground in Ulster and penetrated the towns of Armagh, Belfast, and especially Dublin, which was a ribbon centre before 1820.[30] Dublin Castle was perturbed by these stirrings and devoted considerable resources to undermining the society in the early 1820s. In 1822 a police agent named Michael Coffey penetrated the Dublin branch, where he worked as the secretary to a leading ribbonman for nine months. His information about the society's inner workings led to a series of arrests and convictions.[31] At the ribbon trials, the crown prosecutors laid bare what they had learned about the society, which was known to its members as the Society of St Patrick or Sons of the Shamrock. It was an oath-bound society, based on a network of lodges at the parish level, with a hierarchical structure of representation at the baronial, county, provincial, and national levels. In this it bore a close resemblance to the systems of organization that had been adopted by the Defenders and the United Irishmen thirty years before.[32]

According to Coffey's testimony, twenty-five ribbon delegates had attended a meeting of the national committee in Armagh in March

1822. Based on this figure and on the society's strict rules of representation, Tom Garvin has surmised that fourteen counties had "at least nominal Ribbon organizations affiliated to the national level."[33] By all accounts, the 1822 trials crippled the ribbon society; within a few years, it had split into two rival boards, one based in Ulster (the Northern Union), and the other in Dublin (the Irish Sons of Freedom).[34] The Dublin branch, which served as the nerve centre of the movement, was finally "wrecked" in 1839 with the arrest of its secretary, the beleaguered Richard Jones, who was sentenced to seven years' transportation.[35] The evidence introduced at the major ribbon trials in 1822 and 1839 indicates that although the Dublin leadership had an insurrectionary intent and debated various strategies of rebellion, these plans had never advanced beyond the realm of discussion.[36]

Rural ribbonism was a more recognizable descendant of the protest societies of the eighteenth century, such as the Whiteboys, Rightboys, and Steelboys.[37] In his 1836 study of disturbances in Ireland, George Cornewall Lewis struggled to draw a distinction between ribbonism and traditional Whiteboyism. Where ribbonism had the character "of an armed and well-organized association, with religious and political objects," he wrote, Whiteboyism was "local" and "reactive" and proceeded from an instinct of self-defence.[38] Yet Lewis admitted the "minute shades of difference" between the movements and agreed that in practice they could not readily be distinguished: "Ribbonism is sometimes used to comprehend, not only the religious and political party opposed to the Orange lodges, but also the Whiteboy associations against rent and tithes."[39] The confusion existed "not only in language, but in reality, as the one system appears in some instances to pass insensibly into the other, or rather the one is connected with the other."[40] In some cases, the ribbon oath was used for swearing in Whiteboys. A seized copy of one oath, entitled "Oath of a Whitefoot," began thus: "I solmly sware to be loyall and true to this New Ribbon Act."[41]

One of the earliest ribbon trials took place at the Trim assizes in the summer of 1815, where a man named James Reilly was charged with taking the ribbonman's oath. Reilly had made a confession on his arrest, providing details about the movement and the oath he had sworn, which was written on a slip of paper and recovered from under his hat.[42] The oath was imbued with religious imagery. It began "In the Name of the Father, the Son and the Holy Ghost, Amen" and was sworn on a Catholic prayer book. No Freemason or Orangeman could be admitted to the fold – "none but pure Catholics."[43] According to Reilly, members swore that they would not consort with Protestants, Freemasons, or Orangemen or trade with Protestant dealers at fairs and markets where Catholics could provide the same goods as cheaply;

not to testify against a fellow member when he was prosecuted by a Protestant; and to "attend at all true causes, and if not shall give true account for your non-attendance; that you are to stand for each other in all true and lawful causes, until death."[44]

This oath is similar to the one described by Hugh and Peter McGill, who revealed the purpose of the "Ribbon society" in their statement to the Forkhill magistrate in 1837: "The said society's rules and regulations and to which each member swears go to the determination of resisting by every means the payment of tithes in any shape and against the Protestant religion by injuring the Protestants in every way by night and by day – they are not to deal with or lay out any money with Protestants whilst they can get any Roman Catholic to deal with, and never to refuse when called upon to perform any act directed by the committee against Protestants."[45]

The sectarianism of ribbon membership and the spirit of anti-Protestantism that was manifest in the oath and in the alleged purpose of the society fuelled Protestant fears of a conspiracy. The clandestine and ritualistic elements of ribbonism, which were revealed in the statements of informers and in testimony at ribbon trials, sharpened their anxiety further. It was known that the ribbonmen held secret meetings, known as "the markets," where business was discussed and where passwords and signs for the quarter, known as "the goods," were communicated. The precise nature of ribbon business remained shrouded in mystery, and the statements of informers about the objectives of the society were often vague. In this chapter, we will examine a series of episodes involving ribbonism that took place in and near Forkhill during the tithe agitation of the 1830s. Each one provides a different angle on "outrage," and together they present a different picture of the purpose, character, and operations of the multifarious and much-feared ribbon system.

THE TITHE AGITATION: A CASE STUDY IN OUTRAGE, 1832–1836

Grievances against taxation had been a staple of agrarian agitation in Ireland since at least the mid-eighteenth century.[46] Rates due to the established church were a keen source of resentment among the lower orders of both Protestants and Catholics, and had inspired such movements as the Oakboys, Rightboys, and Whiteboys since the 1760s.[47] These eighteenth-century protestors had not demanded the abolition of the tithe but its abatement, which suggests that they did not object to the tithe in principle; they objected to its excess.[48] Before 1830 most contemporary witnesses corroborate this view – that tithes were a burdensome nuisance to everyone and that the grievances were based on economic grounds, not religious ones.[49]

The tithe war that began in County Carlow in 1830 was different. This time, the protestors demanded not the reduction of the tithe but its abolition. Their tone was defiant, and their resistance was more violent than any previous agitation over these payments to the church.[50] There were several reasons for this. First, there was residual tension between Catholics and Protestants in the wake of the emancipation campaign. Ill feeling remained, and the defeat of the Protestant interest in 1829 sharpened the sectarian dimension of the tithe agitation.[51] Yet the impetus behind the resistance in the 1830s remained primarily economic. The shift from pasturage to tillage during the early nineteenth century had brought more land under the tithe composition, and an increasing number of people simply could not afford to pay it. The passage of the Tithe Composition Act of 1823 meant that the tax was levied twice yearly at a fixed rate. This was intended to spare resident clergymen the burden of an annual valuation of crops, but by 1830 the tithes were rated according to grain prices that no longer prevailed.[52] Both factors increased the burden on tithe payers, making them more hostile to its collection. As Michael O'Hanrahan has observed, the tithe was attacked "because it was levied in an arbitrary and uneven manner between different parishes, between different types of farmers and between different years; and because it had to be settled in cash, which, for the poor was a particular inconvenience."[53]

In Forkhill, the tithe agitation began in February 1832 when the resident magistrates Hunt Walsh Chambré and Major Arthur A. Bernard reported that shots were frequently fired in the neighbourhood at night. They feared that a large portion of the Catholic population was illegally armed – a fear shared by other Protestants in the area.[54] In early summer the Protestant inhabitants of Forkhill were "dreadfully alarmed" by "armed bands ... parading and patrolling" the countryside at night, and their fears prompted the deposition sworn before Chambré in June 1832.[55] On 21 July a meeting was held in the Catholic chapel at Mullaghbawn for the purpose of petitioning Parliament against tithes.[56] The meeting was chaired by Arthur Johnston, MD, the Protestant landlord of the townland of Maphoner in Forkhill. A series of resolutions against the tithe and church rates were adopted unanimously, and the crowd dispersed peacefully.[57]

In August 1832 the Reverend James Campbell reported that a "large portion" of the inhabitants of Forkhill were refusing to pay the tithe and that he had been "forced to distress" for the rate with the aid of the local constabulary.[58] That same month Archibald Murdock, the tithe proctor for Forkhill, and two special constables, Thomas Gracey and Owen Macan, were confronted by a mob as they entered the townland of Aughanduff.[59] They were greeted by the sound of horns and saw a crowd gathered on the surrounding hills armed with pitchforks and graips (dung forks). Several shots were fired, though none of the men was injured. A thirty-five-year-old farmer named Peter Pyar stood atop a ditch and dared Murdock to approach, telling him that all the men against whom he held decrees were assembled. Meanwhile, Murdock and the two constables were threatened in "bad language": "Damn them, stick them and don't let a beast with them" and "Come up Archy Murdock if you dare."[60]

The next month a detachment of the Forkhill police travelled to Aughanduff under orders to arrest Pyar on the charge of firing at the special constables.[61] When the police arrived at Pyar's farm, they discovered that he had fled. They made a quick search of several neighbouring cabins, but on finding that all the male inhabitants were missing they reluctantly gave up the pursuit. As they made their way back to the barracks, they were startled by shouting and the sound of horns. Looking up into the mountains, they saw a crowd of men, at least two hundred strong, running towards the road. As the mob came near, several shots were fired at Sergeant King and the six constables, who returned the fire. Intimidated, the country people ceased the attack and let the police pass along the road, though they fired a few warning shots into the air.[62]

Agitation over the tithe kept the borderlands in a state of unrest throughout the fall of 1832. In October the *Newry Telegraph* reported that a massive assembly of ten thousand people had paraded through the town of Carrickmacross, in County Monaghan, carrying sheaves of straw on the end of poles and shouting, "No tithes," "No high rents," and "Down with absentees." When they reached the house of the tithe proctor, they made a grave at his gate and buried one of the sheaves, crying out, "Thus shall tithes be buried."[63]

In November 1832 the trustees informed Campbell that they would undertake the future payment of all tithes chargeable on the seventeen townlands of the Forkhill estate, though it is not clear how this arrangement affected the tenantry.[64] The fact that the tithe agitation did not abate suggests that despite the altered arrangement, tithes were still being levied and collected in the parish, though against stiff resistance. On 10 January 1833 a meeting of Armagh magistrates was held to discuss the "spirit of opposition" in Forkhill against the collection of tithes.[65] The disturbances were considered sufficiently serious to warrant the addition of nine policemen to the Forkhill constabulary, increasing the local force to fifteen men.[66] The auxiliary force had been in the parish for less than a day when it was faced with a disturbance.

On the night of 15 January 1833, well after dark, a large number of men were seen proceeding through the parish, evidently on some urgent business.[67] They were moving "in quick time" and "speaking to each other to come on," said a witness. James Tuft, who lived in the townland of Shanroe, saw the party pass by his house between ten and eleven o'clock that night, on the road to Thomas Gracey's house. He believed it was "an illegal party," and for the next three-quarters of an hour he kept a discreet watch on the group, which remained "stationed upon the road at and convenient to ... Gracey's," but he could not see what they were doing.[68]

Thomas Gracey was a Protestant farmer who had served as a special constable enforcing decrees obtained for non-payment of the tithe in the autumn of 1832. He told the magistrates that on the night of 15 January his house had been violently entered by a band of armed men and he had been confronted in his bedchamber by no less than twenty of them. One of the party, a man whom he believed to be the "captain" or "leader" and who wore a white band or scarf on his hat, seized Gracey by the hand, clapped the muzzle of a pistol to his breast, and "demanded all the Tithe Decrees and Firearms in his possession."[69] Terrified, Gracey surrendered close to fifty decrees for property and three or four tithe decrees for the parish of Forkhill. He also handed over his only firearm, a double-barrelled pistol. "After the decrees were taken, the Captain still holding the hand of [Gracey] desired him to go down upon his knees, and he there administered an oath ... forbidding him to engage in any tithe business whatever, and declared that he, the Captain, would soon return with his party again, and at same time ordered [Gracey] never to impeach or accuse any person with whatever was done."[70] After breaking the windows of the house, the crowd went on its way.

The group next went to the house of Owen Macan, who worked as a porter for the Reverend James Campbell. Macan had also served as a special constable during the tithe collection the previous autumn. Finding Macan away from home, the men exchanged words with his wife Catherine, broke one window in the house, and took a sword and some candles away with them.[71] Unknown to them, Macan, who was stationed at his post at Campbell's house in the glebe, had witnessed their progress up the road.[72] Macan later told the magistrates that there were about one hundred men in the party, that many of them were armed, and that he heard them fire shots into the air.

The marchers paid three other visits that night. They stopped at the house of Philip Trainor in Tullydonnell, beat him badly, and ordered him to "swear on a book" that he would give up a piece of ground that had come into his possession.[73] They threatened him with "greater abuse" if they had to visit him again. In the parish of Creggan, they visited James Trainor, broke in the door and windows, and dragged Trainor out of his house "in a state of nakedness." They "beat and abused him in a cruel manner" and pressed their blunderbusses against his chest, putting him in fear of his life. According to the men, they were punishing him for his friendliness towards the landlord's bailiff, who had been seen "resorting to or calling in" at Trainor's house.[74] They searched his house for firearms but went away empty-handed. Their fifth stop that night was at the house of Charles Rafferty in Carriff, where they gave him a severe beating and took away a gun.[75]

According to the testimony of several witnesses, all of the men were strangers to the area and were possibly from "a distant part of Louth." Catherine Macan said that the men had spoken a "nice English," and she was impressed by their manners. She told the chief constable that her house had been "entered by 10 men whom she at [first?] believed to be the Police." Although only a small party had come into the house, she had seen a much larger crowd on the road outside.[76] Her husband Owen, who had seen the group pass through Mullaghbawn from his post in the glebe, said that they were speaking "in some kind of cant or gibberish."[77] Many of them wore white bands on their hats, and the leader's horse was distinguished by a white ribbon or cloth on the saddle.[78] The chief constable for Ballybot forwarded the deposition of the witnesses to Dublin Castle, along with a letter summarizing his own impressions: "I am informed that they all spoke good English, and the leaders particularly appeared to be of the better class of people, altho' disguised in shabby dress. Everything was conducted by them with the most perfect regard to order and discipline, the words of command being obeyed with promptitude, and silence kept with the greatest rigour."[79]

One month later, on 21 February 1833, a crowd of between eight hundred and two thousand assembled about two miles from Forkhill village, on the Armagh-Louth border. According to witnesses, many in the crowd were from the Forkhill townlands of Carrickasticken and Carriff. The crowd was planning to intercept the parties of police and military who were on tithe-recovery duty and to prevent them from seizing goods or livestock.[80] The next day, a party of police who were serving summonses in the neighbourhood were startled by the sudden appearance on the hills of several hundred men, armed with pitchforks, pikes, and guns. Others came running from all directions to join them. When the mob determined that the police were not engaged in the recovery of tithes, they allowed them to pass unmolested.[81] Although this incident passed without violence, it was undoubtedly serious. A similar confrontation between police and a country mob near Keady in December 1834 turned suddenly violent when a policeman attempted to wrest a gun from one of the men; at this, the crowd rained a volley of stones on the policemen, also attacking them with pitchforks, spades, and bludgeons – and their intentions were deadly. The surgeon who treated the wounded policemen remarked on the brutality of their injuries, especially the wounds to the head, which had been administered with violent force. One of the officers was left badly mutilated, his face opened by the prongs of a pitchfork.[82]

The tithe agitation in the parish lasted into the winter of 1835–36. At a riotous gathering at Forkhill in November 1835, the police were confronted by a number of country people and were forced to make a hasty retreat.[83] Trouble flared in the neighbouring parish of Killeavy in December, where a mob armed with pitchforks gathered to resist the collection of the tithe. This protest was organized by a man wearing a red cap who carried a white pole of "extraordinary length."[84]

On 28 December 1836 a tithe proctor named James Morris was dragged out of his house near Jonesborough, a village several miles from Forkhill, by a gang of six or seven men. His wife tried to stop them but was struck on the head with a spade. The party uttered not a word during the attack. A short time later the woman found her husband dead, with "a large stone on his body."[85] A report in the *Newry Telegraph* claimed that Morris's body was "pierced in the heart, and in seven or eight other places, with a sharp instrument, supposed to have been a cane-sword."[86] Morris was a Catholic, though "of Protestant extraction," and had served notices on two of his neighbours earlier in the day.[87] The following night, 29 December, several men burst into the home of Hugh and Peter McGill in Forkhill and assaulted them.[88] It was two weeks after this attack that the brothers appeared before a Forkhill magistrate and announced their membership in the ribbon society, offering to inform against their former associates.[89]

Each of these episodes represents a slightly different configuration of rural outrage. The spontaneous gatherings near Peter Pyar's farm in August and September 1832 and the outdoor meeting in February 1833 were provocative displays of strength that demonstrated the level of local support for the anti-tithe campaign. By massing in such large numbers, the protesters sent a message about the universality of the community's opposition to the tithe, and by arming themselves ostentatiously with pitchforks and graips, they indicated how far they were willing to go to enforce this opposition. Their message was not directed solely at the tithe proctors and their assistants; it was also directed at the apparatus of law enforcement that assisted proctors and bailiffs in discharging their duties. The crowd of many hundreds that assembled on the outskirts of Forkhill in February were apparently making plans to intercept the police wherever they were engaged in tithe-collection duty. The violent clash between the country people and the constabulary at Keady in 1835 demonstrates the seriousness of their intention. This type of outrage – which pitted members of the community (the farmers and labourers) against the forces of outside authority (represented by tax collectors, bailiffs, and the constabulary) in a highly public manner – can be considered "extramural."

The other acts of outrage – the murder of James Morris and especially the midnight march through the parish – were "intramural." On that night in January 1833, a large crowd of men (apparently strangers to the area) travelled through the parish, stopping at the homes of five men, two of whom – Gracey and Macan – were involved in the recovery of tithes. By participating in the collection of tithes and collaborating with the civil authority, Gracey and Macan had defied the will of influential elements in the community that had taken a stand against the tithe. As the nineteenth-century historian W.E.H. Lecky observed, "the tithe farmer ... was much more hated than the clergyman," and the same spirit of opposition had provoked repeated attacks on the Forkhill tithe proctor in the early 1790s.[90] The disciplinary action taken against Gracey was not a punishment but a warning – a threat of more severe treatment if he did not refrain from collecting tithes.[91]

This system of administering at least one warning, whether by visiting the transgressors in person or sending them threatening letters, was a common practice among secret societies. On the surface, giving a person the opportunity to desist from his obnoxious behaviour was simply "fair play"; if he chose to ignore the warning, he would get what was coming to him. But on another level, the practice betrayed a consciousness of due process that was almost prim. This characteristic was observed by George Cornewall Lewis in his 1836 study of the Whiteboys and other agents of rural unrest: "In their threatening letters they affect the form and phraseology of legal notices, thereby intimating that they administer a law subsidiary to, or rather substituted for, the law of the state."[92] The ribbonmen were known to hold mock trials at which transgressors would be tried in absentia before a sentence of death could be passed. William Steuart Trench, a land agent in County Monaghan, was targeted for assassination by ribbonmen in the early 1850s. He learned later that he had been tried by the local ribbon lodge, and in his memoirs he provided a vivid account of the proceedings as they had been revealed to him. The trial had been held in a large barn, where fifteen members of the society were seated around a long table that had been brought in for the occasion. Whiskey in abundance oiled the proceedings, and when all were "steeped in liquor," the president opened the proceedings:

"Well, boys, can anyone say anything in his defence?"
There was a short silence, then one of them spoke up:
"He gave me an iron gate."
"May your cattle break their necks in it!" replied the president.
"He gave me slates and timber to roof my house," said another.
"May the roof soon rot and fall!" said another.
"He gave a neighbour of mine wine for a sick child," observed another.
"The child died!" said the president.
All were again silent.
"Guilty," said the president. "Boys he must die."[93]

Near the end of the meeting, one of the appointed assassins asked whether Trench would get "fair notice" that the death sentence had been passed. The president was dismissive, but the man pressed him: "I will never consent to his death until he be fairly warned; it is the rule and the law, and notice I say he must get."[94] And so a warning was drawn up and on 23 May 1851 it was posted on all the Catholic chapels in the district.

The murder of James Morris in 1836 demonstrates the deadly seriousness of such warnings. Morris had almost certainly been served with a warning but had not heeded it; he had persisted in his duty. This was his unforgivable offence. Thus, the attack on him in December was not a punishment beating that went too far; Morris had been sentenced to death. As the *Newry Telegraph* observed, "The fact of the wretched man having received so many and various wounds is accounted for, when we remember that the system in Ireland is that when a multitude proceed to deprive a fellow-creature of life, every one of the party is required to take part in the homicide in order to make all equally culpable, and, therefore, less likely to turn King's evidence."[95]

If the testimony of Hugh and Peter McGill can be relied on and if the ribbon system in the parish in the 1830s was primarily engaged in resistance to the tithe, then it is reasonable to infer that the midnight march and the murder of James Morris were orchestrated by ribbonmen. Morris's murder – essentially an execution – was carried out silently, deliberately, and almost ritually. Similarly, the nighttime march through Forkhill was well ordered and carried out in "rigorous silence." It will be recalled that many of the marchers wore white bands on their hats, and a white ribbon was attached to the saddle of the horse ridden by the leader.[96] The wearing of ribbons can be found in reports of organized outrage from virtually every part of Ireland during nearly every outbreak of disturbances since the early eighteenth century – though, as noted earlier, the name ribbonmen probably stemmed from a clash between Catholics and Orangemen around 1810.[97]

The practice of wearing similar articles of clothing as a show of solidarity and for the purpose of identification was very common. In 1792 J. Byrne described a party of Defenders who had assembled for a fight wearing handkerchiefs around their bodies "as a mark to know each other in the dark."[98] At a funeral near Newry in 1812, about seventy young men, "wearing the same kind of handkerchief round the neck ... separated from the Crowd and went to a field where they fell into Ranks and march'd and exercised."[99] In 1814 the Threshers operating in the neighbourhood of Keady wore "bands on their hatts [sic] to distinguish themselves as such."[100] And the members of one of the Forkhill factions (the Red the Roads, or Rednecks) were known for the red handkerchiefs they wore around their necks.[101] Certain wardrobe details often distinguished the leaders of these parties from the regular membership. For instance, the tithe agitation in Killeavy in 1835 was organized by a man wearing a red cap and carrying a long white pole.[102] And during the tithe war in Kilkenny, one of the local leaders was "distinguished by a military cap and a red and yellow sash across his shoulders."[103]

The practice of wearing ribbons had long been associated with various festivals and special events in the Irish cultural system. One of these was the tradition of May Day (derived from the Celtic festival of Bealtaine), which marked the beginning of summer. The first of May was also the day on which tenancies began and ended, and when the hiring fairs were held.[104] May Day celebrations included parades, sports, dancing, and revelry. The whole population turned out for the celebrations, and the young people dressed in costume – often one that was knotted with ribbons. A note in the *Ulster Journal of Archaeology* of 1855 describes the May Day celebrations in eighteenth-century Carrickfergus, where large numbers of young men assembled "wearing white linen shirts over their other dress, decorated with a profusion of lively ribbons tied in knots."[105] Similar scenes took place in Derry, where the May boys paraded through the neighbourhood, "dressed in shirts over their clothes, and ornamented with ribbons of various colours."[106]

The ribbon, particularly the white ribbon, was also associated with St Brigid and had a hallowed place in rural Catholic culture. Throughout much of Ireland, it was common for people to place a silk ribbon (*brat*) on the windowsill on Brigid's Eve (31 January). According to a tradition in Munster, the *Brat Bríde* would lengthen during the night and was used as a remedy for headache; it was "drawn around the patient's head three times, saying each time the invocation, 'in the name of the Father, and of the Son, and of the Holy Ghost, Amen,' after which it is knotted around the head."[107] Elsewhere, it was believed that the saint, going about the country on the eve of her feast, touched these ribbons and endowed them with healing powers. The powers varied widely, depending on the local tradition, but included the assistance of women in childbirth, the cure of sick animals, the protection of children from fairies, and the repulsion of evil.[108] As Kevin Danaher explains, the *brat* might be a ribbon, a piece of linen or other cloth, a sash, a scarf, or a handkerchief. Anything that was believed to have been touched by the saint would protect the wearer from harm. It was worn by fishermen, who attributed their safe passage through storms to the wearing of the *brat Bríde*. Migratory labourers wore the *brat* when crossing to England and Scotland, and emigrants wore them when travelling to North America.[109]

The belief that the *brat* had protective powers might explain why rural protestors and "midnight legislators" often adorned themselves with ribbons, as well as with sashes, kerchiefs, and caps. An early incident of ribbon wearing dates from 1711–13, during an outbreak of disturbances in Galway. A group of eight men on horseback "dressed in white shirts with white linen bands tied about their heads" had been observed riding into a park, where they killed several sheep.[110] White ribbons were worn in south Armagh during the tithe agitation,[111] and Lord Gosford had noted the same practice at a funeral near the village of Keady in 1833.[112] Two years later, several police constables witnessed a funeral procession through the village of Crossmaglen and observed that the mourners were marching "with rods and white tape tied to the end of each rod."[113] All of these men, from Galway to Crossmaglen, may have believed that the white bands they wore accorded them a supernatural protection as they discharged their duty of upholding the unwritten law of the countryside. They believed that they had right on their side, and the wearing of a ribbon, band, or kerchief may have served as the outward mark of that conviction.

The role of ribbonism in the boisterous assemblies at Pyar's farm, in the mass gathering on the outskirts of Forkhill, and in the other demonstrations in 1835 is harder to discern. These acts were public rather than private; they were conducted in broad daylight rather than under the cover of darkness; and they were challenges to external authority rather than cases of internal discipline. However, to ask precisely what role ribbonism played in such public demonstrations is to ask the wrong question. Ribbonism was at once a system and an expression of rural consciousness; it existed formally and informally, and behaved in a manner that could be either organized or spontaneous. It had varying degrees of organization, coherence, commitment, and support, all of which depended on its location and leadership and on local circumstances. It was notoriously shape shifting. On this account, the attempts of contemporaries and historians to pin down ribbonism –

whether geographically, chronologically, or philosophically – have often foundered.[114] The efforts of George Cornewall Lewis to unravel such nineteenth-century secret societies led him to the following observation: "That the natural and most useful propensity of mankind to pry into what is hidden, sometimes leads to the attributing of too much weight to the knowledge of men's secrets, when their motives are sufficiently apparent from their acts ... Furthermore, it is to be remembered, that when men's interests impel them to use violent and illegal means, and to form secret combinations, in order to gain certain ends, we are not to suppose that those ends are always distinctly conceived, or that the purposes of the Whiteboy association are as clearly defined, for example, as those of a geological or an astronomical society."[115]

Although both the existence and the activities of secret societies depended heavily on the sanction of the community (which was itself a strange admixture of sympathy and terror), not all young men wished to be associated with them. The Monaghan novelist William Carleton, who claimed he had been sworn as a ribbonman without his knowledge in 1814, was most scornful of the society. He condemned the ribbonmen as "ignorant" and connected with the "very lowest dregs" of the population.[116] He believed the society had been provoked into existence by the Orange Order but was afterwards sustained through the manipulation of schemers, purely for their own profit. He claimed that it was not only difficult but dangerous to avoid involvement in the ribbon confederacy, since anyone who resisted its overtures might be waylaid and beaten.[117] This was the story told by John Kerr of Armagh, who was arrested for an agrarian outrage in November 1815. In an effort to "save his own life," he provided a detailed confession, which included a description of his enrolment in the secret society. Kerr claimed that he had been walking home one evening when he was met on the road by three men he knew. One of them "pulled out a book and said if John Kerr would not swear what he was going to put to him, he would blow out his brains, and then pulled out a pistol."[118] Against his will, Kerr took the oath. Undoubtedly, a certain amount of intimidation was used in the secret societies, particularly when they were short of numbers or firearms, and the tactics were not only physical. In March 1859 the unnamed author of a letter to the chief secretary stated that in a recent discussion with the Catholic archbishop of Armagh, the Most Reverend Joseph Dixon, on the subject of the secret societies and their hold over young men, Dixon had said that those going "temporarily to England for employment ... told him that if they did not join associations of this kind they could not procure work in England"; and Dixon had "alluded to the association called the Hibernian, which [was] well-known to exist in Glasgow and Liverpool."[119]

The tithe agitation arose from an ostensibly "religious" issue – the resentment of the majority of the population at being taxed to support a church to which they did not belong. The religious divide created by the tithe war might be expected to have produced sectarian rancour in mixed communities, but in fact its sectarian character was ambiguous in several respects. In February 1832, while the agitation was still in its infancy, an anti-tithe meeting was held in the village of Camlough, several miles from Forkhill. The purpose of the meeting was to petition Parliament for the "total abolition" of tithes: "Your petitioners have long laboured under the infliction of this oppressive tax, which, they are convinced, checks the spirit of agricultural industry among all class of farmers, and bears down, with overwhelming pressure, on the poorer."[120] The meeting was much the same as the one held in Forkhill several months later, except that those present were Protestants: Church of Ireland parishioners and Dissenters. And when the anti-tithe meeting was held in Forkhill in July 1832, it was chaired by Arthur Johnson, a local Protestant landlord.[121]

In November 1835 several threatening notices were posted throughout the parish of Creggan, cautioning landholders "of every creed and persuasion" against payment of the tithe: "Whoever pays that impost called tythe shall be in a short time freed from all worldly cares by him who has slumbered these many days but has now recovered from his drowsiness – therefore we beseech you have not a hand in your own deaths. We are nameless but not without authority." An 1835 outrage report recorded that the principal resisters of the tithe were Protestants and that the resident clergyman, Charles Atkinson, had recently served writs on several wealthy landed proprietors in Creggan who had declined to pay their tithes. The situation had been boiling for several years: "In 1827 the parishioners compounded for £1050 per year and at the vestry the Roman Catholicks were more friendly towards the doctor than either the Protestants or Presbyterians and voted £50 more than he expected. Doctor Atkinson seems to have acted [word obscured] by the people and left off all attempts at collecting his tithe till the last moment, and I believe has no reason to apprehend much opposition from any but Protestants and Presbyterians. Three priests whom I was speaking to on the subject said Dr Atkinson is a very good man and he ought to be paid his tithe ... It is to be regretted that from the wealthy Protestants and Presbyterians he has received so much trouble and opposition."[122]

The leading Protestant landowners in Armagh ignored such grievances and insisted on the sectarian character of the disturbances, sounding shrill warnings to anyone who would listen. In October 1834 more than fifty leading Armagh gentlemen signed a letter requesting the high sheriff to call a meeting to address the "dangers which threaten the Protestant Religion."[123] The signatories included several prominent landlords and magistrates from Forkhill and the surrounding area, including Hunt Walsh Chambré, John Foxall, Powell Foxall, Major Arthur Bernard, and Jonathan Seaver. The high sheriff, Charles Brownlow, replied crisply that he did not have "the slightest doubt" that the type of meeting they proposed would be a "religious and party affair" that would run the risk of arousing fatal dissension, and he could not for a moment sanction such a proceeding.[124] "I think it very wrong," he wrote, "when the people are in the cultivation of industrious and friendly intercourse, to check their growing union, and to endanger the peace of a mixed population by the excitement of crowded meetings assembling ... under religious distinctions."[125] The agitation eventually subsided with the passage of the Tithe Rent Charge Act of 1838, which made the tithe a rent charge payable by landlords.

The petition which the group of Protestant farmers from Forkhill had presented to the government in 1832 had been inspired by fear of action by their Catholic neighbours. Yet this perception of collective action by the Catholic peasantry as lawless, unpredictable, and sectarian was misconstrued. Although lawless, the attacks in the parish followed a particular code of behaviour that was unwritten but widely understood. In fact, the pattern of outrage in the countryside was thoroughly predictable, because of the ribbonmen's practice of warning transgressors of the rural code before visiting punishment upon them. The tithe agitation revealed the somewhat ambiguous sectarian character of the outrage and the fact that it was largely intramural, directing the greatest degree of intimidation and violence against members of its own community.

Acts of outrage occasionally extended beyond the system of discipline and community regulation, finding expression in other ways. Chief among these was the long-standing tradition of faction fighting, which was carried on in Forkhill with some ferocity in the 1830s. Faction fighting has been described as a form of "recreational violence" that filled a void of amusement in the countryside, although this term should not obscure its deadly nature.[126] Factions were usually based on extended families' kin groups, which aligned themselves against other factions over local quarrels. The feuds were passed down from one generation to the next.[127] In Limerick, two rival factions known as the Three Year Olds and Four Year Olds battled for decades, their names having originated from an argument over the age of a colt or cow.[128] In Tipperary, the dispute between the Caravats and Shanavests had originated at the hanging of a man named Nicholas Hanley in 1806. At the foot of the scaffold, one of Hanley's detractors, a man named

Connors, had mocked the doomed man's elegant cravat, and Hanley had retorted with a biting comment on Connors's old waistcoat. This exchange had inspired the formation of the two enduring factions.[129]

Occasionally, animosity between rival parties was revived, a challenge was issued, and an appointment for a fight was agreed upon. A witness before the 1835 inquiry into the disturbances in Ireland described the circumstances behind a typical faction fight: "It very often arises in this sort of way, that at a fair, or at any public meeting, some of the peasantry get intoxicated, a quarrel ensues ... One party prepares his friends and his faction to meet the other party ... at the next convenient place of public meeting, at a fair or market, and there they who have a strong faction attack this party, and beat and ill-treat them, and in some instances lives have been lost; the faction increases, the other party then recruits for the next place, and, at last, it becomes a most serious matter; almost the whole of the peasantry in a fair I have seen engaged in fights in this kind of way."[130] A formal faction fight could involve several hundred men on each side and usually began with the ritual of "wheeling," through taunting and insults. Faction fights could be wickedly violent, the combatants arming themselves with sticks, stones, iron bars, cudgels, old swords, and muskets studded with nails.[131] Severe injuries were commonplace, and many fights led to numerous deaths.

On 28 June 1835 a violent fight broke out at a bonfire near the Catholic chapel at Mullaghbawn in Forkhill, between two parties that were attending a celebration in honour of St Peter's Eve.[132] Witnesses claimed that five hundred people were involved in the affray, all of whom were Catholics. (These details were repeated in a story that appeared on the front page of the *Times* of London on 6 July.)[133] Many of the combatants had been wounded seriously, and the lives of a few were despaired of. One of the wounded, Redmond Hanlon, who lived in the townland of Tullymacreeve, was found "in a most dangerous state," and a doctor in attendance did not think he could survive his injuries.[134] In one of the houses where the injured were being tended, a constable investigating the incident encountered a young man who introduced himself as a divinity student. The student said that the matter was now "in the hands of the church" and would be settled without the interference of the magistrates, and he told the wounded man not to give the constable any information.[135] According to the magistrate, the battle was not the result of "party spirit" in any religious or political sense; it arose "from a long cherished spirit of revenge ... between two families or 'factions' in this part of the country."[136] The Forkhill factions were known as Red the Roads and the Fine Morning.[137] Their rivalry was long-standing, and there had been an equally serious battle between them several years earlier. (An oblique reference to Red the Roads was made in the *Newry Telegraph* in 1828 when describing a dispute between two Forkhill men who had agreed on a boxing match to settle the argument; during the fight, one of them had been egged on by bystanders to "red" the other.)[138]

Faction fighting was recognized as a showcase for honour and revenge.[139] Its members were "typically vain of their superiority in strength" and "wished to be superior to the opposite party."[140] Other factors were often involved: tradition, sport, competition, boredom, and frustration, as well as liquor in many cases.[141] For young men especially, association with a faction may have fulfilled a social need, similar to that offered by ribbonism. Men who joined ribbon lodges enjoyed a sense of belonging, which was confirmed through the rites of initiation, the passwords, and a sworn oath to defend their "brothers."[142] Although factions were less formal, they fulfilled the same need to identify oneself with a group and to affirm this identity through violence if necessary. In many places, membership in local factions and ribbon societies overlapped.[143] Indeed, in Forkhill there is evidence that violent disputes between the two rival factions were connected to ribbonism.

In March 1837 Owen Macan stopped in at Bernard Smith's public house in Mullaghbawn for "a drink of spirits."[144] Smith was a suspected ribbonman whose public house was known as a ribbon meeting house. (Later that year, police were informed that a meeting of the ribbon society would be held in "Smith's public house" in Forkhill.)[145] While there, Macan was called on to drink to the health of the Red the Roads men, and when he refused, Smith and several others threw him to the ground and cut his coat to shreds with a knife and scissors. He made his escape and reported the incident to the police.[146] Macan also worked as a gatekeeper for James Campbell, the Church of Ireland rector of Forkhill, and had passed information about the ribbon societies to the police in 1835.[147] When describing the attack on him, he said that Smith had remarked that he "did not like to see any of the Reverend Dr Campbell's servants coming into his house."[148]

Two weeks after this incident, a man named Edward Kelly was waylaid and beaten by a crowd of nearly thirty men as he returned home around midnight from a wake in Forkhill. Kelly belonged to the Red the Roads faction, and he told police that he had been attacked by members of the Fine Morning.[149] Earlier that year, Kelly had been identified as a member of the "Forkhill Ribbon society" by the informers Hugh and Peter McGill.[150]

In April 1837 Loughlin Hanratty from the townland of Tiffcrum was accosted by Andrew Begley and Archibald McNeal at a pub in the village where Hanratty had stopped to buy some bacon. The men dragged him outside, where they kicked and beat him, and he later died of his injuries.[151] Both men were arrested and tried for the murder but were acquitted. Like Kelly, both had been identified as leading ribbonmen by the McGill brothers. Begley was said to be the younger brother of the head committee man, and McNeal was the secretary of the local committee. In May 1839 Begley was beaten as he returned home from the Forkhill fair (though the circumstances of the attack are unknown).[152]

At the national level, ribbonism was a volatile, fractious, and highly disunified movement. The society split and then repaired its breach several times in the 1830s and 1840s, and there was constant infighting between ribbonmen in the major centres of Dublin and Belfast.[153] Within the Ulster network, there was fierce dissension between factions in Armagh and Monaghan, much of it traceable to the pernicious influence of the Monaghan ribbon leader John Rice.[154] It is not difficult to imagine this fractiousness and territorialism replicating itself just as violently at the parish level and expressing itself through wars between existing factions. The Forkhill factions endured until the twentieth century. Michael J. Murphy has recorded several traditions about the Forkhill "Rednecks," so-called for the red handkerchiefs they wore around their necks; their name was later synonymous with the Ancient Order of Hibernians, known locally as the Hibs.[155] In September 1876 the Forkhill fair was the scene of a vicious faction fight between upwards of one hundred men who fought with sticks and stones: the "*melée* had its origin in a dispute between parties termed 'Rednecks' and 'Fenians.'"[156]

OUTRAGE AND THE LAND

In the twenty years between 1821 and 1841, the population of Forkhill rose from the official figure of 6,772 to 8,128, which translated into a population density of 413 people per square mile.[157] Much of this land was of poor quality and proved difficult to reclaim as tillage, even by a diligent tenantry. The anxiety generated by these circumstances was manifested in the tithe agitation of the early 1830s and was compounded by disputes on the Forkhill estate later in the decade. Controversy over the collection of rent and rental charges on the estate had led to proceedings in the Court of Chancery in 1832.[158] In 1838 the Reverend James Campbell informed the landlord, Nathaniel Alexander, that a recent attempt to lease land on the estate had been resisted by the tenantry: An "extremely unreasonable and unjust attempt was lately made to reduce the Rental ... A spirit of combination was to some slight extent raised on the occasion but it has been allayed and almost entirely overcome. The greater part of the Tenants have renewed their proposals and have gladly undertaken to pay the very moderate Rents." However, Campbell added, "A few obstinately stand out and resist any terms in the hope of being successful in obtaining a reduction of rent at a public sale."[159] In view of this, he advised his bishop to have his land agent attend any auction of the lands in order to prevent any reduction in rent.[160]

In the spring of 1840 the tenants on the Forkhill estate were invited to submit proposals for their holdings – a measure that may have been intended as a first step towards the granting of proper leases.[161] Many tenants seized the opportunity to make a claim, writing plaintive accounts of their circumstances and the urgent need for security in their farms. A tenant named Patrick Shevlun[162] wrote to the land agent in April 1840, and his letter was typical:

> Sir, I beg to suggest that I am in occupation of a farm in Levelmor containing 7 acres plantation measure or thereabouts at the yearly rent of £5.4.1 by the late valuation. The former rent being £4.7.10 – which has been raised on me in 1839. I am now going on 8 years in said farm and have expended a considerable sum of money in improvements and have yet to clear a great part of it to make it tillagable ... It may be seen that more than an acre of land is taken up with rocks and other rugged spots – and therefore of little or no use to me – together with the loss my crops sustain every season by the overflowing of the River which occasions me to lose much of my time in repairing the fences on the course after every fall of rain. I therefore pray you will take my case into your consideration and hope you will make some equitable arrangement in my Rent and shall ever feel grateful. I am, Your most obedient Humble Servant, Patrick Shevlun.[163]

It appears that the exercise was in vain. A witness before the Devon Commission in 1844 testified that leases on the Forkhill estate had been promised several years earlier, "and money was sent to pay for them; and the money was sent back again, and they will not grant any."[164]

The Devon Commission was established in 1843 to inquire into the occupation of land and its relationship to "the causes of discontent in Ireland."[165] The commission heard testimony from 1,100 witnesses on all aspects of the land system, including the valuation of land, the tenant right system, rent charges, and the practice of subdivision.[166] Several residents of south Armagh were invited to testify, including Father Michael Lennon, the parish priest of Upper Creggan, who was also familiar with the parish of Forkhill.[167] Lennon reported that the farms in his area were "very small," the majority being under ten acres. In the districts of Forkhill and Killeavy, most holdings were under five acres. Most of these farms were not leased for life but were rented for short terms from middlemen – these middlemen being farmers who rented sizable farms under longer-term leases and then sublet holdings as a way of augmenting their income.[168] Sometimes the undertenant might in turn let some of his ground to another tenant (usually one worse off than himself), a practice that became more widespread as the population increased. In 1844 Lennon remarked that there were "no leases" in the countryside and that the poor people were all tenants-at-will. Thomas Seaver, a Killeavy landlord, confirmed this. "Few landlords in the country give a lease," he testified.[169]

The position of the tenant-at-will was generally very poor. Because he held land on a yearly or even a monthly basis, he had no security of ownership and faced regular rent increases. The rents on farms held at will were typically higher than on land held under a proper lease, and there were always people ready to replace the sitting tenants if they were unable or unwilling to pay.[170] Tenants who could not afford holdings, or who had been squeezed off the land, rented cottages or cabins from small farmers. The rent for such a holding in Forkhill ranged from thirty to forty shillings annually.[171] These tenants settled the rent with labour, working on their immediate landlord's farm for between one and three days a week. To feed their families, they rented conacre ("potato ground"), often at an exorbitant rate. Lennon estimated that the annual rent for conacre was £8 an acre, or £1 for half a rood.[172]

In these circumstances, it is not surprising that the condition of the tenantry, and the labourers in particular, was deteriorating. A series of unfavourable seasons and failed crops, especially of oats and potatoes, had taken a severe toll. Both Lennon and Walter Dawson (another of the witnesses at the Devon Commission) reported that the condition of the poorer classes had worsened during the previous five years (1839–44). Lennon remarked on the hardship caused by the death of pigs and cattle from diseases "hitherto unknown in this country." Dawson referred to the "empty stack-yards" and the fact that tenants had to plead for seed corn, lime, meal, and even potatoes, on credit. "I do not find [the people] improving one bit where they ought to be," he said.[173]

The most compelling aspect of the testimony heard by the Devon Commission concerned the people's attitude to the land. Land was guarded jealously, measured carefully, and defended with violence. Men and women who had been turned off their land became "demoralized," "savage," and "wild." If you touch the farm and turn a man out, one witness said, "the mind gets changed, and there is sure some misfortune to follow from that." Holding land had become a cultural obsession, and the circumstances behind the letting of land in a community were "engraven on the minds" of the local people for generations. Testimony heard before the commission reveals details of an unwritten code governing the occupation, leasing, transfer, and sale of land, a code that was far more significant than the conveyance of legal title.[174] Consider the practice of outbidding a former tenant for his land when his lease expired. Although this was a perfectly legal transaction, the people considered it "land grabbing" – a reprehensible act. As a County Down farmer explained, it was "against the will of the people" for a man to take another man's farm. Dispossession (seizing land from a tenant who failed to pay his rent) was the most serious transgression against this rural code of conduct, and land agents often had difficulty leasing farms that had been seized from former tenants.[175] The possessive attitude to the land described by witnesses at the Devon Commission had been handed down for generations, and it was precisely this pedigree that made it so formidable.

During the late 1830s and early 1840s, this desperation was translated into acts of outrage, many of which are described in the constabulary reports of the period. They provide a detailed view of the practice of outrage in the nineteenth century.[176] The following cases are drawn from the Outrage Reports for south Armagh between 1835 and 1840. On the night of 6 February 1836, the home of Francis Kearns in the parish of Creggan was entered by a number of armed men. Kearns, along with a few of his neighbours who were in the house, "made to have a stand against this illegal mob" and succeeded in driving them off. "It is reported they killed one of the ruffians by hitting him on the head with spades and that he has been privately buried and another of them has been dangerously wounded by stabs of a pitchfork."[177] The report assigned the motive for the attack to a land dispute: "The Reason Kearns has been attacked is that ten or fifteen years ago he purchased from his father-in-law an acre of land which his brother-in-law now wishes to get back without making any allowance to Kearns either as remuneration for Purchase money or Improvements."[178]

In July 1836 a Forkhill man, Terence Groogan, was severely beaten by five men yet refused to provide information to the police. The resident magistrate, Major Bernard, noted that both the victim and the attackers "were of one religion."[179] In August the home of Michael McTeague, a Catholic and a pensioner from the Royal Navy, was attacked by several men who broke the windows and threw large stones onto the bed where he and his wife were sleeping. "It is supposed that the children of his landlady want the land back, now that he has improved it."[180] Later that month, a rood of turf belonging to

Michael McConville was destroyed during the night: "It is generally supposed that this outrage occurred owing to a dispute over land."[181]

On 9 March 1837 at around four o'clock in the morning, John McAleavy heard shots fired near his house in the townland of Shean in Forkhill. When he rose from his bed, he saw coals on fire near one of his hayricks. The previous year, McAleavy had testified at the assizes against several local men who had been charged with riotous assembly.[182] In September 1837 Owen Rice and his wife were "burst upon" in the middle of the night by a mob with blackened faces. Rice managed to escape, "though in a complete state of nudity," and sought refuge in a neighbour's house. He was quarrelling over land with another family in Killeavy, and he suspected that the attack was related to that dispute.[183] In February 1838 a Creggan man named James McNulty was seized by a mob and beaten "and obliged to promise on his knees that he would not offer more than one pound an acre for land."[184]

Most of the outrage reports carefully recorded information about the nature of the attack, the relationship of the victim to the suspect (if known), the religion of the parties involved, and speculation about the motive. Owing to the speculative nature of the reports and the fact that many outrages went unreported because of the prevailing system of intimidation, it is impossible to provide an accurate statistical analysis of outrage in the countryside during these years. But an unscientific sample of 141 outrages drawn from the reports filed in south Armagh between 1835 and 1840 suggests that nearly 40 per cent of the outrages were traced to disputes over land – more than any other single suspected cause (and the true figure is probably higher).[185] In 130 cases, the religion of both the victim and the suspect was given. This breakdown reveals that 100 outrages (73 per cent) were committed against Catholics and fully 97 per cent of them were committed by fellow Catholics.[186] Of the thirty outrages committed against Protestants, 90 per cent arose from disputes over property.

These estimates confirm the findings of the Devon Commission, which had asked witnesses to comment on the extent to which the "revenge about the ground" proceeded from sectarian motives. A series of witnesses testified that Protestant and Catholic offenders of the land code were treated in a similar manner, though some believed that a Protestant would be treated more harshly. Others said that sectarian prejudice was almost never the motive for an attack and that justice was administered impartially. Virtually all of the evidence presented before the commission agreed on one point – that agrarian protest movements defended local rights to the land against anyone who dared interfere, whether Catholic or Protestant.[187]

The extent to which these assaults on land and person were connected with the ribbon system is difficult to determine because of the secrecy of the society and because of the notorious reluctance of victims and witnesses to provide information to the police. But there is little doubt that ribbonism was a vital force in the parish in the late 1830s.[188] As already noted, there were strong suggestions that the society was involved in the tithe agitation between 1832 and 1836, and the McGill brothers had confirmed its existence in their statement to the magistrates in 1837. That same year, a number of altercations were reported between members of the Fine Morning and Red the Roads factions in Forkhill; the latter appear to have been involved with the ribbon system. In December 1837 police interrupted a gathering, held at an unlicensed pub in the townland of Cloghinny, which they suspected to be a ribbon meeting. They searched the men for seditious papers and found, in the pocket of Pat Rafferty's trousers, a slip of paper containing a printed set of passwords. The first password read: "May the Day star of Erin appear more clear / And Brighten our Prospect Each succeeding year." The second password was for safe passage at night: "The stars Look Dim / A gale from the north would refresh them."[189]

The ascension of ribbonism coincided with the surge of outrages in the parish in the late 1830s, many of which were traceable to disputes over land. This coincidence suggests that the regulation of the land system was a key part of the ribbon agenda and that the ribbonmen were active in disciplining those who transgressed the land code. Indeed, they had done as much in January 1833, when the ribbon procession through Forkhill had stopped at the house of Philip Trainor, beaten him severely, and ordered him to give up a piece of ground that had lately come into his possession.[190] Some years later, the witnesses before the 1852 Select Committee on Outrages, which convened in the wake of serious unrest in the districts of south Armagh, north Louth, and north Monaghan, emphasized this preoccupation of ribbonism with the land.[191] The ribbonmen, one witness asserted, are "against the proprietary of the land; their principal object is to get the rents down."[192] The "tenure of the land" was the "favourite object" of the ribbonmen, said another, and ribbon outrages were "almost always connected with land in some way."[193] When the same witness was asked if the ribbon system had any "religious or political object," he replied that he had "not considered [the system] in that view."[194] The land agent William Steuart Trench agreed: "The main object of the ribbon society was to prevent any landlord ... from depriving a tenant of his land...The second object was to deter, on pain of almost certain death, any tenant from taking land from which another tenant had been evicted."[195]

Circumstantial evidence also suggests that the men in Forkhill who were ribbonmen would have been attracted to a society that defended rights to the land. In their statement to police in 1837, the McGill brothers supplied the names of twenty-three local men who, they claimed, were members of the ribbon society.[196] Sixteen of the men lived in the townland of Tiffcrum, six others lived in the neighbouring townlands of Carrickasticken and Cloghinny, and one was from Shean. Twenty of these men can be located with some certainty in the 1821 census.[197] Although most of them had been quite young in 1821 and were still unmarried and did not have farms of their own, the amount of land held by their fathers (or widowed mothers) can provide some indication of the social and economic circumstances – and, more important, the prospects – of these alleged ribbonmen.

Eighteen of these twenty men had lived at home in 1821, and the average size of the homestead was 3.7 acres (less than the parish average of 4.3 acres). Five of the men were the sons of labourers, four were the sons of widows, and the remainder were the sons of small farmers. There were no tradesmen, merchants, teachers, or professionals among their ranks. In 1837 the men ranged in age from twenty-one to forty-nine, and the average Forkhill ribbonman was thirty-one years old. If the information supplied by the McGill brothers is correct, we can conclude that the typical Forkhill ribbonman was a labourer or small farmer, with little or no land of his own and little prospect of coming into a holding in the near future. Consequently, he was more likely to feel the pressure of the developing crisis over land in south Armagh and was perhaps more easily moved to resistance – and even violence – in response.[198]

OUTRAGE AFTER THE FAMINE

The famine of 1845–49 changed the picture dramatically. Between 1841 and 1851 the population of Forkhill declined by more than one-quarter, and the acute pressure of population on the land that had fuelled nearly two decades of outrage was swiftly and painfully remedied. Anxieties over the ribbon system persisted, however. In April 1851 Widow McEleavy's house in Forkhill was broken into by a party of several men. They forced Mrs McEleavy and her daughter Bridget onto their knees and compelled them to swear that they would not prosecute James Nugent at the next petty sessions. If they did, "they would be shot."[199] The intruders fired a warning shot in the house before departing. Bridget was able to identify two of the men (one of whom was Nugent himself), and both were charged with assault. But at their trial in August, Bridget refused to incriminate them, and they were acquitted. Widow McEleavy "rejoiced [that] her daughter had perjured herself and liberated the prisoners, for a clergyman could absolve her from the sin of perjury, but had she to tell the *truth* and the two prisoners was transported, she would never be forgiven."[200]

In early January 1852, several prominent Armagh landlords signed a memorial attesting to the "disorganized and fearful" state of the country which, they said, was riddled with a "deep and wide-spread conspiracy ... by which murder has been reduced to a system."[201] According to these landowners, the climate of disturbance, violence, and general lawlessness had made the enforcement of the law, the levying of rates, and the protection of civil rights virtually impossible.[202] In May 1850 Lindsay Mauleverer, a land agent for the Hamilton, Tipping, and Jones estate, was murdered near Crossmaglen. He had been struck on the back of the head with a blunt object and was found lying face down at the side of road.[203] In December 1851 Thomas Bateson, a land agent and magistrate, was beaten to death. Shortly afterwards, on Christmas Eve, there was an attempt to murder a Louth landlord, James Eastwood.[204]

That same month another landlord, the Killeavy magistrate Meredith Chambré, had received a letter threatening his life.

> To all this concerns, and Beware of General Avenger. I am not Fools. I am giving you timely warning, all Tyrants and oppressors of the Poor. Its like the Thief of the Gallows, its over you particular landlords, particularly in the seed time, if they don't give their tenants Seed Oats to put in their land, and lower their rents, it will be measured with their corpse. And their is Mr Chambrie, a Beggarman, he had better keep close, for if he does not, he may have his coffin ready; but we will bury him when he will neither have coffin or shroud around him, for its too Good for an oppressor of the Poor, as an idle-hearted rascal; besides, who prides in the downfall of his country men, we need not wonder – he is no Irishman ... I am, General Vengeance.[205]

On the evening of 20 January 1852, Chambré left the petty sessions court in Forkhill, where he had spent the day presiding over the local sessions, and set out on the short journey to his home in Killeavy. As his coach passed through the townland of Drumintee, about a mile from Forkhill village, shots rang out. Chambré was struck in the head, face, and neck. He leaped from the coach, blunderbuss in hand, but collapsed at the side of the road. Travelling with him were his brother Hunt Walsh Chambré and his butler David Cole. They carried Chambré to a nearby cabin and sought assistance. The inhabitants were "ominously incommunicative and sulky," but after some difficulty the wounded man was admitted. When the doctor arrived, he managed to extract two pellets, but the victim remained in a precarious state. A statement was released the following evening and printed in the *Newry Telegraph*: "Poor Chambré is in a deplorable state, with little hopes of recovery. His left eye is smashed. He has been almost unconscious ever since."[206]

The newspaper speculated that Chambré had been targeted for his role in the arrest, prosecution, and conviction of local ribbonmen, and it harped on the sectarian dimension of the attack. Like Alexander Berkley before him, Chambré was depicted as the blameless victim of the exclusively Catholic and deeply sectarian ribbon society.[207] The *Telegraph* described him as a generous landlord, committed to the social improvement of the poor people on his estate by finding employment for his tenants and building a school for their children.[208] But the Irish folklore manuscripts give a far more negative impression, presenting him as a parsimonious landlord and belligerent Orangeman.[209] Stories of Chambré abound. During the famine, he had been accused of seducing his tenants by offering them money and food if they sent their children to the Protestant school on his estate; he was said to require every household on his estate to feed and fatten a goose through the winter (at the household's own expense) and to surrender it to him in the spring; and he was accused of charging excessive rent and of refusing to give his tenants seed to plant their crops.[210]

A massive police effort was undertaken immediately after the attack on Chambré, and by 24 January thirteen men had been arrested. One of them was a labourer from Drumintee named Francis Berry, who was arrested at his mother's house on the evening of the shooting. A small quantity of powder was uncovered in the thatch of the roof, and some percussion caps were found in his pocket.[211] The report noted that Berry's face was scratched "as if by briars" and the knees of his trousers were muddied. His boots, which were drying by the hearth, were confiscated by the police and later tested against footprints at the scene. They matched. While Berry was being held in Forkhill police station, his sister brought him some bread and cold meat wrapped in newspaper. Recalling that pieces of newspaper had been recovered at the scene of the crime and that some paper had been used to stuff the blunderbuss that fired the shots, the police confiscated the wrapping. They compared the newspaper recovered at the side of the road with the wrapping on Berry's sandwiches, and they too matched.

The next day, Berry confessed to involvement in the plot to murder Chambré and admitted that he had been at the scene of the shooting with two other men, who were strangers to the parish. His job had been to identify Chambré's coach to the men. "Well I shall tell the truth whether I shall die or no," he said. "I was one of them men myself that was at that gather [fair] and two more me [i.e., two others] from Cross or Glassdrummond said two men asked me would I show the mark and I replied I would and I would not go near hand them for this man Chambré would know me, they said very well."[212]

Berry claimed that he had taken off over the fields before the shots were fired and had heard the report of the gun from a distance. At his trial in July 1852, he wore a tweed frock coat and dark trousers, and looked about twenty-seven years old. He pleaded not guilty but was convicted of the attempted murder and sentenced to death. He was hanged at Armagh in August 1852.[213] Berry's body was taken by hearse to his uncle's cabin near Camlough, where a wake was held on the Saturday night, and he was buried on the Sunday in the Old Killeavy cemetery.[214]

The attempted murder of Meredith Chambré earned nothing less than the reproach of Queen Victoria. In the Speech from the Throne in February 1852, she denounced the disturbances that kept the borderlands in a state of unrest: "It is with much regret that I have to inform you that certain parts of the counties of Armagh, Monaghan and Louth, have been marked by the commission of outrages of the most serious description. The powers of the existing law have been promptly exerted for the detection of the offenders, and for the repression of a system of crime and violence fatal to the best interests of the country. My attention will continue to be directed to this important object."[215]

The government responded to this apparent surge of unrest by appointing a committee to inquire into the nature of the disturbances in the Ulster borderlands. The Select Committee on Outrages consisted of eighteen members, including the attorney general and the solicitor general for Ireland, and convened between 22 March and 18 May 1852. A parade of witnesses testified that the Ulster borderlands, particularly the region around Crossmaglen, were the most lawless parts of the country. Captain Warburton, who had taken up residence in Forkhill in early January 1852, reported that the district had "a system of intimidation carried on that I had never seen before."[216] Another testified that the ribbon system in south Armagh was better organized "than ever I knew it to be in any other part of the country I was ever in."[217] A third witness claimed that the neighbourhood around Crossmaglen was "probably the worst part of the country."[218]

Many of the witnesses who gave evidence before the select committee in 1852 testified that a "new" system of ribbonism had infiltrated the countryside, a deadlier system than before. Reading through the report, I was puzzled by the witnesses' emphasis on this point and their sense that the disturbances were a recent phenomenon. South Armagh had suffered disturbances throughout the 1830s and early 1840s, and most of the outrage reports are concentrated in the period 1835–45. As far as I can determine, the ribbon system had not become particularly violent or better organized by 1850, though it is true that conditions in the countryside had been transformed by the famine. Perhaps when pressure on the land was eased somewhat, the ribbonmen became more outward looking and less preoccupied with their own ground. This might explain why their targets assumed a higher profile during the post-famine years.[219] The murder and attempted murder of prominent landlords and agents may have captured the attention of the witnesses because these men were so like themselves – mainly Protestant magistrates and government officials, most of whom were substantial landowners.

Nevertheless, virtually every one of the witnesses who appeared before the select committee testified that the ribbonmen targeted Catholics as regularly and deliberately as Protestants. The ribbon system in south Armagh "acted as much against Roman-catholic proprietors as against Protestant proprietors," claimed Captain Warburton.[220] Edward Golding agreed, pointing out that the largest Catholic landowner in the district was shot in his own front hall as he passed through it: "I do not believe that the tenants of Roman-catholic proprietors are a bit less likely to be mixed up in the ribbon conspiracies than the tenants of Protestant proprietors; there is not the least difference."[221] The testimony of Captain Fitzmaurice made the same point. When asked if the ribbonmen spared Catholics, Fitzmaurice replied that "where they infringe[d] on the rules of the society," they had no mercy; the system of outrage targeted all classes "without distinction of creed."[222] Moreover, he claimed that popular sympathy with these outrages was not confined strictly to the Catholic population but was "participated in very generally speaking by all."[223] Similarly, James O'Callaghan said that it made no difference what creed a man professed, for "they are very impartial."[224]

If, as Fitzmaurice suggested, some support for the ribbon mandate could be found among the Protestant population, the opposition of the Catholic hierarchy remained implacable. As a body, the Catholic Church was vehemently opposed to the ribbon societies and regularly denounced them from the altar. Known ribbonmen were denied Holy Communion and the last rites, and were forced to recant their oaths in confession before they could be admitted to the sacraments.[225] Although the sympathies of some priests lay with the movement, most evidence indicates that the majority of the clergy were staunch enemies of ribbonism.

In the 1850s and 1860s, the surge of Catholic missions to Ireland targeted the ribbon societies and sought to loosen their hold on the people. An Austrian priest and Redemptorist missionary who travelled through Ireland in the early 1850s claimed great success in suppressing the secret societies. "The Ribbonmen," he wrote, "came to us in masses and abjured their membership and accepted the Holy Sacraments."[226] In 1853 Nicholas Hughes, the Catholic parish priest of Forkhill, wrote to the archbishop of Armagh in reference to a recent murder attempt by "ruffians from Forkhill." He praised "the Providence of God ... who employed so humble an instrument as I am to assist in saving human life and handing over to the vengeance of the law two members of that bloody conspiracy which continues rampant and merciless as ever, spreading terror and dismay among the poor ignorant peasantry ... One satisfactory feature in the deplorable event is that the enemies of our church cannot renew the oft repeated charge that we connive at Ribbonism."[227]

Ten years later, the clergy in Forkhill were still at war against the ribbon system, although they remained confident of victory. James Malone, parish priest of Drumintee, reported that the parish mission in June and July 1864 had been most successful. "I think Ribbonism is crushed in this part of the country," he wrote.[228] "During the Mullaghbane Mission a great number of the party men came in and resigned the system, a good number too have come in since. There is one parish master who still obstinately persists in this evil system – if I once had him I think Ribbonism would be almost dead here."[229]

A NEW OUTLOOK ON OUTRAGE

During the past forty years, social historians have made great strides in the study of protest and the objectives of unrest, with a particular focus on Western Europe during the eighteenth and nineteenth centuries. Historians have become more attuned to the consciousness of protestors and to what their agitation was intended to achieve.[230] Instances of violence, vandalism, and intimidation are no longer dismissed as irrational or criminal, though elements of the irrational and criminal are sometimes present. In Ireland, this development has been impeded to some extent by the sectarian dimension of the conflict. For much of modern Irish history, outrage has been characterized as an expression of sectarian animosity (whether latent or overt), particularly when disturbances occurred in mixed communities and especially when Catholics were engaged in some form of collective action.[231] The recent historiography of protest and rural violence in Ireland has been a valuable corrective in this regard. The Whiteboys, Rightboys, Defenders, and ribbonmen are now understood as movements that operated according to codes of behaviour that were often rational and predictable (if self-interested) in pursuit of particular sets of objectives that were widely understood – all of which elevated them above an impulsive banditti.[232]

However, these arguments are made with greater confidence in those parts of Ireland where the population was predominantly Catholic and where outrage was de facto "intercommunal." Approaches to the subject of outrage in mixed communities, such as the frontier zones of Ulster, have been less sure-footed. The concept of the "moral economy" is applied less readily here, perhaps because the circumstantial evidence for the sectarian character of outrages is frequently persuasive. In south Armagh, where the majority of the population was Catholic and where lawful authority was concentrated in the hands of a Protestant minority (landlords, magistrates, judges, and constabulary), the sectarian character of confrontations often appeared self-evident. This impression is reinforced by contemporary testimony from landlords, magistrates, yeomen, and clergymen, especially during periods of supposed "upheaval" (1790s, 1814–17, 1832–35, 1851–52). As property-owning Protestants in positions of authority, they were personally threatened by the stirrings of discontent among the Catholic population.[233] Many of them regarded any collective action by Catholics as a threat to their security and were quick to raise the sectarian alarm. In the absence of other witnesses, the opinion of the Armagh gentry on the subject of rural outrage has carried considerable weight. Even recent historical accounts of unrest in Ulster slip into generalizations and exaggerations about the essential sectarianism of eighteenth-century Defenders and nineteenth-century ribbonmen.[234]

Yet even in the frontier zone of south Armagh, outrage in the nineteenth century rarely proceeded from sectarian impulses. The truth of this assessment can be found in the ambiguity of the sectarian character of many of the disturbances, in the blindness of attacks on transgressors of the ribbon code, and in the exceptional degree of violence within the Catholic community. Rather than viewing outrage in south Armagh as sectarian, it should be understood, as it has been understood elsewhere in Ireland, in terms of a specific canon that regulated social and economic relationships in the countryside. It arose from the collective rural consciousness and an instinct of self-preservation, and was justified on the basis of its claim to a greater legitimacy. Ultimately, the purpose of outrage was the enforcement of legitimacy: from rent levels to the collection of tithes and cess, to the occupation of the land. Dispossession, eviction, land grabbing, and "drawing straight lines" were clear violations of the rural code of conduct. Raising rents beyond fair levels, underpaying labourers, charging excessively for conacre and potato ground, charging excessive fees for grinding corn – all these were considered unjust. Taxes, whether the cess or the poor rate, were generally not considered illegitimate in principle, but excessive taxation was. In the early 1830s, payment of the tithe was outlawed entirely, and punishment was visited upon stubborn tithe collectors. Nor was the Catholic Church immune to such scrutiny; the rates levied by the Catholic clergy for baptisms, marriages, and burials provoked opposition when they were considered excessive.[235] In 1842 Father McParlan, a Forkhill priest, was ordered not to charge more than a certain rate of cess.[236]

A contemporary observer described ribbonism as a "self-constituted tribunal, to settle the various affairs of the country people on almost all subjects," and in some cases this extended to the enforcement of social mores. In 1838 a crowd of men "armed with firearms and swords" entered the home of John McAtavry, a Catholic living in Creggan, and assaulted him and his wife. It was alleged that McAtavry's son Patrick was the father of a child born out of wedlock to a woman named Peggy Woods, although the young man denied the charge. "An illegal mob endeavouring to establish this have left the child in the residence of the old man with the directions to have it taken proper care of; they also went to oblige Pat McAtavry to marry the mother of the child and have promised further acts of violence should their orders not be obliged."[237] A witness before the 1852 Select Committee on Outrages confirmed that a number of marriages had been "enforced or prevented" by the society.[238]

The founding principle of its essential legitimacy found expression within the structure and operation of the ribbon system. The organization of the society was rigidly hierarchical; the expansion of the lodge network proceeded (on paper, at least) according to a rigorous formula based on figures of enrolment; the rules that bound its members were pervasive and controlling; the swearing of the ribbon oath was a formal ceremony that, with its invocation of Our Lord and the Virgin Mary, approached a holy sacrament.[239] The practice of giving victims three warnings before an attack, the mock trials carried out in the ribbon lodges to "convict" offenders, and the rumoured system by which every man took part in the crime by stabbing or beating the victim in turn in order to apportion blame – these were all examples of the ribbon system conferring legitimacy on itself and thus justifying the enforcement of its own peculiar brand of fairness. This spirit is manifest in the society's written communications – the threatening letters that were sent to obnoxious individuals or posted in public places. These letters were written in a tortured legal language that was meant to sound fearsome, impressive, and (most important) invested with the highest authority. Summoning the forces of "justice," "the law," and "the banner of trooth," they would put down all "tyrants," and "oppressors."[240] Often the notices were signed by Captain Rock, or Captain Fearnought.

Far from being lawless, the people of south Armagh were profoundly legalistic and, when the opportunity arose, litigious. Preserved in the Public Record Office of Northern Ireland are the surviving order books for the petty sessions court in Forkhill, dating from 1852.[241] The ledgers record a staggering number of cases that were brought before the petty sessions court in the 1850s and 1860s. Some of these cases were prosecutions made by the constabulary and magistracy for offences such as public drunkenness, petty theft, working on the Sabbath, possessing guns without a licence, and allowing dogs to go "unlogged"; as well, the landlords Henry Alexander of Forkhill and John Foxall of Killeavy occasionally brought charges against tenants for theft of timber and turf from their demesnes. But the vast majority of cases were civil proceedings among the people of the parish themselves – between employers and employees, between neighbours, and between family members.

On 20 March 1855, Bernard Smith of Mullaghbawn charged Hugh and Rose McCann with cutting down and carrying away "a portion of a fence, property of complaintant." Stephen Murphy of Mullaghbawn charged James Murchan of Tullymacreeve with "holding forcible possession of a field of land" that belonged to Murphy. James Morrison charged Bernard Murphy with allowing four head of cattle to wander on the public road. Arthur McCormick charged John McCoy with failing to pay his poor rate, which amounted to two shillings.[242]

On 7 August 1855, Arthur Bennett of Ballykeel charged Edward Cosgrove with allowing his pigs to trespass on Bennett's lands, injuring his potato crop, and "refusing to pay the ten shillings awarded by the appraiser for this injury together with one shilling in fees." Anne Begley of Shean charged Thomas Brooks of Shean with allowing his horses to trespass on her lands several times during July, damaging her corn crops, and of refusing to pay the seven shillings awarded by the appraiser together with one shilling in fees. Arthur McShane of Shean lodged a similar complaint against Brooks. Hunt Walsh Chambré charged Anne Connelly of Armahain with trespassing on his property and stealing carrots.[243]

These squabbles do not account for all the cases that were heard each day. Indeed, they barely scratch the surface. Although it is difficult to establish what degree of litigation might be considered normal in a nineteenth-century rural parish, the sheer volume of cases brought before the Forkhill petty sessions court (many of a trifling nature) suggests that the people were exceedingly litigious. Unfortunately, I do not know when the petty session court was established in Forkhill and thus cannot determine whether the high volume of cases brought before it in the 1850s was normal or represented a sudden increase.[244] The petty sessions courts had been created with the passage of an act in 1828 but were not adopted everywhere right away. Forkhill did not have its own court at the time of the Poor Inquiry in 1836, when the nearest petty sessions court was in Meigh, roughly four miles away. When the commission inquired if there was a Manor Court in the district, it was informed that there had once been such a court at Forkhill but it had not been held for the past seven years.[245] The petty sessions court was established sometime after 1836, and judging from the volume of cases it adjudicated in the 1850s it soon became indispensable.

Yet this is not to suggest that the scores that had once been settled under the old system of outrage were now being relocated to the petty sessions court and that local recourse to justice had suddenly become civil. At virtually every session, the court heard cases of violent assault, threats, and trespass, and frequently these cases involved disputes over property and land occupancy ("of taking forcible possession of a portion of ground"). In October 1852, Peter Donnelly of Shean accused Patrick Hamill of Shean of following him with a pitchfork and threatening him violently respecting the possession of the land.[246] In November 1853, Cormack McElevy of Shean accused Francis McElevy of Shean of entering his house and "assaulting himself and family and abusing his cow and acting in other respects in an outrageous manner."[247] In April 1854, Alexander Murdock (who was the son of the tithe proctor in the 1830s) complained that Thomas Brooks, Henry and Terence Burns, and Peter Begley, all of whom lived in the townland of Shean, trespassed on a portion of his ground "and wilfuly injured it by placing a quantity of stones thereon, and by taking forcible possession of said ground and making use of violent threats towards complaintant's men." Clearly, elements of "the system" endured.

The rising number of cases heard before the petty sessions court was partly a reflection of the changing times. For example, the people now had a facility with English which they had not had fifty years earlier. The shift may also have been effected in part by the legal and political reforms at mid-century, including the widespread extension of the franchise. With the passage of the Irish Reform Act of 1850, the voting population leaped from 45,000 to 163,546. K.T. Hoppen has called this act the "single most important legislative influence upon the make-up of the electorate and the course of electoral politics in nineteenth-century Ireland."[248] Nevertheless, the vital element behind the popularity of the petty sessions court in the 1850s was the opportunity it allowed for the public airing and redress of grievances. While the organized system of outrage had not been swept away, its most powerful undercurrent (the determination to see right done) had found a new theatre of expression.

A SIMPLE MURDER

Peter McGill was the Forkhill ribbonman who, along with his brother Hugh, had turned against his fellows and become an informer in 1837. Their statement to the magistrate was made in the strictest confidence, for they claimed that "if it were known or suspected that said Deponents gave information thereof or made such acknowledgement, they firmly believe that they would be murdered, or otherwise have to leave the country."[249] The revelations cannot have come to light, for in 1845 Peter McGill was still living on a small farm in the townland of Tiffcrum and working as a day labourer for his neighbour, a farmer named Christopher Jordan. In April 1845 Jordan was murdered near his home, and his body dumped in a bog-hole. He had last been seen in the company of McGill, who was arrested shortly afterwards and charged with the murder. Peter's son Owen, a sailor nearly twenty years old, was also arrested in connection with Jordan's death but was freed when he agreed to serve as a witness against his father.[250] In his statement at the trial, Owen McGill provided a chilling account of the events on the night of 1 April:

> When his father [Peter McGill] came in he had Christopher Jordan with him ... They had sat down, and began to speak of crops of oats, and such things; this conversation lasted for an hour; there was no room in the house but the kitchen; the prisoner called witness out and told him he had got some meal from the deceased, two years before, and that he had no means of paying for it, except by giving up possession of his land for the ensuing crop, and that now he was going to the bog to raise a stick for the deceased, and that when there he would put an end to his life; the prisoner asked witness to go with him; witness refused to go; the prisoner then pulled a hemp rope out of his pocket and showed it to the witness; he was afraid and consented to go; the prisoner went to the end of the house and took a stone, three or four stones weight, with him; saw him go towards the bog, carrying the stone ... The prisoner came back without the stone; witness followed him into the house; deceased was there still; they sat down for a quarter of an hour and smoked; they were talking Irish; but witness does not understand much of that; at the end of a quarter of an hour Jordan said "Peter, 'tis time to go to the bog"; prisoner said it was, and they then went out; Jordan had a gray frieze body coat and a black felt hat on him; witness followed them at a distance of about two perches ... and saw Jordan on a half stoop, as if measuring with a rule; saw the prisoner take deceased by the neck or collar and knock him down;

> saw the deceased give three moans; at the time of the murder it now not dark or bright, but the moon was shining; saw his father stamp with his boot on the breast of the deceased; he had heavy nailed shoes on; saw the prisoner take the stone ... and tie the stone with the rope he had shown witness to the body, and fling all into the bog hole.[251]

There was only a handful of cold-blooded murders in Forkhill in the nineteenth century, and this was one of them. Although the murder of Christopher Jordan was an aberrant act, it serves as a reminder of the occasional acts of violence and lawlessness that took place in the countryside – acts that were in no way connected to the organized system of outrage and were merely brutal. The case against Peter McGill collapsed at the summer assizes in 1845 and again at the spring assizes in 1846. In a memorial to the court, McGill claimed that he could not afford the cost of another trial. He had been reduced to the "extremest degree of poverty and [had] been deprived of all means of earning a livelihood by his labour for now twelve months."[252] McGill was eventually convicted of the murder and sentenced to transportation.

7

Famine, 1845–1850

A man named Connor had the giving out of potatoes in Forkhill, and a poor man came along looking for food.

"I have none for you," said Connor.

"No, but you had them for the Big Fellow," the poor man said, referring to a well-to-do Protestant farmer.

"Well," says Connor, "haven't you got the land?"

"I can ate the land?" the man replied.[1]

The series of potato crop failures in Ireland between 1845 and 1849 reduced the population to a wretched state of existence. Although it is difficult to determine the number of casualties of starvation and disease caused by the collapse of the country's principal food source, it is believed that more than one million people did not survive the five seasons of want, and it is estimated that more than a million others had emigrated from Ireland by 1851.[2] The famine, they say, "cleaned the country."

The population decline varied considerably in the different counties, parishes, and townlands of Ulster.[3] Between 1841 and 1851, the populations of Antrim and Down decreased by 9 and 15 per cent, respectively, a figure below the national average. This can be attributed in part to these counties' economic diversity and greater prosperity.[4] But in congested mountain districts, where small farming was the principal occupation and where the potato remained the staple food source, the destitution took a more serious toll. The population of Counties Cavan and Monaghan fell by 28 per cent, a figure on par with the worst-affected areas of the country. Parts of south Armagh experienced a comparable rate of decline. Between 1841 and 1851, the population of Forkhill fell by 27 per cent owing to relocation, emigration, starvation, and death from illness and disease.[5] In order to appreciate the impact of the famine on Forkhill and the surrounding countryside, we will examine the correspondence generated by the Relief Commission, the Distress Papers, the Board of Guardians records, parliamentary papers, and local newspaper reports. But to understand how an airborne spore brought a country to its knees, we must first take a close look at the potato.

THE POTATO

The potato was introduced into Ireland in the late sixteenth century as a supplementary food source, though its advantages as a staple crop soon became apparent. It flourished in the damp and sunless Irish climate. In wet seasons, when cereal crops suffered, the potato made a fine substitute for oats and barley and helped stave off famine. It yielded far more food per acre than cereal, came in a number of hardy varieties, and was an excellent single source of energy and nutrition.[6] Upon analysing the vitamin content of ten pounds of potatoes and one pint of milk, the historian K.H. Connell concluded that this daily intake represented a nourishing diet for an adult male.[7] Data on British army recruits between 1800 and 1815 reveal that Irish-born recruits were generally taller than those from England and Wales, despite unfavourable economic comparisons between the countries. Historians have concluded that this apparent anomaly was partly the result of a monotonous but nutritious diet.[8]

Throughout the eighteenth century, the potato grew in popularity among the labouring classes until it became the staple food of the small farmer for most of the year, though he continued to supplement his diet with herrings, turnips and grains. However, between 1810 and 1845, these alternate food sources largely disappeared from the labourer's mainstay, and Ireland became heavily dependent on the potato. Contemporary estimates indicate that an adult labourer's average daily intake of potatoes in 1841 ranged between twelve and fourteen pounds. Women, and children between the ages of eleven and fifteen, consumed between nine and ten pounds of potatoes a day, while young children consumed between four and five pounds a day.[9] Under such pressure, the fault lines of the single food source economy began to appear. Dependence on the potato created an unrelenting cycle of want. The pressure of population on the land, combined with the gradually declining yield of the potato crop in the years before the famine, compelled many people to eat portions of their seed crop for the following year. With part of the seed crop gone, the next year's yield was lower, making the demand even greater. More dangerous still was the fact that the people had no food source to fall back on if the crop failed. Twenty years before the famine, an anonymous observer had warned of the danger of the situation. When wheat and beer constitute the principal part of the labourer's diet, he remarked, the labourer can resort to cheaper articles, such as oats and potatoes, when his main food source becomes scarce. "But when he is habitually and constantly fed on the very lowest species of food, he has plainly nothing to resort to when deprived of it." Labourers in such circumstances can sink no lower and teeter on the "verge of existence."[10]

The late P.M.A. Bourke, who did pioneering research on the subject of the blight and the famine, argued that under the twin conditions of extreme population pressure on the land and dependence on a single food source, disaster was inevitable.[11] Both of these conditions prevailed in south Armagh to an acute degree on the eve of the famine. The county had the highest population density in Ireland in 1841, supporting 511 persons on every square mile of arable land. The parish of Forkhill supported a population of 8,128 on 12,590 acres, not all of which was arable, a ratio that proved unsustainable when faced with the potato failure later in the decade.[12]

LIVING CONDITIONS IN FORKHILL ON THE EVE OF THE FAMINE

In 1835 the House of Commons commissioned an inquiry into the state of Ireland's poor in advance of the institution of the national poor law system. The commissioners sent a lengthy questionnaire to prominent local residents, clergymen, magistrates, and gentry in parishes throughout the country, soliciting information on various aspects of life in rural communities. They inquired into the working of the conacre system, relations between landlords and tenants, the state of agriculture, labourers' earnings, the employment of women and children, provisions for the elderly, medical relief, the extent of illegitimacy, patterns of emigration, the quality of food, clothing, and housing, and the prevalence of alcohol. In short, the survey was a comprehensive examination of rural life on the eve of the famine.[13] The respondents for Forkhill were the Reverend William Smith, the resident Church of Ireland curate; the Reverend Daniel O'Rafferty, the Catholic parish priest; and Major Arthur A. Bernard, the resident magistrate. All three lived and worked in the parish.

According to them, most of the families in Forkhill in 1835 were labouring families. They scraped out a living on their small farms or "potato gardens" while also working for hire, rearing poultry or pigs for market, and selling turf. The annual rent for a small cabin ranged from £2 a year with some land to £1 with no garden.[14] Many labourers, fathers and sons alike, sought seasonal work in England or Scotland, or in other parts of Ireland.[15] At one time, women had earned good money at the linen trade as spinners and weavers, but those days had passed. Children were often sent out to household service as soon as they were able to work, and their wages supplemented the family income. The principal source of this income was the wage earned by the head of the household, which ranged from £5 to £11 a year.[16]

Given the meagre family income, in general the diet, clothing, and furnishings of labouring families were miserable. Potatoes were their main source of food, supplemented occasionally with salt herrings, oatmeal, or buttermilk.[17] In neighbouring Creggan, Father Michael Lennon claimed that his parishioners frequently survived on potatoes alone, with a little milk when they could get it. He pronounced their diet "miserable indeed."[18] Every single one of the respondents from the parishes of Creggan, Forkhill, and Killeavy reported that the labouring classes survived principally on potatoes in 1835.[19]

In addition to the economic unsoundness of dependence on a single food, this lack of diversity in the labourers' diet was a source of health problems. In his statement to the Poor Inquiry, the doctor at the Forkhill dispensary remarked that the heavy concentration of potatoes and meal in the diet of farmers and labourers caused frequent problems of indigestion ("derangement of the bowels"), a concern echoed by doctors in nearby Meigh and Crossmaglen.[20] In 1842 the Forkhill doctor recorded more than thirty ailments treated during the previous twelve months that were specifically related to intestinal disorders, including anasarca, anscites, gastritis, odema, dysenteria, colica, and dyspepsia.[21] Symptoms included severe indigestion, stomach inflammation, and fluid retention, and the cases ranged from mild to severe. Many of these "diseases" were caused by nutritional deficiencies. In a study of dietary patterns in north Louth and south Ulster in the 1830s, Margaret Crawford found that labourers endured a particularly monotonous diet, which she called "exceptionally poor."[22] They were heavily dependent on potatoes, and unless their diet was supplemented with buttermilk or whole milk, they probably suffered from nutritional deficiencies. Crawford referred to the region as a corridor of "marked dietary deprivation."[23]

Despite the inadequate provisions, the people were fortunate to have medical care under a responsible surgeon. The dispensary at Forkhill had been established in 1821 with funds from Richard Jackson's trust.[24] It was a small building, two storeys high, with a waiting room and a dispensary, although without provision for lying-in patients.[25] The doctor attended the dispensary on Tuesdays, Thursdays, and Saturdays between the hours of eleven and three o'clock, though acute cases and accidents were admissible at all times. For his services, the doctor, Samuel Walker, drew a salary of £50 per annum from the trustees.[26] According to the dispensary register, 6,664 people had been treated in the three years prior to the survey, a much higher figure than was reported for the dispensaries of more densely populated neighbouring districts; on the day of the survey, twenty patients were waiting to see Dr Walker.[27] He treated a variety of cases, mainly of a chronic nature, though accidents, fractures, and fevers were common. Women in labour were generally attended by midwives or other experienced women, but the doctor was expected to assist at difficult births. He is said to have administered "vaccinations" to all who applied, observing that "the poor have great confidence in them."[28] Yet he did not vaccinate against smallpox, since it was not common in the district at the time.[29]

In the 1830s the poor made their own clothing out of frieze, corduroy, and coarse linen. They tried to keep some decent clothes for Sunday, but during the rest of the week their dress was "miserable," described by one respondent as a "variety of shreds and patches."[30] In the first years of the famine, many paupers pawned their clothes for a pittance to buy grain, but by 1847 most articles of clothing were so filthy and worn that they would not be taken in pawn. For want of decent clothing, many people were ashamed to attend either church or chapel.[31]

The living conditions of the people were an equally stark reflection of their poverty. Most families lived in one-room cabins built of stone and clay, rudely furnished, with a dirt floor covered in straw.[32] Father O'Rafferty provided a list of the few contents: "A chest, small table, two pots, a few inconvenient sorts of stools, some straw, a blanket, which, together with the clothes they wear, serves for their covering at night. No bedsteads."[33] The cabins of labourers were uniformly miserable throughout the whole of south Armagh.[34] In some instances, two or more families shared a cabin; O'Rafferty reported that there were "many" such cases in the parish.[35]

An alternative to the desperate overcrowding and lack of employment was emigration. O'Rafferty and the two other Forkhill men reporting to the 1835 inquiry all said that some families had recently left the parish and most of them were bound for North America. The Reverend William Smith knew of four families that had emigrated since 1831, all small farmers.[36] O'Rafferty knew of fifty-three emigrants, whom he classified as "labourers, mechanics, and women." Major Bernard claimed that between ten and twelve people "of the best description of farmers and of the best character" had left the parish in the past few years.[37] These comments underscore the diversity of Ireland's emigrant stream, particularly in the years before the famine. Still, the rate of exodus from the parish in the early 1830s was low, and emigration remained the exception rather than the rule. The decision to emigrate had to be supported by sufficient capital for passage and provisions, and few people were able to save money for such a venture.[38]

At the end of the Poor Inquiry's questionnaire, the commissioners asked if the general conditions of the poorer classes had improved since the "Peace of 1815." The responses varied. Smith and Bernard reported that the condition of the Forkhill poor had indeed improved; their farms were better cultivated, the people were more civilized, and they were much more industrious: "The face of this parish has been entirely changed within those few years, from being all bog and heath, it is now all tillage, except at the top of the mountains."[39] Father O'Rafferty was more pessimistic. "Condition of the poor deteriorated," he wrote. "The population is greatly increased and increasing."[40] Under these conditions of acute pressure on the land and utter dependence on the potato, the parish encountered the blight ten years later, in 1845.

THE BLIGHT

The first definite reports that the potato blight had reached Ireland from continental Europe came on 6 September 1845.[41] The blight blackened the potato fields of Armagh that month, and the results were felt immediately. On 11 October the master of the Newry workhouse reported that the potatoes provided by the local contractor were of very bad quality. He could not serve them to the paupers and had been forced to feed them extra helpings of meal instead.[42] Richard Pennefather, who served on a relief committee in Newtownhamilton, a village ten miles north of Forkhill, described a diseased crop in a stricken field in his neighbourhood on 20 October. The potatoes were blemished with dark reddish spots: "The tuber is found nearly black and of a watery substance, and when boiled, totally unfit for use, and in some instances an objectionable smell proceeds from them when broken."[43] Still, some poor people were eating the blackened potatoes for want of other food, and the diseased crop was selling locally for one penny per stone.[44] The extent of the destruction to the potato crop soon became apparent. By November, close to one-third of the crop in Crossmaglen had been lost. Virtually every variety of potato had suffered, especially the "white species," the Lumper, which was the cheapest and most common variety.[45]

Alarm at the potato failure was general. An emergency meeting was called in Forkhill on 9 December 1845 to consider the state of the crop, the availability of food for the winter, and the best way to combat "the evils of scarcity." The groundwork was laid for a relief committee composed of local clergymen, resident landlords, and substantial farmers.[46] William Smith was elected secretary of the committee.[47] The members took a number of prudent measures at the meeting; they undertook to collect information about the potato failure, to monitor the parish food supply throughout the winter, and to devise measures for relief and employment if the situation deteriorated.[48] In January 1846 the Forkhill poet Art Bennett described the effects of the blight in a letter to an acquaintance, Robert MacAdam. He was tired and weak, he wrote, for his "last spark of life threatened to be extinguished with hunger by the failure in the potato crop."[49] The effects of malnutrition, even over the short term, became starkly apparent in February when a grieving Bennett informed MacAdam that his fifteen-year-old daughter had died of convulsions related to fever.[50]

The Forkhill relief committee met again in May 1846, to address the problem of subsistence during the coming spring and summer. July and August were traditionally known in Ireland as the "meal months," when the year's potato supply had been exhausted and the people resorted to a meagre diet of oatmeal and barley until they could harvest the new crop of potatoes. The lean summer months would be much leaner in 1846, and the parish relied on emergency aid to get through them. The landlord of the Forkhill estate, Henry Alexander, responded to the distress by granting £300 to purchase meal for the relief of his tenants.[51] It was not a gift, however. Alexander stipulated that the meal would be issued at cost, and loans were to be repaid during the coming autumn and winter. John Foxall, a resident gentleman, distributed £200 among the local people to enable them to purchase food, and several smaller sums were subscribed by other local residents. By June 1846, £525 had been subscribed locally by landlords and clergymen.[52]

Every shilling and every bushel of grain helped, and the people managed to scrape through the meal months in anticipation of an abundant crop at the end of the summer. They survived on turnip champ and a dish known as "brawlum," a mixture of meal and cabbage, which "had the guts run out of them."[53] In May 1846 the Forkhill constabulary reported that 1,682 acres had been planted with potatoes that spring; this was somewhat less than the 1,996 acres planted in 1845 but was a sizable crop nonetheless.[54] The worst possible news came in August, when the potato blight resurfaced in the countryside, more virulent and widespread than before. The *Nation* reported the total failure of the Irish potato crop on 20 August, and confirmation of this poured in from across the country.[55] In Newtownhamilton virtually the entire crop was stricken with blight by mid-August. The stalks were withered, the potatoes were thin on the ground, and most had gone black with disease. Not more than one-third of them were fit for consumption, and many farmers predicted – correctly – that there would not be a sound potato in the district in two months' time.[56]

By September 1846, the people of south Armagh had been surviving on starvation rations for months, and the prospect of another failed crop put them beyond despair. "The distress is rapidly and fearfully increasing every day," Father Lennon wrote from the parish of Creggan. "It is really heartrending to listen to the lamentations of the poor people crying out for work that they may be enabled to purchase food."[57] The extent of the crisis was confirmed by Lieutenant Griffith, an officer based in Upper Fews and Upper Orior during the autumn of 1846. In November he remarked on the "absolute devastation," "destitution," and "famine" in those regions.[58] The poorer class of farmers and cottiers were "generally ... in a state approaching starvation."[59] All farm operations in the area had ceased, and Griffith feared that many people would perish if not immediately provided with food. Although the people were patient, there were murmurings of discontent and threats of an uprising: "[They] meet in crowds about the doors of the Relief Committee-rooms ... and loudly declare that they must provide food from the stack-yards, if not otherwise immediately supplied."[60] The distress had already accelerated the spread of fever in the region. In September 1846 the superintendent of the Forkhill dispensary, Dr Stanley, presented a memorial to the Forkhill trustees expressing the "great inconvenience" that was experienced in the parish from the want of a fever hospital; the nearest one was twelve miles away.[61]

During the winter of 1846–47 the distress reached a terrible peak. In January Father Lennon sent a despairing letter to the relief commissioners. Several people in his parish had perished and hundreds more were wasting away, he wrote. "The people are becoming frantic with hunger, and God only knows what may be the terrible consequences."[62] On 16 January, Lieutenant Griffith confirmed that two people had died recently from starvation in Upper Orior and many others were in a "dying state."[63] The following week he reported that the people were suffering from "unparalleled destitution" and had "arrived at the extremity of endeavouring to support themselves on sea-weed; bran and turnip, where they can be had."[64] The letters of both Griffith and Lennon gave the same warning – that the people were starving, had exhausted all means of subsistence, and if they did not get help immediately, they would die. This alarm was raised across the country in the winter of 1846–47, forcing the government to take immediate aid measures.

THE RELIEF EFFORT

The famine relief had five main components: local subscriptions, government grants, public works schemes, workhouse charity, and outdoor relief. In most districts, resident landlords, magistrates, clergymen, and farmers subscribed money or provisions towards relief – to be distributed by local committees or dispensed among the people directly. Beginning in early 1846, resident Forkhill landlords put money towards corn and meal, allowing the tenants to buy cheaply and on credit. At this early stage, everyone hoped that the crisis would pass, that the crops would revive, and that interim loans would be quickly repaid. In the wake of the second crop failure, however, grim resolve set in. A special meeting of the board of trustees was held at Forkhill on 26 November, and the trustees recorded their "great regret that a large portion of the Tenantry on the Forkill Estate has been visited with much distress and severe privations in consequence of the failure of the potato crop." [65] They granted £200 gratis for the purchase of provisions to last through the winter, most of which was spent on seed corn.[66] Close to £1,000 was raised from private subscriptions before the end of 1846.

Where money was subscribed, the government committed to match the donations through grants-in-aid. This system proved to be an administrative nightmare, and in many cases the grants failed to come through. On 30 May 1846, William Smith sent a letter to the office of the Relief Commission in Dublin, enclosing a copy of the Forkhill relief committee's resolutions and requesting a grant-in-aid.[67] The commissioners replied that they needed a complete list of local subscriptions before the application would be considered. The Reverend James Campbell, treasurer of the committee, drew up the list and submitted it to the Relief Commission on 5 June; once again, the application was rejected.[68] Reading between the lines, it appears that the officers of the Relief Commission were not convinced that the Forkhill committee had canvassed widely enough for local charity. The commissioners wanted to see a list of the landlords who had refused to make any charitable contribution, a request that Smith declined.[69] He continued to send the commissioners reports of the parish committee meetings for a further six months, though it is unclear if the funding issue was ever resolved.[70] Meanwhile, the Forkhill committee continued to receive charitable subscriptions from private donors in the amounts of £10, £20, and £50, and this allowed the committee to purchase meal, which was sold cheaply to the tenants.

In the summer of 1846, the government introduced public works schemes, paying labourers a daily wage for building roads, draining land, and breaking stones. By March 1847, close to 750,000 people were engaged in these schemes, but the system was imperfect. There was too little work, it was redundant, and the pay was a pittance, amounting to only threepence or fourpence a day. In 1846 Henry

Alexander offered employment to a number of labourers to drain a tract of land in the mountains around Forkhill, but neither he nor any other local landlord could devise enough work to employ several thousand men indefinitely.[71] In January 1847 the Forkhill relief committee complained that only one-tenth of the district's 1,220 labourers were employed on public works.[72] At the Extraordinary Presentment Sessions for Upper Orior later that month, some farmers expressed resentment at the inactivity of the landlords during the crisis. The Forkhill priest Father McParlan declared angrily that many landlords "had not set the people to work as they should have done."[73] He was sharply rebuked by one of the gentlemen present, who insisted that the landlords were doing "all in their power" to alleviate the distress. Some had even mortgaged their estates rather than demand rents from their tenants, he claimed.[74] Ultimately, the meeting decided to reserve more than £14,000 for the barony, most of which would be put towards works projects. But public works projects were not designed to sustain a large population over a long period. As the months wore on, the men were simply too weak to work, and many projects were left half done.[75] The government pressed on with these schemes past their usefulness because of its reluctance to initiate outdoor relief programs and increase funding to the union workhouses; it feared that the masses would cease to work and become dependent on charity. But in view of the scope and duration of the disaster, the workhouses became essential (though inadequate) sources of food, shelter, and clothing.

The Irish Poor Law of 1838 had divided Ireland into 130 poor law unions, each with its own workhouse, which offered direct relief to the destitute in the form of shelter, food, clothing, and medical attention. Forkhill was divided into the unions of Newry and Castleblayney; the closest workhouse was based in Newry town and opened in June 1839.[76] The union workhouses had been designed to relieve the distress of a poor country during normal times and were not equipped to respond to the scale of the disaster in the wake of the potato failure. By late summer 1846, conditions in the Newry workhouse were critical. The Poor Law commissioners recorded their "deep regret" that the situation in the local union was so "unfavourable," and they recommended that the Newry guardians immediately renew their stock and supplies in preparation for a surge in the workhouse population.[77]

The number of people in the Newry workhouse swelled throughout the fall and winter of 1846–47, and in January 1847 the resident medical officer sent a grim report to the Poor Law Commission: "I am sorry to state that fever, dysentery and afflictions of the chest, are much on the increase in the workhouse, owing in my opinion to the following causes. First, the majority of those admitted during the last two months being in a wretched state of destitution on admission, and many of them labouring under disease. Secondly, the very crowded state of the House and the absolute necessity of it *now* being better ventilated ... Thirdly, the want of mere clothing for the infants, children and delicate adults, and fourthly the straw received for bedding not being sufficiently dry ... From the state of the House I consider it would not be prudent to admit any more at present."[78] In March 1847 the Poor Law Commission learned that the paupers in the Newry workhouse were "lately in the habit of throwing bread over the walls of the Institution and receiving money as a consideration in a similar way."[79]

The failure of the public works schemes and the inadequacy of the workhouses to hold starvation and disease in check had become alarmingly clear. In late January and early February 1847, the government rushed through legislation to provide rations of food to the destitute at government-sponsored soup kitchens. The Relief Commission was determined to impose order and accountability on this new level of bureaucracy, however, and this slowed down the procedure.[80] Many relief committees had anticipated local need and established soup kitchens themselves, drawing on donations of money and meal from farmers, landlords, the Society of Friends, and other private sources.

In January 1847 the Forkhill relief committee began distributing free meal to the most afflicted classes, as well as to widows, orphans, and the elderly.[81] The committee members were overwhelmed by the demand. On the first day, they managed to provide small amounts of meal to 450 impoverished people but were forced to turn away at least the same number of destitute.[82] Early in 1847 the committee opened a soup kitchen in the centre of the parish, and several other food stations were established locally.[83] The Forkhill soup kitchen was located on the first floor of a building known as "the boardroom," where the trustees held their quarterly meetings. (The two-storey building is still standing along the main road out of the village, not far from the Protestant church.) A huge iron boiler, two yards wide and two yards deep, was built into the lower floor of the boardroom. From this old boiler, the charity workers served porridge in the morning and soup in the evening. The people came with tins to carry the soup home to their families, a practice known as "bottling the soup."[84]

The government's response to the crisis and the efforts of local relief committees constituted the "official" response to the famine. Popular response to the crisis ranged across an even wider spectrum, from deliberate strategies of survival to impulsive, desperate acts. An old woman in Forkhill told a heart-rending story about people who had travelled a good distance to get holy water from the priest to shake over the rotten potatoes. "They mightn't have bothered," she said,

The boardroom of the trustees of the Forkhill estate, Forkhill, County Armagh (photograph by J.E. Madden)

"every priddie rotted."[85] Unrest was an early symptom of the growing destitution, and it grew more serious after the second potato failure. Food riots and obstructions were uncommon in Ireland, but these were not normal times, and the situation was desperate enough to arouse aggressive action. In October 1846 a crowd of four hundred labouring poor entered Newtownhamilton carrying spades and shovels, demanding employment, money, or bread, and crying out that they "must be supported." The local clergyman collected some money from the merchants and distributed it among the crowd, which dispersed peacefully.[86] A similar scene took place in the town of Armagh in December. A crowd of fifty people carrying spades and shovels proceeded through the streets, calling at the bakers' shops and demanding bread. They dispersed when the bakers met their demand, but they warned that they would be back and would take food by force if necessary.[87] In the nearby village of Loughgall, a crowd of thirty or forty men marched with sticks demanding "bread or work" from the well-off farmers and gentlemen.[88] In Newry, several merchants received letters from "Molly Maguire," warning them not to ship any meal out of the country, under threat of a visit from Molly herself.[89] In the same month, port authorities in the coastal town of Carlingford were alerted to an attack planned on a ship that was being loaded with oatmeal bound for Scotland. A crowd of country people were preparing to take the meal off the ship by force, and they planned to line the roads with armed men to protect the carriers as they made their escape.[90]

An unprecedented number of prisoners were called before the Armagh assizes in the spring of 1846, mainly for theft of clothing, turf, fowl, and potatoes, having been driven to steal out of want.[91] A considerable trade in firearms had sprung up in the baronies of Upper Fews and Upper Orior, another symptom of the growing unrest.[92] Major Bernard and the Reverend James Campbell responded to the discontent by appointing additional policemen to patrol the parish.[93]

In December 1846, Patrick Sands's home on the outskirts of Forkhill was forcibly entered by two men who beat him as he lay in bed. His attackers stole bills, silver coins, a watch, and a silk handkerchief, as well as two bags of oats and barley. Some of the grain had spilled to the ground as it was carried away, leaving a trail which the police later followed to the doorstep of Michael Farrell in the nearby townland of Shean. Inside Farrell's cabin were bags of meal and a four-stone weight of flour, which Farrell confessed to have stolen as well. Other bags of meal were found concealed in the house of Hugh Cunningham, who also was arrested for the attack on Sands. Hugh's wife Bridget told police that she had heard Farrell convincing her husband to go with him to Sands's house to rob him of meal. She added that when she had advised against the idea, Farrell had told her to hold her tongue and said that "if she was his wife he would knock her head against the wall."[94] One month later, Thomas Murphy's house in Mullaghbawn was raided by three men who waved a gun and demanded money from the family. The men stole some cash, along with a box of meal. Under the cover of darkness, Murphy followed two of the men, whom he had recognized as Laurence Gollogly and Patrick McCann, and trailed them to McCann's house a short distance away.[95] He reported them to the police and both were later arrested.

Survival strategies ranged across a wide spectrum. If the registry of baptisms can be taken as a rough indication of the number of infants born to the Catholic population of Forkhill, it would seem that the regular pattern of births was interrupted during these years. The Catholic baptismal register begins in 1845, a year in which 170 baptisms were recorded in the parish. The number fell to 143 the following year, fell again to 89 in 1847, and reached a decade low of 46 in 1848.[96] There are several reasons why the number of births may have fallen during this period. First, the entire population declined by 27 per cent between 1841 and 1851, mainly because of emigration and death from disease or malnutrition; as the overall adult population decreased, the number of births would naturally decline as well. Second, the collapse of the community's principal food source, and the accompanying vitamin depletion and malnutrition among women of child-bearing age, may have affected their ability to bear children, at least temporarily.

There is another factor that may explain the steep decline in births during the famine years: infant death. Even in normal times, a sizable proportion of infants born in pre-industrial societies died soon after birth, despite the best efforts of their mothers to nurse them to health. The circumstances into which babies were born during the famine years made their chance of survival even more remote; and in some cases, knowing how difficult it would be to sustain them, it is possible that their mothers did not fight so hard to keep them alive. Infanticide was the most unspeakable of famine horrors, and although there were occasional reports of mothers who wilfully neglected their children or who smothered their infants, the practice was not spoken about, and its true extent is unknown.[97] Similar stories were reported during and after the Bengal famine of 1943–44, which was in other ways comparable to the experience of famine in Ireland. In her book *Darkening Days*, Ela Sen writes that a "large number of women became bereft of their sense through privation and want, and rather than watch their children die slowly and in pain, they would put them out of their misery – in the same way an animal will not allow a decrepit offspring to live."[98]

During the famine years, the number of marriages also fell sharply. The Catholic register of marriages in the parish of Forkhill records forty-five marriages in 1845, nineteen in 1847, and eight in 1848–49. In the years of greatest scarcity (1847–49), the marriage rate was practically nil;[99] there was not a single Catholic marriage recorded between August 1848 and February 1849 or between July and December 1849.[100] The decline in the number of births and marriages may represent a survival strategy engineered deliberately, or intuitively, in the face of disaster. At some point, perhaps as early as the first failed potato crop, the people must have realized that having a child during a time of scarcity would be a tremendous burden. Any addition to the household taxed the energy and resources of the entire family. Precisely how this reduced birth rate was effected – whether through abstinence from sexual relations, contraception (*coitus interruptus*), or impairment from malnutrition – is impossible to determine. But it made sense to wait until the crisis had passed, and between 1846 and 1850, resources and energy were concentrated on survival.

Others did not wait out the disaster. During the 1840s, many people simply gathered up a few of their belongings and left their homes to travel the roads, often ending up in Belfast or Dublin. Such people could not afford to emigrate, at least not right away, but neither could they afford to remain on the barren land any longer. An old woman interviewed by the Irish Folklore Commission (IFC) in the 1940s stated that by 1850 there were more houses than people in the parish. When people came wandering into the mountains, she said, they were told to take shelter in an empty house, for there were any number of them along the roadside.[101] The question of depopulation through eviction is a thorny one, and there is no reliable local record of evictions to draw upon. Around Crossmaglen, several notorious landlords were accused of evicting tenants en masse in order to clear and consolidate their lands. I have found no similar complaint of evictions on the Forkhill estate during the famine, though rents were in arrears by 1846. This was a symptom of the crop failure, since the people had no produce to exchange for cash. But by spring 1847 the trustees were beginning to lose patience with the situation, and they sent a stern letter to Henry Alexander, reminding him of "the absolute necessity" of the "immediate payment" of the balance of rent on the estate.[102]

SOUPERISM IN FORKHILL

Accusations of proselytism during the relief effort is one of the most contentious issues in famine scholarship. The transcripts of the IFC contain numerous references to proselytism in south Armagh by landlords, clergymen, and farmers in Forkhill, Killeavy, and Jonesborough.[103] Alleged attempts to wean Catholics from their faith ranged from the insidious to the fantastic. The Protestant charity workers in Forkhill were accused of "putting on a big feed" of beef and soup on a Friday, with "plenty leftover to take away," despite the fact that Catholics were not supposed to eat meat on Friday. Some Protestant landlords reportedly provided Catholics with money, food, employment, and contracts for relief – on condition that they renounce their faith.[104] According to legend, strict conditions were imposed on people who accepted relief from Protestant sources, ranging from attendance at Sunday services to explicit denial of the tenets of Catholicism. In Jonesborough, a man named Benson gave out soup (known locally as "Benson's gravy"), but it was said that "you had to twist yourself over to get it – and all you'd get anyway was one cupful."[105] "Twisting yourself over" meant that you converted to Protestantism for promises of food and charity. In Crossmaglen, the story was told of a man who was weak with fever and unable to work; the local Protestant clergyman offered to till the man's land for him if he would come to his church.[106] The most colourful is the story of the soup kichen in Faughart, which had a statue of the Virgin Mary standing near the door. Any poor soul who wished to line up for soup first had to drive a pitchfork through the Virgin Mary.[107]

Much of the evidence collected by the IFC in south Armagh emphasizes the greed of landlords and uncharitableness of charity workers during the famine years. Walter Dawson, a gentleman who lived at Dungooley, supposedly sold rotten turnips to the people at eight shillings a stone and had a man jailed for stealing one of the turnips.[108] Meredith Chambré allegedly threatened to evict any of his tenants who were in arrears unless they sent their children to the Protestant Sunday school. There were complaints about the food, as well. The soup and meal was widely remembered as being of poor quality, and the men in charge of the boilers and depots were criticized for their meanness. People who gave out inferior meal or who gave it out on credit were known as "meal mongers."[109] Thomas Brooks, a Protestant from Mullaghbawn, who was a member of the Forkhill relief committee, earned such a reputation. Brooks allegedly gave out meal only on credit or in exchange for land, and the Catholics who took soup from him were known as "soupers." Indeed, the numerous references to "soupers" and "turncoats" in the folklore manuscripts indicate the severity of the social stigma attached to those who took the soup.[110]

There are several reasons why we must approach these stories with caution. First, the circumstances of the relief operation would have made outright proselytization efforts in Forkhill impractical. The local relief committee operated under the watchful eye of the two local priests, who sat on the committee and were involved in its decisions and operations. Given the contentious history of education in the parish, and earlier accusations of proselytism in the endowed schools, the connection between charity and religious obligation was extremely sensitive, and it was not in the interest of the relief committee to inflame the situation. As for the tales of unscrupulous landlords whose charity was conditional, we must remember that these stories were recorded by the commission one hundred years after the famine and shortly after the most divisive period of modern Irish history. They were told after the Easter Rising of 1916, the civil war, and the construction of the border between north and south in 1920 – events that had profound implications for Irish nationalism. As Niall O'Ciosain has observed, the IFC itself played a role in the construction of famine memory. He argues that the impressions of the famine that were recorded in the 1940s were shaped by the collectors' lines of questioning, which emphasized particular aspects of the famine experience and disregarded others.[111] For example, O'Ciosain suggests that the apparent preoccupation of folk memory with the subject of proselytism was a feature of the questionnaire itself, which inquired specifically about souperism and instructed informants "to distinguish between centres at which proselytism was carried on and those at which it was not."[112] The respondents were thus required to address the issue of proselytism, rather than simply skipping the question if they had nothing to report. As a result, some felt obliged to say something on the subject and responded by recalling stories that took place well outside their native districts.

Accusations of souperism may also have grown out of resentment at the sectarian imbalance of the situation. The relief effort in Forkhill was almost completely undertaken by the Protestant community; the clergymen, the landlords, the doctor, and the substantial farmers who contributed aid were, with few exceptions, Protestant.[113] Even most of the charity workers who ladled out soup and porridge in the boardroom were Protestant. On the other hand, most of the supplicants were Catholic, and appearing before the Protestant charity workers with a begging bowl was a bitter pill for some. This resentment was channelled into complaints about the quality of the food, the stinginess of the charity workers, the greed of landlords who exploited the situation for profit, and the attempts at proselytization – the most indignant charge of all. Perhaps telling such stories relieved the consciences of those who felt guilty for accepting Protestant charity and were angry at being forced into this position. I do not expect there was much humility or gratitude in the line-ups outside the boardroom as the people waited for their empty bowls to be filled with soup. But in the winter of 1847, they took it anyway.

DISEASE AND DEATH

Based on the surviving evidence, it appears that the relief efforts in Forkhill were moderately successful, bridging the gap between destitution, which was widespread, and actual starvation, which was rare.[114] But if the relief effort managed to keep the people from starving, it could do little about a far more deadly problem – the spread of disease. As part of the 1851 census, Sir William Wilde compiled tables on death and disease for the period 1841 to 1851, which provide stark proof of the relationship between severe malnutrition and disease.[115] The major diseases fell into two broad categories: diseases of nutritional deficiency (marasmus, dropsy, scurvy), and famine-induced diseases transmitted by infection (fever, tuberculosis, measles, cholera.) Starvation was listed as a category of disease in Wilde's tables – ironically included under the heading "Violent or Sudden Deaths." Ninety-two deaths from starvation were recorded in Armagh during the decade, reinforcing the point that starvation was an accelerating factor in many premature deaths rather than the ultimate cause.[116]

Nutritional depletion caused by lack of food weakened the immune system and increased the susceptibility of the population to infection.

Cases of smallpox, measles, fever, tuberculosis, dysentery, and cholera increased dramatically during the famine years. Smallpox and measles proved most deadly among infants and young children, while dysentery and fever were more even-handed killers, sparing neither the young nor the middle-aged. Both diseases were highly infectious and spread like wildfire through workhouses, fever hospitals, and soup kitchens, which were veritable breeding grounds for disease. Throughout the winter of 1846–47, hundreds of starving poor beat a path to the door of the Newry workhouse, swelling its ranks and spreading infection. In January, the workhouse doctor reported 36 cases of fever and 105 cases of measles under his care. In an effort to halt the spread of infection, the workhouse shut its doors against the admission of any more paupers.[117] Within a short time, the resident schoolmaster and the master of the workhouse succumbed to famine fever, and the doctor himself fell gravely ill.[118]

"Famine fever" was an umbrella term for two diseases caused by exposure to organisms found in lice: typhus and relapsing fever. Typhus sufferers experienced shivering and delirium and complained of headache and aching pains. Their skin turned a dusky hue – the disease was known in Irish as *fiabhras dubh* (black fever). Relapsing fever, or *fiabhras buidhe* (yellow fever), was accompanied by violent rigour, sickness, and vomiting, followed by sweating and exhaustion; jaundice was often a fatal complication.[119] Evidence from the IFC manuscripts suggests that fever killed more people in south Armagh than dropsy, dysentery, or starvation, though it is impossible to know how many.[120] The fever dead were carried out of their houses, dumped into carts, and hauled away to unmarked graves. They were buried without coffins and within hours of dying, in an effort to halt the spread of infection.[121]

Although the potato blight struck with far less severity in the autumn of 1847, waning confidence in the potato and the shortage of seed produced a drastically reduced yield, thus prolonging the season of want.[122] The blight destroyed a substantial portion of the crop in the autumn of 1848 and reappeared the following year, though to a lesser extent. Beginning in 1847, the disaster of the recurrent crop failure was mitigated by the influx of meal into the country. In January 1848 the Newry Board of Guardians began shipping meal to surrounding rural depots, and Forkhill received between six and twelve hundredweight of Indian meal every week until the worst of the crisis had passed.[123]

One last blast of death came in 1849 with the arrival of cholera from England. Cholera is an intestinal infection, caused by ingestion of contaminated food or water. The Irish term for the disease, *tonn taosgach agus crampaidhe*, translates as "vomiting and cramps."[124] According to the old people, cholera started between the two big toes and worked its way up from the foot, turning the body "as black as behind the fire."[125] Art Bennett reported that the disease took a terrible toll on the people of Forkhill. In 1849 he wrote, "The cholera raised its head with Gorgon terrors in this neighbourhood and carried off countless numbers of the population. Two or three hours was the longest time they lasted. The mortality chiefly fell on the middle-aged people."[126]

Art Bennett (1793–1879) was a farmer and stonemason, born in the townland of Ballykeel. He was schooled at home by his father, and from a young age he took great interest in the literary traditions of south Ulster. Literate in both English and Irish, he wrote passable Irish verse and spent much of his time transcribing Gaelic manuscripts. He appeared on a list of thirty-eight authorities on Irish language and literature that was drawn up in Dublin in 1838.[127] Despite his literary gifts, Bennett struggled to earn a living as a stonemason, for employment was scarce in his trade. "Another addition to my griefs, all these misfortunes, is the worst of employment," he wrote in 1850.[128] He suffered anxiety over his land: "I was obliged to mortgage my little spot of land for £2.0.0, and if I do not redeem it before the 17th of March, I am done with it for 6 years or more, a term I'll never see."[129] And he suffered during the famine: "The rod of affliction has withered the land and a direful calamity hangs over the country."[130] When in 1846 his daughter died of fever, he mourned, "Worse than all I had not in my possession any food or drink or a penny to buy it or bury her."[131]

In the 1840s Bennett came under the patronage of the Belfast Gaelic scholar, Robert MacAdam, who commissioned him to write a history of Ireland in the Irish language, but he quarrelled with MacAdam not long after beginning the project, and their correspondence ended abruptly. The two had argued first over the language of the text (Bennett wished to write it in English, while MacAdam wanted an Irish version), but the final rift was over money and the payment for writing supplies.[132] Some draft sections of Bennett's history have survived, including a description of the famine that had brought devastation to Ireland in the 1740s:

> The destructive waste of famine in 1740 and 1741, a date to be remembered as long as a letter appears on the pages of Irish history. Having consumed their whole stock of provisions they had recourse to dogs, cats, mice, carrion, and all such putrid and nauseous food such as famine usually seeks, and when this wretched sustenance failed, these miserable beings endeavoured to prolong the remains of life by feeding on dockings and nettles, their countenance exhibiting the colour of the weeds on which they fed. They crawled from their cabins into fields in quest of shamrocks … The streets, the highways and the fields were covered with dead bodies where they remained unburied, a prey

to kites and vultures, infesting the air with their putrid exhalation. Fluxes, and malignant fevers invaded every cabin, whole villages were laid waste and 400,000 are computed to have perished. The mortality fell chiefly on the Catholics, being the poorer class who had no means to purchase provisions and whose filthy and wretched cabins were more accessible to the ravages of pestilence than the comfortable dwellings of their taskmasters.[133]

This passage rings with the authenticity of one who had witnessed the horrors it describes, and it is hard to escape the impression that Bennett was not writing about the famine of 1740 but about the one through which he had just lived. Such shocking scenes were recorded by witnesses to the famine of the 1840s in the most ravaged parts of the country.

The sense of injustice that underwrites this passage in Bennett's history struck a chord with his countrymen. In April 1848 Father Mulligan, parish priest of Forkhill, forwarded a petition to the House of Commons. It bore the signatures of 1,500 local people, all praying for a "Repeal of the abominable union" – the parliamentary union with England established by the Act of Union of 1800.[134] Two years earlier, Father McParlan, also of Forkhill, had collected £8 2s 6d locally towards the Daniel O'Connell Compensation Fund – not an insignificant sum during hard times.[135] The cause of Repeal in south Armagh was taken up unexpectedly by Captain Thomas Seaver of Heath Hall in Killeavy, a renegade member of the local Protestant establishment; he presided at a Repeal meeting held in Newry on 17 March 1848.[136]

The theme of injustice and of the culpability of the British government for the ills of Ireland ran through Bennett's history, which was eventually completed under the title *Combric na Gaodhil agus na nGall le cheile* (The Conflicts of the Irish and the Foreigners).[137] His outrage was echoed in the writings of John Mitchel, author of two of the most influential nationalist polemics of the nineteenth century, *Jail Journal* (1854) and *The Last Conquest of Ireland (Perhaps)* (1861). When Mitchel thundered famously that "the Almighty sent the potato blight, but the English created the famine," he raised the question of the inevitability of the disaster with his searing condemnation of Irish landlords and the British administration. Mitchel's vitriol seeped into history. Nearly a century and a half later, the axe of debate within famine scholarship turns on the same question: Was the famine inevitable?

For the several million people who survived the years of blight, an answer to this question did not much matter. Those who emigrated did their best to build new lives for themselves and to make peace with their decision to leave their homeland. For those who stayed behind, the famine had a bitter resonance. Recall that it came on the heels of the disturbances of the 1830s, the almost universal stand against the tithe, and the campaign of outrage waged to regulate the leasing of ground. All this was part of a grassroots effort to control the people's only life-sustaining resource: land. Land guaranteed livelihood and survival. Then came the famine and the expiry of this guarantee. Suddenly, a quarter-acre – or four acres or forty acres – meant nothing when it amounted to a field of rot. The moral of the story that began this chapter is that the famine, a catastrophe and a tragedy, was also a cruel irony. For at the end of the day, you could not eat the land.

8

Religion, 1846–1858

In the 1850s the religious tensions that had formed such a volatile backdrop to the famine relief effort were brought firmly into the foreground. The man responsible was the Reverend Henry Wray Young, a newly ordained Church of Ireland curate who arrived in Forkhill in 1846. Young is remembered in local folklore as a cunning agent of the evangelicals who encouraged Catholics to renounce their faith by offering them gifts of food, money, and clothing. His labours in Forkhill followed a half-century of missionary work in Ireland by British-based evangelical groups such as the London Missionary Society (LMS), the Church Missionary Society (CMS), the London Hibernian Society, and their various auxiliaries. By 1825, there were eighty-eight local associations of the Hibernian auxiliary of the CMS in Ireland, and most of them were in Ulster.[1]

This intensified effort by the evangelical societies to convert Irish Catholics to Protestantism – a missionary impulse based on the Protestant perception of Catholicism as superstitious and idolatrous – was known as the Second Reformation. Its main features were outlined in chapter 5 in the context of the tensions over religious education and the controversy surrounding the Kildare Place Society. The evangelical outreach took place on other fronts as well, through Bible instruction classes for adults, the distribution of Bibles and religious tracts, and the sending forth of itinerant preachers and Scripture readers to spread the gospel. In recognition of the fact that significant numbers of the rural population were Irish-speaking, many Bibles and much religious literature were printed in Irish. The rector of Forkhill, Charles Atkinson, was among the subscribers to William Neilson's *Introduction to the Irish Language*, published in 1808.[2] In 1818 the Society for Promoting the Education of the Native Irish through the Medium of Their Own Language was formed. The Irish Society recruited, trained, and supported

Irish speakers to serve as Scripture readers, visiting homes in Irish-speaking communities and reading the Word.[3] At a meeting of the board in May 1836, the Forkhill trustees considered the possibility of employing a Scripture reader for the parish.[4]

In terms of the lasting conversions that it secured, the Second Reformation in Ireland was not a success.[5] Its chief legacy was the resentment that the evangelical outreach created in the countryside, particularly in the west of Ireland, where the missionary effort was concentrated. The story of the Reverend Alexander Dallas is an instructive example. Dallas was an Englishman who had spent five years in the British army before being ordained in the Church of England. He was said to be a zealot, possessed of a "strange, fanatical mind" and a loathing of the church of Rome.[6] He viewed Catholic worship as gross superstition and believed that the famine had been sent to prepare the hearts of the people to receive the gospel.[7] With the support of like-minded Protestant landlords and clergymen in Connacht, Dallas established a series of mission stations along the Connemara coast in the 1840s. It was here that the spiritual need of the people was perceived to be greatest and where the influence of the Roman Catholic Church was thought to be weakest.

In 1849 Dallas founded the Society of Irish Church Missions (ICM) in Dublin, with the intention of expanding his missionary work throughout Ireland. He immediately considered how he could take advantage of existing evangelical networks and was drawn to the work of the Irish Society, which was one of the most active evangelical societies in the country. Between 1836 and 1849, it spent close to £4,000 a year distributing Irish Bibles and employing the services of Scripture readers. Beginning in 1849, Dallas and his supporters brought great pressure to bear on the Irish Society to join the missionary crusade of the ICM, producing a petition signed by five hundred evangelical clergymen all "pleading" with the Irish Society to join its ranks. The society eventually bowed to the pressure and agreed to an alliance with the ICM for a trial period of three years, beginning in 1853.[8] Under the agreement, the work of the Irish Society would be carried out by representatives of the ICM throughout Ireland (except in the dioceses of Cashel, Cork, and Limerick).

From the outset, the relationship was one of discord. Dallas was an intractable and controlling figure, who had no interest in the traditional and gentler educational approach of the older organization. In the words of one historian, Dallas "never lost the mind of the soldier ... In his reckoning he was enlisted in the army of righteousness opposing the powers of darkness."[9] Where the Irish Society steered away from overt proselytism for fear of a Catholic backlash, the ICM measured its success by the number of souls it saved, and refused to waste its resources on those who were not receptive to the idea of spiritual conversion. The alliance between the Irish Society and the ICM barely survived the trial period, and they parted ways in 1856. Even on its home territory in Connemara, the lasting effect of the society's work was negligible. At its peak, the ICM operated twenty-one churches, eight parsonages, and thirty schoolhouses in the west of Ireland, but there were frequent clashes between representatives of the missions and their opponents. Scripture readers were attacked in the streets.[10] On one occasion, Dallas was stoned by his detractors after preaching a sermon in Galway.[11]

The fortunes of Dallas and his Connemara mission would have been followed closely by Henry Wray Young. He was cut from the same cloth as the ICM founder, was associated with the Irish Society, and later became an agent of the ICM.[12] His arrival in Forkhill in 1846 ushered in a decade of religious controversy that bore many resemblances to the experience of Dallas in the west of Ireland.

RELIGIOUS CONTROVERSY IN FORKHILL, 1852–1856

Born in London, the son of a mathematics professor, Henry Wray Young served for twelve years as curate of Forkhill under the rector James Campbell.[13] Young arrived in the parish during the first year of the potato blight, and for the next four years he moved among a people who were suffering hunger, privation and disease. For a man of Young's evangelical outlook, his placement in the parish at this particular time was no coincidence; he had God's work to do. Dallas, in his memoirs, connected the devastation of the famine with divine providence: "The state of Ireland during the whole of this year [1848] was most appalling: disease, in the shape of fever and cholera, had followed on starvation. Many hearts were thus being prepared to receive those consolations which the glorious Gospel of God can alone impart. The oil of this joy was to be poured in by His missionary servant."[14] The famine was a divine dispensation, he wrote, "a direct judgement from God on the account of the toleration of idolatry."[15] Given the sequence of events in the parish, it is reasonable to suppose that Young shared this view.

Beginning in the early 1850s, Young led Scripture classes that were open to both Catholics and Protestants, at which the Bible was read and discussed.[16] For a time, he also led a "controversial class," though this class had apparently been stopped by 1855.[17] "Controversial" lectures and debates were popular during the evangelical revival and involved the public disputation of points of theology.[18] Young's class was likely in the same vein, questioning and refuting points of Catholic theology that were not supported by Scripture. In addition, he distributed Irish Bibles and invited Bible readers into the parish under the auspices of the Irish Society. Elsewhere, he gave controversial lectures on theological topics, such as the one that took place at the Newry scriptural schools in December 1854. Before a "tolerably good" audience, thinned by inclement weather, he addressed the question: "Is the Church of Rome the Catholic Church?" The lecture was delivered "with much fervour and feeling."[19]

Young's fervour and feeling soon got him into trouble. He was an aggressive proselytizer and, worse, was accused of bribing his listeners with gifts of food and wine, money and clothing. He was also a bristling Orangeman and had married into a prominent Orange family (the Chambrés of Killeavy) in 1852. His father-in-law, the magistrate Hunt Walsh Chambré, was a leading member of the Orange Order in Armagh and was the force behind the construction of an Orange Hall in Killeavy in the 1860s.[20] Some fifteen years after Young left his post at Forkhill, he addressed a crowd of Orangemen at the Twelfth of July celebrations in Stewartstown, County Tyrone. The "only excuse," said Young, that can be given for not becoming an Orangeman, "is a certain moral cowardice which prevails in the minds of many men, and a desire for popularity among the members of a certain religion. They know that once in the Orange ranks they must stand shoulder to shoulder and fight the battle with the main body; and some like to see a Roman Catholic priest nod his head to them and bid 'good morrow.'"[21]

Although this speech came later in Young's career, it gives us some idea of his disdain for Catholicism and its clergy. He clashed with the priests of Forkhill on numerous occasions in the 1850s. On 22 June 1852 the petty sessions court in Forkhill convened to hear Young charge a local priest, James Finnegan, with threatening to assault him. Young claimed that he had been returning home from Forkhill village two weeks earlier when he met Father Finnegan on the Longfield road. The priest approached him, shouting and brandishing a stick, calling him a "d—d Souper" and other names that Young would not repeat before the court. The priest had to be physically restrained, said Young, and he had feared for his safety. Young denied that he had provoked the encounter and "indignantly repudiated the allegation that he had ever put his tongue out at him or any other man [for] he would be incapable of so ungentlemanly an act."[22] The court decided in Young's favour and required the priest to post bail to keep the peace.

A more serious controversy arose the following year. A Forkhill man who had converted to Protestantism under Young's superintendence fell gravely ill. A rumour circulated that the man in question, Hugh Gartlany, had renounced his conversion on his deathbed and had requested the last rites of the Catholic Church.[23] Several witnesses, including members of Gartlany's family and a Catholic cleric, Charles McShane, claimed that the sick man had called for a priest, who had administered the death rites.[24] Further, they claimed that Gartlany had promised to resign any connection with Young and his "swaddling Irish society" if he recovered.[25] McShane corroborated the story, stating that he had "attended" Hugh Gartlany while he was ill, though he did not state explicitly that he had administered the last rites. In a statement printed in the *Newry Telegraph*, McShane reserved harsh words for Young and his confederates, condemning the "unblushing audacity [of] persons connected with that humbugging Evangelical Society."[26]

When Gartlany recovered from his illness, he signed a statement declaring that he had never called for the priest, nor had the last rites been administered to him. Indeed, he said that when he had sent for Young, his relations had thrown him (Gartlany) out of the house, saying that if the curate came, the house would be "thrown down before morning."[27] As the controversy escalated and the contradictory statements of witnesses were printed in the *Telegraph*, Gartlany angrily issued a more explicit declaration: "I never resigned or promised to resign my connexion with the Irish Society; I never sent for McShane or any other Priest of the Church of Rome; nor did I receive for the last five years any of the rites of that church."[28]

Although McShane had visited the sick man, probably at the request of Gartlany's family, the meeting (according to Young), had been brief and ungracious. Gartlany had been asked to sign a document that obliged him to surrender his Bible, and when he adamantly refused, the priest took his leave.[29] Young trumpeted the news in the *Newry Telegraph* in March 1853. "Gartlany was at Forkhill Church last Sunday," he declared. "No well-thinking person doubts for a moment his sincerity or the truthfulness of his declaration … We have reason then to rejoice that in the midst of the greatest poverty – and among the blackest Roman Catholics – poor Gartlany has not surrendered the great map of eternal truth."[30]

The following month, the Forkhill poet and scribe Art Bennett wrote a furious letter to his friend Father Lamb on the subject of Young's missionary labours. "I went to the post office of Forkhill on Good Friday last and there I saw a large multitude of the most wretched fugitives trudging after Mr Young to church. Each of them had an Irish Bible. I was told they attended that synagogue every day during that week and received their communion. These shameful doings had set the feathers on end upon me and prompted me to give vent to my feelings in the foregoing lines ... It's little matter that I would be poor; many and many a time these 20 years past I was promised a high salary if I would join the corrupted system. I'll live and die on the alms of the humane before I bring scandal on my creed and family."[31]

The incensed Bennett wrote a poem in Irish describing the scene, "An Ghleann na Subhailce." The poem demonized Young: "From the demons of yore there now issues forth the lean and crafty deceiver," who has ensnared the people with the "Nets that Hell wove." Bennett reserved his harshest words for the souls who followed the curate like "gaggles of geese," drawn from the most miserable classes of the community: "The mean and the low he makes all his own ... All the tinkers he draws, and old vagabonds ... for a taste of his dainties they trail." Bennett explicitly accused Young of bribing his listeners: "With anger wild, the Great God will reply: 'I will not acquit ye – For the Minister's bribes you shall ever abide in the place of his last retreat.'"[32] Bennett restated the charge in a later poem, "An Ministéar Young," where he wrote: "*Mheall sé corradh a's tri chéad / Le Bioblai Gaeilge is le duais*" (Three hundred and more he did ensnare / With Gaelic Bibles and with gifts).

Several months later, in August 1853, the Protestant church in Forkhill was broken into, some brass fixtures were stolen, and "an attempt was made to injure the melodium."[33] Such an attack on the church was exceptional in the history of the parish. Even during the volatility of the 1790s, when churches of various denominations came under siege, the Protestant church in Forkhill had withstood looters and vandals. In the circumstances, this attack on the most prominent symbol of Protestantism in the parish may be interpreted as a sign of the growing animosity to Young's presence. Still, Young persisted in his overtures and in his encouragement of mission preachers, despite a precedent of local intolerance. In January 1836 a Keady man had been threatened in his home by a band of men who had warned him of the "vengeance of Captain Rock if he did not banish all Protestant Books from his house and return to the true Church of Rome." The victim, Hugh Feighan, had recently become a teacher of the Scriptures in Irish and was "in some measure opposed to the doctrines of the Romish church."[34] Then, in March 1842, a number of Irish-language Scripture readers had been attacked and beaten in the parish of Killeavy "to prevent them reading Scriptures to Roman Catholics."[35] And in March 1846 a party of men (and two women) had kicked in the door of James Toner's house in Creggan, shouting that they would murder him, for he was "a bloody old Irish teacher."[36]

In November 1853 two members of the ICM, Henry Donaghy and Charles Neville, arrived in the parish at Young's invitation and made their way up Slieve Gullion to spread the gospel. Partway up the mountain, they stopped at a cabin, inside which was a woman and her two small children. They sat down and spoke with the woman "of things spiritual and things temporal," until a neighbour arrived and told the men to leave. As they were leaving, the husband, Francis Covey, returned home and confronted the pair. He asked them "what they were about," and when they told him who they were, he lashed out, striking both men and kicking Donaghy to the ground.

Acting on the advice of Young, the two missionaries charged Covey with assault, and Young paid for the summons himself. At the trial, Donaghy and Neville admitted that they had not been invited into the house, but they insisted that they had not forced Covey's wife to listen to them. "We don't force ourselves on anyone," Neville declared. "If they wish to hear the word of God, we read it to them!" The legal counsel for Francis Covey summoned great moral indignation on his behalf, censuring the missionaries and their attempt to corrupt his family: "Covey is a humble man and a poor man, but these are no reason why his faith and that of his family should be tampered with, or the morals of his wife and young children contaminated by instructions such as these men could offer." The court sided in principle with this argument and issued Covey with only a small fine (2s 6d).[37] In the wake of the incident, the *Dundalk Democract* directed an angry editorial against Young and his evangelicals – those "ranting mountebanks of the lowest character, who intrude into the dwellings of the poor, torturing the Holy Scripture into any form and meaning that suits their wicked purposes, with the object of making perverts, hypocrites, liars and apostates of the Catholic peasantry." The newspaper called on Young to quit his proselytizing in south Armagh and devote his energies to heathen England, where "wives are murdered by their husbands, children by their mothers, and where at the coal pits the name of Christ is not known."[38]

Young was unperturbed and continued in his work. In August 1856 he issued an open letter to "the Roman Catholics of Forkhill," framing a set of statements about Catholic doctrine for which (he claimed) there was no foundation in Scripture. The statements, printed in the *Dundalk Democrat*, were:

1 That we are commanded to use the intercession of the Blessed Virgin, and that the intercession of our Redeemer is not sufficient for us;
2 That the Roman Catholic doctrine of Purgatory is true;
3 That it is necessary to confess our sins to a priest;
4 That the sacrifice of the Mass can take away the sins of the living and the dead.

In an audacious gesture, Young pledged that on behalf of the ICM, he would donate the whole sum required to build a new Roman Catholic church in Forkhill to any priest who could find proof in the Bible for these statements. Young called this his "fair offer."[39]

A man known only as J.K.B. responded to the challenge in the pages of the *Dundalk Democrat* in September 1856.[40] He argued that Young's narrow concentration on the Bible and his neglect of tradition (the writings of the Church Fathers, such as Jerome, Basil, and Augustine) were erroneous and unchristian. For nearly two hundred years before the writing of the New Testament, J.K.B. argued, Christians had lived without the written Word and "by the guide of apostolic tradition." Further, "Christ never wrote any of his doctrines himself; and I will feel obliged if you point out where he commanded his disciples to commit any part of them to writing." Was it sensible, he asked, that God's divine law be subject to the draught of a pen? And what proof had Young that "the Father was unbegotten? That Sunday ought to be kept holy? That Easter Day be celebrated always upon a Sunday?"[41] How were the four Gospels selected, and how were others omitted? All these were "traditions," unwritten but accepted by the Protestant Church. The Catholic *Democrat* pronounced Young thoroughly defeated and proclaimed his failure "to run the hearts of the people of Forkhill from Rome to Exeter Hall [despite] blarney and reproof; soup and tracts; money and marbles."[42]

But Young refused to let the matter drop. In the fall of 1856 the curate challenged a Forkhill priest, Father Hugh Mulligan, to a public disputation on points of theology.[43] The priest did not reply, but the invitation was taken up by a man named William McGeough, a former student of the priesthood and a travelling salesman of Catholic religious books. A debate was arranged in the neutral ground of the Methodist chapel at Forkhill, and a crowd gathered for the occasion. According to a newspaper report – and a lively folk memory – the debate went badly for the curate. He was outmatched by the young salesman and showed his discomfiture by blushing and perspiring. Young's wife, who was watching through a window, broke a pane of glass with her umbrella to give him some fresh air. Upon seeing this, McGeough quipped, "I see that your wife is throwing in sharp tokens of surrender." The crowd roared, and the debate descended into a row. Young eventually had to be rescued from the chapel by police.[44]

Several weeks later, the Catholic chapel in nearby Drumintee was broken into, and a statue of the Virgin and child was smashed. Young immediately issued a statement defending himself and the Bible readers, stating that no person connected with the Irish Church Missions was involved in the outrage. In a report on the incident, the *Democrat* emphasized that the community did not suspect the collusion of the Protestant families of Forkhill, whose "high and peaceful conduct" was of long standing – leaving the distinct impression that Young was to blame.[45] Young quit his post at Forkhill the following year and moved to the curacy of the parish of Ardee in County Louth.[46]

UNDERSTANDING THE CONTROVERSY

In 1768 an Armagh poet, Art MacCumaigh, wrote a poem called "An Tagra an Da Theampall" (The Disputation of the Two Churches). The poem was written the year after the erection of the new Protestant church in Forkhill, which had been commissioned and paid for by the landlord, Richard Jackson. The poem takes shape as a dispute between "An Teampall Galda," the newly built Church of Ireland building, and "An Roimhchill," the Catholic chapel in nearby Faughart.[47] An Roimhchill begins the conversation by asking the new Protestant church who had built its sturdy walls: "Was it the Irish ... or the followers of Luther, or the descendants of the Strongbownians?" An Teampall Galda scornfully replies:

> You silly old dame, I would have you forsake
> Your ignorant papish notions
> For all your sliocht Gael are declining away
> From Popery's vain devotion.
> My Protestant states are thriving each day
> Since Rome and they divorced;
> Your church is decayed and ever shall fade
> Under our Lutheran forces.

The next verse rang with superiority:

> In spite of your beads, my English shall reign
> Whilst Irish grows daily odious
> England and Wales have riches in heaps
> To flourish away most glorious.
> My flock has estates, with land and demesnes
> All riding in state in their coaches
> While taxes, arrears, and cesses severe
> Upon your Gaelian broaches.

An Teampall Galda further accused the Catholic clergy of teaching "false doctrine" and of perverting Scripture in order to justify their money grabbing – until Luther and Calvin rescued the church by correcting these abuses. An Roimhchill retorted that Luther was the

The Church of Ireland in Forkhill, erected in 1767, now a private dwelling, Forkhill, County Armagh (photograph by J.E. Madden)

architect of the desecration of the church and the pollution of Ireland with squabbling sects of "New Light nó Seceders, Old Presbyterians, Swaddlers nó Quakers." Calling itself the one true church, An Roimhchill invoked the names of O'Neill, O'Hanlon, and other ancient chieftains who had once ruled the kingdom of Orior, and it forecast the resurrection of the Catholic Church and the downfall of the Protestant interest in Ireland.[48]

"An Tagra an Da Theampall" isolates every element of difference that was perceived to exist between the Protestants and Catholics of Forkhill in 1768: language, political loyalty, social class, and creed. The poem is a slur on the Protestant gentry of Armagh, who were accused of flaunting their estates and riches "in heaps" before the native Irish, who were heavily burdened by taxes and debt, an outdated language, and a "decaying" faith. The relationship between the two communities – presented as confrontational and acrimonious – is underlined by the language of the poem. Where the Protestant Church speaks its lines in English, the chapel retorts in Irish; in other words, they were literally unable to communicate.

The resentment that courses through the poem is the key to understanding Forkhill's response to Henry Wray Young nearly one hundred years later. For Art Bennett, Father Finnegan, Father McShane, and the others who clashed with him, Young was the embodiment of An Teampall Galda: pompous, corrupt, and the messenger of a false gospel. They lashed out at him violently, in person and in print. Yet the fury that Young provoked was entirely disproportionate to the progress of the evangelical movement in Forkhill. In 1834 there were 6,562 Catholics living in the parish and only 479 Protestants.[49] On the occasion of the next religious census in 1861, the Protestant community in Forkhill had dwindled by nearly one half, an erosion that exceeded the rate of decline in the Catholic community.[50] In 1834 Protestants accounted for less than 7 per cent of the parish population; by 1861 that figure had fallen to 4.4 per cent. Given these figures, Young posed no threat to the security of the Catholic community in Forkhill, and the number of lasting conversions he secured could probably have been counted on two hands. So why was the response of the Catholic community so visceral?

I suspect that Young's ministry recalled that of an earlier Church of Ireland cleric who had tried to put his stamp on the parish – the Reverend Edward Hudson, who had been the overseer of Richard Jackson's trust and the man in charge of settling the estate in 1788–92. Like his successor some sixty years later, Hudson had shown no interest in reconciling his ambitions for the estate with the local way of life. His goal was to uproot and replant, "[making] our Savages happy against their wills, by establishing trade and industry among them."[51] By his sweeping changes to the existing system of land tenure, his active pursuit and prosecution of local Defenders, and his affiliation with the Forkhill yeomanry, Hudson soon became the embodiment of everything the people loathed. It will be recalled that he was subjected to a sustained campaign of intimidation waged by local Defenders and was eventually run out of the parish. On some level, the entrance of the brash and determined Henry Young recalled the era of Edward Hudson. The association may have invoked the collective memory of the hostility and uncertainty of the early 1790s, when the community was faced with an influx of settlers and the imposition of an alien authority, and felt that their way of life was under threat. This revival of resentment found vociferous expression in the writings of Art Bennett.

If Young was An Teampall Gealda, Art Bennett was An Roimhchill, the Catholic chapel – downgraded but confident of its imminent resurrection. For Bennett, Forkhill's rejection of Young was imperative, because symbolically it was the rejection of the Protestant Church and English rule, a protest against the defeat of the Gaelic chieftains, the loss of their land, and the imposition of foreign settlers and alien laws. In chapter 7 I quoted a passage from Bennett's history of Ireland in which he described the famine of 1740–41. His history was a searing indictment of the social structure and political system that had created widespread vulnerability to disaster. Bennett returned to the theme in a later section of the manuscript in which he described the oppression and injustice of the penal era:

> The famine of 1756 and 1757, and finally of 1766 ... and the cholera of 1832, all these miseries present but a faint image compared to the sufferings of the Irish Catholics during the infernal existence of the Penal Code ... The historian, the geographer, the chronologer, the antiquarian, the naturalist, the poet, the orator, nay even the observer of human nature in its original simplicity, could not describe their melancholy state. Everything that malice and bigotry could conceive, that craft or falsehood could invent, or that ignorance and national apathy could believe was attributed to the Irish name, language and nation. To describe the savage atrocities, the shocking barbarities, the lawless oppression, the unrelenting cruelty by pains and penalties, the brutal massacres, midnight assassinations of members, fines and imprisonment, and the enforcement of martial laws in the midst of profound peace, would require the silent study of Diogenis and the glowing pencil of Tacitus. Scotch Puritans, Cromwellian veterans and itinerant Quakers were alike encouraged and naturalised, and the Irish language and its professors were made aliens in their native soil.[52]

This passage rings with an indignation that was almost personal. Although Bennett was ostensibly writing about the injustices and persecutions committed against the Irish Catholic nation by its English overlords (along with those "apostate Catholics who had sacrificed their cause on the altar of hatred to the religion they deserted"), his account in fact contains parallels with his own life. By the late 1850s, Bennett was an embittered man. Having lost his fifteen-year-old daughter to fever in the first year of the famine, he had then watched the rest of his family live on the verge of starvation. Over the next few years he struggled to find work as a stonemason and worried that he might lose his plot of land, which he had been forced to mortgage to meet his debts; he worried constantly about his health, and in the latter days of the famine he feared he was close to death. In addition, he was a difficult personality, arrogant and irritable. His countryman and fellow Gaelic scholar Father Patrick Lamb once warned a colleague that Bennett was "of a very singular and odd disposition," "very fond of his own opinion," and liable to react impetuously to any perceived slight.[53]

Bennett's quarrel with Robert MacAdam, who had commissioned the book, was very much in character – even his refusal to write it in Irish: "As for the compiling of the Elizabethan Wars etc. in Irish, I would not undertake it upon any consideration."[54] When he reconsidered and sent an early extract to MacAdam in the spring of 1850, the latter was unimpressed and sent him only token remuneration. An angry Bennett wrote back to MacAdam in March 1850: "I acknowledge the receipt of your letter inclosing a few sheets of paper and 2s 6d. I can't say (altogether) that you made little of my proposed work. It was as much as the Redeemer of the World was sold for."[55] It was not surprising that correspondence between them ceased and that Bennett had to find another patron – the Newry stationer Edward Augustus Maginnis.[56]

A strain of pessimism is evident in many of Bennett's personal letters, his historical writings, and much of his poetry.[57] As noted above, he identified with the sufferings he described in his book and may have located within the "cruelty" and "melancholy" of Irish history the origin of his own personal struggles. Although he had not suffered directly under the strictures of the penal code, he was a victim of the strains on the landlord-tenant system and of the worst excesses of the famine, which John Mitchel traced to the indifference and corruption of the political administration. Indeed, the writings of Mitchel (which were from the same period) display a similar parallel between the life of the individual and the history of the nation, one that Mitchel acknowledged in his *Jail Journal* (1854). "The general history of a nation may fitly preface the personal memoranda of a solitary captive," he wrote, "for it was strictly and logically a consequence of the dreary story here epitomized, that I came to be a prisoner."[58] In the same way, Bennett's harrowing experience of famine had an impact on his understanding of Irish history, and on his opinion of the Reverend Henry Young.

Ultimately, the famine is the context for understanding Young's ministry and the response he provoked in Forkhill, for he merely electrified an atmosphere that was already highly charged. In her study of famine literature, Margaret Kelleher ponders the question of the adequacy of language to describe the "unspeakable" suffering wrought by famine.[59] The term "unspeakable" might be understood to imply the dumbness or awkwardness of contemporary observers who struggled to find words to describe the shocking scenes of suffering that they witnessed. But it also implies the silence of those who suffered, both during the famine and afterwards. There is no historical record of the unspoken. Perhaps that is why so little is known about the mental toll that the famine exacted from those who lived through it. Mental suffering could be expressed in various ways: as grief for loss, as guilt for the inability to provide for one's family; as shame for having to accept charity; or as frustration at one's helplessness in the face of crisis. I wonder if the outbursts against Young in the 1850s can be understood partly as the unleashing of this emotion, which had been unexpressed in the years since the famine but was still raw.

The controversy over Young was also influenced by developments outside the parish in the 1850s. This decade marked the impressively swift consolidation of the Catholic Church in Ireland with the appointment of Paul Cullen to the archbishopric of Armagh in 1849 and his accession in 1852 to the archbishopric of Dublin. Over the course of twenty-five years, Irish Catholicism was transformed as Cullen imbued the church with a coherence and unity it had not previously possessed. The lax discipline, low mass attendance, pagan customs, and irregular practices that had distinguished Catholic religious life in pre-famine Ireland were thoroughly reformed. The church building (rather than the home) became the centre of religious life; rituals and devotions, such as perpetual adoration, the rosary, and novenas, were encouraged; and missions were held throughout Ireland to encourage lay receipt of the sacraments.[60] Cullen was a dynamic religious leader, but there is no doubt that he was aided enormously by the social circumstances of Ireland after 1850. The indiscipline and laxity that had characterized the pre-famine church were the result of overextension: the population had simply been too large for the church to manage. In 1840 there had been roughly 2,150 priests in Ireland, or one priest for every 3,025 people. By 1850 there was one priest for every 2,100 Catholics, and the ratio steadily improved during the next half-century.[61]

In April 1855 the Fathers of St Vincent de Paul held a three-week mission in the village of Crossmaglen, not far from Forkhill. Between 7,000 and 8,000 people received Holy Communion during the mission, and on the closing Sunday 1,200 attended mass, which was celebrated by the Reverend Dr Joseph Dixon, archbishop of Armagh.[62] Throughout the mission, the preachers emphasized the importance of forgiveness and reconciliation, and urged the people to set aside petty quarrels and family disputes and to forget past resentments and injuries. More than twenty priests from Creggan and the surrounding parishes heard confessions. The *Dundalk Democrat* contrasted the piety of the Armagh priests with the "bigotted ... itinerant declaimers against Catholicity who are prowling around the country in these latter days," in a clear rebuke to the Reverend Henry Young.[63]

Young's "fair offer" to finance the building of a new Catholic chapel in the parish of Forkhill was rejected outright, and the people vowed to pay for the construction of one themselves. A charity sermon was held in May 1857, and the proceeds were put towards the cost of remodelling the old building at Mullaghbawn until a new chapel could be erected.[64] Work on the new building began in the summer of 1861, and St Mary's Church at Mullaghbawn was dedicated to divine worship by the archbishop of Armagh in October 1862. On that day, High Mass was celebrated by the Reverend Father Nicholas Hughes.[65] Father Hughes was the son of Bridget Hughes, who, it will be recalled, had been keeping house for her uncle, Father Nicholas McIvor, at the time of the 1821 census. Bridget had had two boys at the time: Bernard, who was four years of age, and Nicholas, an infant.[66]

9

An Astronomy Lesson

During his work for the Irish folklore commission in the 1940s and 1950s, Michael J. Murphy recorded a local version of the story of Alexander Berkley, the Forkhill schoolmaster and linen weaver who was attacked and mutilated by a gang of Defenders in 1791. In this twentieth-century version, entitled "Bartley and the Boys of Mullaghbawn," the schoolmaster was tied to a tree in the Protestant churchyard, and his tongue and fingers were cut off. He later attempted to write down the names of his attackers "with a pencil between his toes."[1]

The story had been retold more violently in a history of Orangeism published in the 1930s. In that version, Berkley was thrown to the floor by his assailants and stabbed repeatedly. After "removing the four fingers and thumb of his right hand with some clumsy instrument, [they] left him in utter helplessness and suffering on the floor. Mrs. Barclay's tongue was cut out, and the four fingers and thumb of her right hand were amputated in the same barbarous way. She was afterwards beaten and battered in a terrible manner, while one of her breasts was cut away. In her case, death came as a happy end to her sufferings. Her brother, a boy of thirteen years, had come from Armagh that morning on a visit, and he was the third victim. The miscreants cut out his tongue, and hacked away the calves of his legs. This revolting outrage on three Protestants was the cause of public exultation. No effort was made to conceal the crime. On the contrary, the perpetrators marched along the road, carrying torches in defiance of everyone."[2] This description of the attack is based on the account in Richard Musgrave's *Memoirs of the Different Rebellions* (1801), though with the addition of even more lurid details.[3]

In the history of Forkhill, the 1791 attack was the equivalent of an earthquake. Its aftershocks were experienced over a vast area and lasted for more than a hundred years. In the introduction, I described the importance of this event in the history of Ulster Protestantism and the still virulent sense of horror and indignation that accompany its description, whether recounted by Richard Musgrave in 1801, Colonel Verner in 1840, or an anonymous member of the Orange Order in the 1930s.

Within the parish itself, the memory of 1791 had a profound impact on successive generations of Protestants. At certain moments it is possible to detect a bristling and regrouping within the Protestant community, particularly during periods of rural unrest. Three moments come to mind. The first was in 1796, when Colonel Ogle forwarded the petition to Dublin Castle "expressing the Sentiments of 88 of the principal inhabitants of the parish of Forkhill," who wished to establish a local yeomanry corps to counter the disaffection that was spreading through rural Ulster on the eve of the rebellion.[4] The next was in April 1803, when the Church of Ireland vestry in Forkhill, registering alarm at the persistence of local unrest and the rumours of a regenerated Defenderism, appointed twelve men to "superintend the police of this parish ... [and] exert themselves to suppress all illegal meetings."[5] Finally, in 1832, three Protestant farmers swore an affidavit stating that they were "in dread and fear that the lives and properties of themselves, their Protestant brethren and neighbours are daily in danger of being destroyed"; they were chiefly alarmed by the behaviour of the "whole Roman Catholic population," who were "flying through the country, calling at every house and giving what deponents conceive to be a watchword and from which they apprehend some serious consequence may arise."[6]

In each case, the defensive posture assumed by the Protestant community was a response to stirrings among the wider Catholic population, represented by the Defenders and United Irishmen in 1796, the "resurgent" Defenders in 1803, and the tithe agitators in 1832. The rationale for their response was clear. Outrage was perceived as an unpredictably violent weather system that might touch down at any moment, and its rational and predictable elements often were not recognized or acknowledged. Moreover, any collective action by Catholics was regarded as subversive and, if unchecked, as a potential precursor to indiscriminate sectarian violence.[7] In Forkhill, these assumptions constituted the unmistakable legacy of the brutal attack on Alexander Berkley and his family in 1791.

Edward Hudson's arresting accounts of that night, recorded in his letters of 29 January and 3 February 1791, bring us closer to this event than any other known documents. Yet despite Hudson's proximity to the event (and perhaps because of it), he spread the wrong story. The version of the attack that crystallized immediately in the minds of

Protestants throughout Ulster was that Alexander Berkley had been singled out for torture by a band of Catholic savages on account of his Protestantism, and that "those like him" had reason to fear a similar reprisal. As I explained in chapter 2, the expression "those like him" did not refer to Protestants generally but to informers and other obnoxious individuals who had opted to prosecute local men for their misdeeds.

Yet the sectarian explanation of this story is so widespread and so mainstream that it has never been investigated or seriously questioned. I heard the story when I was growing up, and I accepted it as a grisly tale of sectarian hatred in the lawless republic of south Armagh. There seemed no reason to doubt it, and when I began to research the history of the settlement of the Forkhill estate in the 1790s, I expected that these sectarian attitudes would be violently showcased. But expectations are dangerous things for a historian to carry around. In his book *The Shape of Irish History*, A.T.Q. Stewart makes the following observation: "The phrase 'contrary to all expectations' rings through the story of the progress of human knowledge. It was 'contrary to all expectations' that the Earth was found to be revolving round the sun, and not the other way round, and that a mould growing in one of Dr Alexander Fleming's dishes was found to be capable of destroying bacteria. When in 1989 the spacecraft Voyager 2 got close enough to the planet Neptune to take detailed pictures of the surface, they were 'contrary to all expectations.'"[8]

Contrary to all expectations, Catholics willingly attended the staunchly Protestant schools sponsored by Richard Jackson's charity, beginning in 1790, and they attended in numbers for more than forty years. Although the proportionate attendance of Protestants was higher throughout the period, Catholic pupils, both boys and girls, far outnumbered their Protestant neighbours in the Forkhill schools.

Contrary to all expectations, the families of Catholics and Protestants in Forkhill in 1821 were almost exactly the same size; and their size was modest, which was also contrary to expectation. Likewise, there were many poor Protestants in Forkhill in 1821, living on small farms and struggling to make a living on the land and at the loom. They were just as gravely affected by the decline of the weaving industry and the increased competition for ground in the years before the famine as their Catholic counterparts were.

Contrary to all expectations, tensions over land produced a far higher degree of violence within the Catholic community than was ever experienced between Catholics and Protestants. Indeed, the ribbon society – that "deeply sectarian" movement devoted to the extirpation of Protestantism in Ireland – was surprisingly even-handed in its treatment of Catholics and Protestants, and punished both with impartiality.

Contrary to all expectations, outrage in the countryside rarely proceeded from overtly sectarian impulses, and the most infamous "sectarian" outrage of the period, the attack on Alexander Berkley in 1791, was not motivated by his Protestantism. The misinterpretation of this incident cast a false shadow over the nineteenth century and predisposed the Protestant gentry to perceive the conflict in sectarian terms.[9]

The Catholic community in Forkhill was not exempt from such predispositions, and this is most apparent in its view of its own history. There is a degree of amnesia on the subject of early education in the parish, the regular attendance of many Catholic children at the Protestant schools funded by Richard Jackson's trust, and the extent to which this attendance, over the course of nearly fifty years, was voluntary. Instead, local memory, sustained by oral traditions, highlights only discord. A recent history of the parish described the building of the first Jackson schoolhouse in the townland of Shean in 1790, remarking in an aside that "the lands for this school ... [had] been reputedly confiscated from the Hearty Family of Shean."[10]

Local experience of the famine offers another example of the selectivity of historical memory. The famine hit Forkhill hard: crop failure was general and destitution was widespread; both Catholics and Protestants were counted among the suffering. The relief effort, which originated in the Protestant community, staved off mass starvation and bridged the gap between suffering and death. Yet there is no graciousness in the recollection of these years, and local memory of the famine records a legacy of resentment and blame. The stinginess and proselytism of the Protestant community are what live on in the popular memory; their charitable response merits barely a footnote.

In contrast, local tradition has allowed ample room for the memory of the Reverend Henry Wray Young, the unpopular curate who served in the parish from 1846 to 1858. An old woman living in the parish in the 1950s told Michael J. Murphy, the folklore collector, that she had "heard of Young. He was a tract dropper and proper villain."[11] Local historians can recount in detail how he was soundly defeated in the theological debate in the Methodist meeting rooms in 1856. This one man and his failed missionary endeavour have commanded a disproportionate amount of attention in the oral history of Forkhill. I suspect this is because Young – and his attempts to win over local Catholics with gifts of Bibles, food, and wine – represented a caricature of Protestantism that was easy to despise and reject, particularly in the painful decade after the famine. The charges of proselytism that were levelled against Young in the 1850s echoed those that were made against the charity schools in the 1820s and 1830s by the parish priests, who accused the trustees of "seducing the [Catholic] children to attend their schools" by giving them a penny a week merely for showing up.[12] The charges were repeated recently in a historical account of education in the parish; the authors described the condition of the people in the 1790s as "extremely poor," stating that the Jackson schools had "exploited this poverty by giving a penny or two pence per week to every child."[13]

But it appears that many Catholics felt comfortable sharing in the endowments of the Jackson trust and even felt entitled to its benefits. Their attendance at the charity schools is the obvious example, but the work of the Forkhill trust extended beyond the sphere of education. In his will, Jackson had reserved an annual donation for the infirmaries in Dundalk and Armagh, and had put money towards "decent provision for honest old decayed tradesmen or farmers" on his Cavan and Armagh estates.[14] He left £100 to buy looms for his poorest tenants, and he left a hundred greatcoats to the hundred oldest tenants at the time of his death.[15] On 1 November 1791, twenty-five old men were asked to come before the board of trustees "for selection or rejection" to determine if they were eligible to benefit from the fruits of the charity, and the list of recipients was updated regularly over the course of the next fifty years.[16] In August 1817, during a period of scarcity following a failed harvest, the trustees, moved by the "unexampled distress of the poor," gave £30 to the rector, Charles Atkinson, to purchase meal for the tenants.[17] A more generous gift was made in 1846, during the second year of the famine. In 1837 a loan society had been established in the parish "for the benefit of the industrious," and although it was not administered by the trustees, they authorized their treasurer to lend money to the society from their floating balance, free of interest, up to £300.[18]

In the early 1840s the trustees found themselves with a surplus of funds, owing to the increased rental income from the estate. They considered increasing their annual endowment to the overseas missions, which had been one of Richard Jackson's abiding concerns; in his will, he had earmarked a considerable sum for "propagating the religion of our blessed Saviour, particularly in the East, by adding to the number of Danish and other protestant missionaries."[19] Upon learning of the trustees' deliberations, the tenants of the estate drafted a petition in which they respectfully requested that the additional funds be applied to charitable concerns in the parish instead of being "sent away from them to Hindostan ... [for] it grieves them to have so much money the produce of their industry given to strangers in a distant part of the Globe with whom they can have no sympathies and whose social condition is in many respects far superior to that of your petitioners."[20] The petition was signed by 126 men, both Protestants and Catholics.[21]

In the tenants' view, the Jackson trust was not just a charitable organization but a stock in which they, by their labour, invested and from which they were entitled to benefit; the term "charity" did not carry the uncomfortable associations that it would several years later.

And there were other mediations. The 1821 census, which recorded the names of all 6,313 people living in the parish, shows that Catholics and Protestants adopted many of the same Christian names, drawing mainly on the books of the Bible, the roll of saints, and the royal family. But there were some conspicuous differences. Fewer than one percent of Catholic men were named William, which was a popular name among Protestants; and of the nearly four hundred women named Bridget, all but one of them was Catholic. This does not explain the number of Catholic girls in Forkhill named Susanna. Susanna was the name of the surviving sister of Richard Jackson and the heir to a considerable portion of his estate. In a codicil to her complicated will in 1803, Susanna Barton stipulated that a premium of £10 would be awarded to every Forkhill family that bestowed her name on one of its daughters.[22] Of the fifteen families in the parish that appear to have accepted her offer, nine were Catholic.

Since I have studied only a single parish, I cannot claim that the shifting and sometimes ambiguous nature of the relationship between Catholics and Protestants in Forkhill was representative; local studies would need to be conducted in other places in order to permit such a generalization. And although I have argued that the concept of sectarianism may have been dulled beyond usefulness as a tool for understanding Irish history, there is no question that religion remained the primary badge of identification in nineteenth-century Ulster. This made certain cultural behaviour (such as the community's response to Young in the 1850s) understandable and even predictable. Less well understood is how that system of identification worked, when and why it was invoked, and when and why it was ignored. But as we have seen in the preceding chapters, sectarian impulses did not determine most of the decisions or interactions in the lives of these people, and there is evidence of their integration in virtually every decade – from the identification of local rebels with the cause of the United Irishmen, to the participation of Catholic children in the Protestant charity schools, and to the generous dispensation of famine relief. Even in a sectarian atmosphere that was sometimes highly charged, the motives and circumstances that determined people's behaviour were not always determined by their religion. This would have made life in mixed communities utterly unworkable, and it wasn't.

Several thousand years ago, when navigating across open water or across the desert, people tracked their progress by watching the night sky and tracing the stars. The sky was their compass and their calendar. To make the sky easier to read, they grouped the brightest stars into recognizable shapes of birds, insects, and people, and named them accordingly. We know these shapes as our modern constellations. Our effort to impose order on the historical past involves a similar exercise in imagination. The moments of recorded history are like stars scattered through a vast galaxy. The brightest stars in this galaxy draw our gaze and we join them, one to another, creating historical narratives that are constellations unto themselves. The structure that these narratives provide helps us make sense of history, but the system is not flawless. It could be argued, for example, that much of recorded history is the history of exceptional moments – it was on account of their exceptionalism that most events were written about – and that it documents not the ordinary but the extraordinary. Likewise, the essential subjectivity of these narratives, and the fact that they are constructed by us, must be acknowledged; if not, we risk allowing them to assume a degree of permanence and unassailability that they do not deserve.

The impulse to identify the extraordinary as the ordinary and to blur the distinction between the past and its narrative bedevils modern Irish history. We can easily forget that sectarianism is a persuasive historical narrative – not a gravitational force acting upon history. As a means of explaining the peculiar course of Irish history since the Reformation, the sectarian narrative is probably irreplaceable, but it should never be a substitute for closer scrutiny. Rethinking the prevailing narrative of Irish history is not simply a matter of revising our understanding of conflict, however. Sectarianism is expressed not only through violence and by hooligans, but insidiously and unconsciously. Historically, it has conditioned our expectations of how Catholics and Protestants relate to each other and how we expect them to behave among themselves. But as we have seen a number of times in the foregoing chapters, these assumptions do not leave room for observing what is "contrary to all expectation," just as they did not leave room for understanding what was meant by "those like him."

APPENDIX

A Ribbon Oath

I, A.B., with the sign of the cross do declare that I come here and promise of my own free will to join my R.C. Brothers the knights of St P[atrick] or Son[s] of Shamrock in all things appertaining thereto,

2nd That I will not buy or purchase any article or commodity from an O.U.B. or T if a brother or RC disposes of the same article as good and as cheap as they do,

3rd That I will be ready at 2 hours warning to aid and assist my true and loyal Brethern [sic] when they or any loyal calls upon me if I am not prevented by sickness or business or distress,

4th That I will not knowingly or willfully provoke, challenge or fight with any true and loyal Brother if I know him to be as such, And if a brother be unjustly treated or ill spoke of I will espouse his cause if it be just, but if a Brother be in fault I will advise and save him if possible to do so,

5th That I will not allow any person of an ill famed character into this board of Eternal trust and that I will propagate brotherly love and friendship to all such of my acquaintances as may be thought worthy of our trust,

6th That in Town and Country I will give the preference of my dealings to my true and loyal Brethern as reasonable as to any other if I know them to be attached to our National Interests,

7th That I never will see a Brother short taken or in distress for the amount of a shilling or sixpence, a meal's meat or night's lodging if possible I can relieve him,

8th That at the place of our meetings I never will drink to intoxication so that any person might know my mind or for fear of disobedience or mentioning the name of any member,

9th That I never will discourse of any of my true and loyal Brethern if I was hanged, beheaded and quartered,

10th That I never will injure a true and loyal Brother, his wife, sister, daughter or mother, except in the lawful bonds of matrimony,

11th That I will be true and loyal to our holy — the RC Church, dedicated to God by St Patrick our holy apostle and patron of Ireland in all things lawful but not otherwise,

12th That I never will discover of any of my true and loyal Brethern or of my Committee's name or any one here present except on certain or lawful occasions if I were hanged up in chains to dry before the Sun.[1]

Notes

ABBREVIATIONS

APL	Armagh Public Library
BNL	*Belfast News-letter*
CSORP	Chief Secretary's Office, Registered Papers
DD	*Dundalk Democrat*
FJ	*Freeman's Journal*
HJ	*Hibernian Journal*
IFC	Irish Folklore Commission
NAI	National Archives of Ireland
NL	National Library
NS	*Northern Star*
NT	*Newry Telegraph*
OFLA	O'Fiaich Library and Archive
PRONI	Public Record Office of Northern Ireland
RIA	Royal Irish Academy
RLFC	Relief Commission Papers
SOC	State of the Country Papers

CHAPTER ONE

1 Edward Hudson to Francis Dobbs, 29 January 1791, Charlemont MS 12 R16, no. 51, Royal Irish Academy (RIA). Hudson served as rector of Forkhill from 1779 to 1795 (Leslie, *Armagh Clergy and Parishes*, 302–5).

2 Letter of the Forkhill trustees, 3 February 1791, reprinted in Musgrave, *Memoirs of the Different Rebellions*, 51–2.

3 Ibid.

4 Thomas Prentice to Charlemont, 14 February 1791, Charlemont MS 12 R16, no. 56, RIA.
5 Musgrave, *Memoirs of the Different Rebellions*, 53.
6 William Drennan to Samuel McTier, 5 February 1791, in Chart, ed. *Drennan Letters*.
7 *Report from the Select Committee Appointed to Inquire into the Nature, Character, Extent and Tendency of Orange Lodges, Associations, or Societies in Ireland, with the Minutes of Evidence and Appendix*, [377], HC 1835 (hereafter cited as Orange Lodge Inquiry), 15:29.
8 Gowan, *Orangeism*, 125–6; Dewar, *Orangeism: A New Historical Appreciation*, 92; *Orangeism in Ireland and Throughout the Empire*, 1:276–7.
9 Dewar, *Orangeism: A New Historical Appreciation*, 92.
10 Conversation with Kevin McMahon, a local historian in south Armagh, 1997.
11 Stewart, *Narrow Ground*, 181–2.
12 Ibid., 26.
13 Farrell, *Rituals and Riots*, 6.
14 See, for example, Hirst, *Religion, Politics, and Violence in Nineteenth-Century Belfast*, 19: "The sectarianism of [certain districts of Belfast] during this period [1813–34] was due to the importation of conflict from the Ulster countryside ... Migrants from the Ulster countryside brought with them their sectarian fears and hatreds and this was reflected in the establishment and growth of the Orange and Ribbon societies in Belfast."
15 Exceptions include A.T.Q. Stewart's study, *The Narrow Ground*, which is a unique analysis of the patterns of conflict in Ulster, though it retains a predominantly sectarian outlook. See also D.H. Akenson, *Small Differences*, a quantitative analysis of Irish immigrant populations in North America, Australia, and New Zealand. Akenson compares the socio-economic profile of first- and second-generation Catholics and Protestants in the New Worlds, and discovers that they assimilated in much the same way, with similar degrees of success. In *The Catholics of Ulster*, Marianne Elliott destroys the idea of a northern Catholic monolith. She emphasizes the peaceableness that has characterized the majority of northern Catholics throughout their history, though she does make some exception for historic frontier zones such as south Armagh.
16 Gillespie, "An Historian and the Locality," 20.
17 Gregory, "*Is* Small Beautiful?" 104–5.
18 Gillespie, "An Historian and the Locality," 20.
19 There were sixty-one Presbyterians in Forkhill in 1834 ("Returns of Religious Denominations in the Several Parishes of the County of

Armagh in 1834," Tenison Groves MS, T/808/14943 Public Record Office of Northern Ireland [PRONI]); O'Kane, "A Statistical Return of Armagh Diocese in 1836," 181–9. See also the visitation reports for Forkhill in the Armagh Diocesan Registry Papers, DIO/4/9/8/1–33, PRONI. An entry in the diocesan visitation records for Forkhill in 1804 noted that "the Dissenters [had] quarrelled much amongst themselves ... [which] had attracted many to the established Church." The rector was encouraged to take advantage of this dissension because it might "bring more over every day" ("Report, Lower Diocese of Armagh, 1804," Armagh Diocesan Registry Papers, DIO/4/29/1/1/, PRONI).

20 Lewis, *Topographical Dictionary of Ireland*, 633.

21 "Returns of Religious Denominations in the Several Parishes of the County of Armagh in 1834," Tenison Groves MS, T/808/14943, PRONI.

22 Much of Ireland's townland framework was in place by the twelfth century. William Reeves has described townlands as "the earliest allotment on the scale of Irish land divisions" (quoted in Connell, Cronin, and O'Dalaigh, eds., *Irish Townlands*, 10).

23 The estate in fact consisted of seventeen townlands, but one of these, the townland of Lisnalee, was in the barony of Lower Orior.

24 Cullen, "The United Irishmen," 21–2.

CHAPTER TWO

1 Most of Forkhill lies in the barony of Upper Orior, although a small part of the parish is in Lower Orior.

2 The 1612 indenture for the lands that made up the Forkhill estate is part of the Chambré Papers, T/529/1, Public Record Office of Northern Ireland (PRONI). For descriptions, see the letters of the Reverend Edward Hudson to the Earl of Charlemont, Charlemont MSS 12 R14–27, Royal Irish Academy (RIA); Lewis, *Topographical Dictionary of Ireland*, 633; Day and McWilliams, ed., *Ordnance Survey Memoirs of County Armagh*, 45.

3 Story, *Impartial History of the Wars of Ireland*, 15.

4 Hill, *The Plantation in Ulster*, 312–14; Robinson, *The Plantation of Ulster*, 48–77; O'Sullivan, "Land Confiscations and Plantations in County Armagh," 333–80; Crawford, "The Reshaping of the Borderlands," 95.

5 Gillespie, "The Transformation of the Borderlands," 81. The poll-tax return (census) of 1659 recorded the number of males and unmarried females over the age of sixteen.

6 Tenison Groves MS, T/808/14929, PRONI.

7 Richard Jackson was a freemason and a fervent Protestant who bequeathed a generous legacy to further Protestant missionary work in

India. He served as high sheriff of County Armagh in 1760 and was appointed deputy master of the Masonic Lodge in Ulster in 1768. Jackson died in 1787 at the age of sixty-five (papers relating to Jackson and his Forkhill estate, T/1722, PRONI); *Freeman's Journal* (*FJ*), 11 June 1768.

8 The Right Honourable Richard Jackson was one of the original trustees of the Forkhill estate and attended their first meeting on 1 August 1789. He died shortly afterwards and was replaced by Walter Synnot (1 August 1789 and 3 July 1790, Minutes of the Proceedings of the Trustees of the Charitable Donations of Richard Jackson of Forkill, Esq. [hereafter Minutes of the Forkhill Trustees], vol. 1, 1789–1830).

9 Crawford, "The Reshaping of the Borderlands," 99.

10 *Belfast News-letter* (*BNL*), 3 January 1764, November 1765, and 11 October 1771.

11 Byrne, "Impartial Account," 104–5.

12 The will of Richard Jackson, the draft bill of the act of Parliament, and related documents are part of the Chambré Papers, T/529/16, PRONI. Jackson's will is reprinted in Miller, ed., *Peep O'Day Boys and Defenders*, 91–3.

13 These words appear in italics in the original document (Chambré Papers, T/529/16, PRONI).

14 Edward Hudson to Charlemont, 7 December 1789, Charlemont MS 12 R15, no. 67, RIA.

15 *BNL*, 17 October 1787.

16 *BNL*, 8 August 1788.

17 Byrne, "Impartial Account," 104–5.

18 Edward Hudson to Charlemont, 7 December 1789, Charlemont MS 12 R15, no. 67, RIA.

19 Ibid.

20 Some of the indentures were shared among leaseholders, and in a few cases (3%) they appear to have been shared between Catholics and Protestants. For these cases, I created a third group of mixed leaseholders and did not include them in the profile.

21 There were 25 Protestant leases, 13 Catholic leases, and 1 mixed agreement.

22 Catholics leased only 12.5% of the land, with average holdings of 26.2 acres. The principal Protestant leaseholder on the estate was Thomas Read, Esq. Read controlled 1,015 acres, much of it in the mountains, and his interest in the estate inflates the overall strength of the Protestant leaseholders. When his lands are excluded from consideration, Protestant control of the land falls from 86 to 78% and

Catholic control of the land rises to 20%. Even with this adjustment, Protestant farms remain, on average, twice the size of Catholic farms.

23 There were 55 leases: 15 Protestant leases, 37 Catholic leases, and 3 mixed agreements. The average size of a Protestant farm fell to 29.2 acres, bringing it closer to the size of an average Catholic farm.

24 There were 94 leases: 40 Protestant leases, 50 Catholic leases, and 4 mixed agreements. When Read's interest in the land is excluded from consideration, Protestant leases account for 58% of the land and Catholic leases for 38%.

25 Edward Hudson to Charlemont, 7 December 1789, Charlemont MS 12 R15, no. 67, RIA.

26 Ibid.

27 *BNL*, 17 October 1787.

28 Robert Stevenson's "View of County Armagh" (1795), D/562/1270, PRONI.

29 This additional £5 would be considered as "compensation" in place of a holding on the estate (Will of Richard Jackson and related documents, Chambré Papers, T/529/16, PRONI).

30 Coote, *Statistical Survey of the County of Armagh*.

31 Musgrave, *Memoirs of the Different Rebellions*, 51–3. At a meeting of the Forkhill trustees in July 1790, a motion was introduced to allow an abatement in the previous year's rent in order to compensate the tenantry for "the extraordinary losses they have sustained during the late disturbances" (3 July 1790, Minutes of the Forkhill Trustees, vol. 1).

32 The following discussion is based on evidence in the Armagh Assize indictment records. For some background on using the assize records as historical documents, see Garnham, "How Violent Was Eighteenth-Century Ireland?" Although the indictment books do not identify the home parish or townland of the parties involved, I have been able to identify the names of some Forkhill leaseholders and tenants by using the leases in the Chambré Papers and newspaper accounts. The County Armagh Crown Book [Indictments] General Assizes (1737–97) is held in the Armagh Public Library. The Armagh Assize Indictments for this period are cited hereafter as AAI (1737–97). The County Armagh Crown Book [Indictments] General Assizes (1797–1822) is held in PRONI and is hereafter cited as AAI (1797–1822), ARM1/2A/1, PRONI.

33 Edward Hudson to Charlemont, 26 August 1789, Charlemont MS 12 R15, no. 61, RIA; *BNL*, 5 January and 20 August 1790.

34 Edward Hudson to Charlemont, 28 April 1791, Charlemont MS 12 R16, no. 62, RIA; AAI (1737–97), Lent 1791; *FJ*, 21 April 1792. The two other targets of the conspiracy were Richard Johnston and

Thomas Lee; Johnston assisted in the arrests of the Murphy brothers for the Berkley outrage in 1791, and Lee was a member of the Louth Grand Jury who was active against the Defenders (Official Papers 18/2, National Archives of Ireland [NAI]; *BNL*, 12 April 1791).

35 AAI (1737–97), Lent 1789, Summer 1789, Lent 1791, Lent 1792, Summer 1792; *BNL*, 3 May 1791 and 30 March, 3 April, and 28 August 1792.

36 *BNL*, 3 April 1792.

37 AAI (1737–97), Summer 1789, Lent 1790; *BNL*, 13 April 1790.

38 R. Power to Lord Gosford, 11 April 1790, quoted in Miller, ed., *Peep O'Day Boys and Defenders*, 103.

39 AAI (1737–97), Lent 1791; *BNL*, 28 August 1792.

40 *FJ*, 23 August 1791.

41 The best-known contemporary work on the origins of the Armagh Disturbances and the early Defenders is Byrne's "Impartial Account" of 1792, and reprinted in Miller, ed., *Peep O'Day Boys and Defenders*. See the correspondence of the Earl of Charlemont during this period, in Charlemont MSS 12 R14–18, RIA. See also John Ogle to Edward Cooke, Rebellion Papers, 620/24/37, NAI; anonymous letter to Dublin Castle, Rebellion Papers, 620/26/51, NAI; William Richardson to the Duke of Abercorn, Abercorn Papers, D/623/A/156/4–5, PRONI.

42 Miller, "The Armagh Troubles, 1784–1795," passim; Miller, ed., *Peep O'Day Boys and Defenders*; Cullen, "Late Eighteenth-Century Politicization in Ireland," passim. Miller and Cullen debate the topic in *Irish and Economic Social History* 23 (1996).

43 Miller, "The Armagh Troubles, 1784–95," 157.

44 Byrne, "Impartial Account," 105.

45 Cullen, "Political Troubles of County Armagh: A Comment," 20–3: "The south of the county was different from the northern half: remote, upland, largely Catholic, and the centre of a sustained process of recolonisation from the 1760s. The Jackson will and the Barkely [sic] mutilations fit into that context. The region's troubles, such as they were, were very different from the events, either purely rural or political, elsewhere in the county … [Yet] the region was far from being untouched by the radical issues of the 1780s and 1790s. The story was obviously different because it had two centuries of resistance, with some success, to encroachment, to which its primitive economic condition and the survival of the Irish language both bore eloquent testimony. However, precisely because it was largely Catholic, the region had a small Catholic middle class with some ties to the close-by urban centres of Newry, Dundalk and Carrickmacross. There is a story to be told which, while not ignoring the Jackson/Barkely [sic] affair, should be set in a much wider context."

46 Reprinted in Musgrave, *Memoirs of the Different Rebellions*, appendix 2. Hudson referred to these documents in a letter to Charlemont (Hudson to Charlemont, 15 February 1795, Charlemont MS 12 R18, no. 65, RIA).

47 Edward Hudson to Charlemont, 11 July 1789, Charlemont MS 12 R15, no. 54, RIA; Hudson to Charlemont, 7 December 1789, Charlemont MS 12 R15, no. 67, RIA; Hudson to Charlemont, 10 January 1790, Charlemont MS 12 R16, no. 37, RIA.

48 Smyth, *Men of No Property*, 33–7. "Conacre" referred to land rented for the taking of a single crop, usually potatoes. Competition for conacre among agricultural labourers was keen, and it accounts for a good deal of the rural unrest in the pre-famine period.

49 Lewis, *On Local Disturbances*, 94–5.

50 The parallel has also been observed by other historians, including L.M. Cullen, S.J. Connolly, and Eamonn O Ciardha. See O Ciardha, "Toryism and Rappareeism in County Armagh in the Late Seventeenth Century," 381–2.

51 Hobsbawm, *Bandits*, 26.

52 Ibid., 17–26, 47, 63–7.

53 Edward Hudson to Charlemont, 7 December 1789, Charlemont MS 12 R15, no. 67, RIA.

54 1 August 1789, Minutes of the Forkhill Trustees, vol. 1.

55 Smyth, *Men of No Property*, 34; Dickson, "Taxation and Disaffection in Late Eighteenth-Century Ireland," 52–9; Simmons, *A List of Peculiar Words and Phrases*, 3.

56 Lewis, *On Local Disturbances*, 66–7; Smyth, *Men of No Property*, 33–7; Beames, *Peasants and Power*, 114–18.

57 O'Hanrahan, "The Tithe War in County Kilkenny," 482.

58 Ibid.

59 Lewis, *On Local Disturbances*, 66–7.

60 Lecky, *A History of Ireland in the Eighteenth Century*, 2:31.

61 O'Hanrahan, "The Tithe War in County Kilkenny," 482.

62 The spelling of Alexander Berkley's name presents some difficulties. He has been referred to as Barclay, Barkley, and Berkley, and Hudson spelled it Barkeley. I have opted to use Berkley, since this is how he signed his own name on his lease in 1789 (Lease of Alexander Berkley, Chambré Papers, D/294/12, PRONI).

63 The attack on Berkley, his wife, and her younger brother was described in contemporary letters and newspaper articles and in Byrne's "Impartial Account" (1792). See Hudson's letters to Charlemont, in Charlemont MS 12 R16, nos. 5, 56, 59, 63, RIA; William Drennan to Samuel McTier, 5 February 1791, in Chart, ed., *Drennan Letters*; Petition of James Davitt in Official Papers, 18/2, NAI;

Hibernian Journal (HJ), 2 February, 20 April, 4 May 1791; *BNL*, 3 May, 13 September 1791; *FJ*, 21 April 1792, 26 March 1793. The attack was also discussed in many nineteenth-century documents and publications, such as Musgrave, *Memoirs of the Different Rebellions*, 51–3; Gowan, *Orangeism*, 125–6; and Lecky, *History of Ireland in the Eighteenth Century*, 3:422–4.

64 Letter of the Forkhill trustees to the bishop of Dromore, 3 February 1791, reprinted in Musgrave, *Memoirs of the Different Rebellions*, 52.

65 Ibid., 53.

66 Byrne, "Impartial Account," 104–8.

67 Ibid., 106.

68 Miller counters this argument in "Politicisation in Revolutionary Ireland: The Case of the Armagh Troubles," 3–10.

69 Cullen, "Late Eighteenth-Century Politicization in Ireland"; Miller, "Politicisation in Revolutionary Ireland," 1–17; Cullen, "The Political Troubles of County Armagh," 18–23.

70 On 3 February 1791 the Privy Council issued a proclamation offering a reward of £500 for information leading to the arrest of anyone involved in the attack, and several arrests were made shortly afterwards. One of the men involved in the attack, James Davitt, turned approver and informed on the Murphy brothers. Charges were brought against several other men in 1792, but no other convictions were secured (Petition of James Davitt of Dundalk, Official Papers 18/2, NAI).

71 Edward Hudson to Francis Dobbs, 29 January 1791, Charlemont MS 12 R16, no. 51, RIA. In his letter to Dobbs, Hudson referred to "Barkeley who was stabbed by Donnelly." For prosecutions, see AAI (1737–97), Summer 1789 and Lent 1790; *BNL*, 13 April 1790; Byrne, "Impartial Account," 106. "Mr D—n" was William Duncan, who had shared the prosecution with Alexander Berkley. Explanatory footnotes inserted into Byrne's 1792 pamphlet by T.G.F. Paterson identified him as James Dawson. Dawson was a well-known figure in Forkhill but was not the man to whom Byrne was referring.

72 *Journal of House of Commons of Ireland* (1792–94), vol. 15, app. 5, p. 5.

73 *BNL*, 19 August 1796.

74 In 1815 a yeoman who was active in the parish of Creggan received a threatening letter warning him that "his tongue would be cut out" (Henry Stewart to —, 15 December 1815, SOC 1711/24, NAI).

75 Lewis, *On Local Disturbances*, 258–78.

76 *HJ*, 20 April 1791; Smyth, *Men of No Property*, 50.

77 On scarring and mutilations, see Beames, *Peasants and Power*, 79–80.

78 Musgrave, *Memoirs of the Different Rebellions*, 52. The trustees reserved the sum of £40 per annum for Alexander Berkley and £20 per annum for Nathaniel Thompson, his young brother-in-law (2 May 1791, Minutes of the Forkhill Trustees, vol. 1). In 1796 Berkley sent a letter to the trustees from Santo Domingo (1 November 1796, Minutes of the Forkhill Trustees, vol. 1).

79 The "Forkhill Tragedy" and the ensuing trial was described in a history of the Orange Order published in the 1930s. According to this version of the story, the injured boy (Nathaniel Thompson) was carried into the court in Armagh and laid on a table. "Asked whether he saw anyone present who had been at Barclay's house on the night of the outrage, the boy laid a rod on the head of one of the men in the dock, and, when questioned as to the clothing that prisoner had worn, he pointed to a person outside the dock. This man was a brother of the accused, and, it appeared, they had exchanged coats in the jail that morning" (*Orangeism in Ireland*, 277).

80 Edward Hudson to Charlemont, 28 April 1791, Charlemont MS 12 R16, no. 63, RIA.

CHAPTER THREE

1 Foster, *Modern Ireland*, 280; Wilson, *United Irishmen, United States*, 30.

2 For background to the rebellion, see Madden, *Antrim and Down in '98*; Elliott, *Partners in Revolution*; Gough and Dickson, eds., *Ireland and the French Revolution*; Smyth, *Men of No Property*; Dickson et al., eds., *United Irishmen: Republicanism, Radicalism and Rebellion*; Curtin, *United Irishmen: Popular Politics in Ulster and Dublin*; *The Turbulent Decade*; Whelan, *Tree of Liberty.*

3 William Drennan to Samuel McTier, 21 May 1791, in Chart, ed., *Drennan Letters*, 54.

4 For discussion of the connections at the leadership level among the various Catholic associations, see Smyth, *Men of No Property*, 116–20; Whelan, *Tree of Liberty*, 40–9; Elliott, *Catholics of Ulster*, 243–9. See also Edward Cooke to Thomas Pelham, 4 December 1795, Pelham Transcripts, T/755/2, Public Record Office of Northern Ireland (PRONI).

5 Smyth, *Men of No Property*, 63–6.

6 Curtin, *United Irishmen: Popular Politics*, 49–50.

7 Smyth, *Men of No Property*, 75.

8 Curtin, *United Irishmen: Popular Politics*, 50.

9 Ibid., passim; Smyth, *Men of No Property*, chap. 7.

10 Bartlett, "Defenders and Defenderism in 1795," 373–94.
11 Miller, ed., *Peep O'Day Boys and Defenders*, 113–29.
12 Elliott, *Catholics of Ulster*, 225–6.
13 Senior, *Orangeism in Ireland and Britain*, 18–19.
14 Quoted in Curtin, *United Irishmen: Popular Politics*, 164.
15 Smyth, *Men of No Property*, 157–61.
16 Davies, "The *Northern Star* and the Propagation of Enlightened Ideas," passim.
17 General Lake to Thomas Pelham, 26 April 1797, Pelham Transcripts, T/755/4B, PRONI.
18 James Coigly to —, 27 July 1796, Rebellion Papers (hereafter cited as Reb Papers), 620/24/59, National Archives of Ireland (NAI).
19 Edward Hudson to Charlemont, 3 August 1794, Charlemont MS 12 R18, no. 19, Royal Irish Academy (RIA).
20 Edward Hudson to Charlemont, 2 March 1794, Charlemont MS 12 R18, no. 5, RIA.
21 Pamphlet enclosed in letter from Edward Hudson to Charlemont, circa July 1794, Charlemont MS 12 R18, no. 17, RIA.
22 Madden, *Antrim and Down*, 97.
23 Ibid., 116; information of John Conellan, 10 June 1798, Reb Papers, 620/3/32/8, NAI; Armagh Court Martial, 12 July 1798, Reb Papers, 620/2/10/2, NAI.
24 Madden, *Antrim and Down*, 98.
25 Smyth, *Men of No Property*, 63–6.
26 Keogh, *Patriot Priest*, passim; Elliott, *Partners in Revolution*; McEvoy, "Father James Quigley," passim; Miller, "Politicisation in Revolutionary Ireland," 1–23; Cullen, "The Political Troubles of County Armagh."
27 Keogh, *Patriot Priest*, 1–8.
28 Smyth, *Men of No Property*, 117; Cullen, "The Political Structures of the Defenders," 129–30.
29 Colonel Ogle to Edward Cooke, 25 March 1798, Reb Papers, 620/36/66, NAI; General Nugent to Edward Cooke, 7 August 1797, and General Nugent to Marquis of Hartford, 12 August 1797, Reb Papers, 620/1/4/2–3, NAI.
30 C.M. Warburton to Dublin Castle, 29 May 1798, Reb Papers, 620/37/212, NAI; C.M. Warburton to Bishop of Ferns, 7 June 1798, Reb Papers, 620/38/77, NAI; 21 June 1798, Downshire Papers, D/607/F/260, PRONI. The "priest McKoin" identified by Warburton was probably Father Patrick Quinn, who served as the parish priest of Lower Creggan. Quinn is a phonetic English spelling of McKoin, just as Quigly is the English version of Coigly.
31 C.M. Warburton's allegation about the priest's involvement in the Berkley outrage was not explained further and cannot be

substantiated. Both Cullen and McKoin were arrested in Dundalk shortly after Warburton supplied this information to Dublin Castle.

32 Edward Hudson to Charlemont, 30 November 1798, Charlemont MS 12 R20, no. 52, RIA. Local tradition records that a group of yeomanry who attempted to capture the priest were drowned in a bog near Forkhill (Murray, "Shanroe Barrack, Mullabawn," 28–9).

33 Percy Jocelyn to Dublin Castle, 4 June 1803, Reb Papers, 620/65/107, NAI.

34 Corry, *Odes and Elegies*, passim.

35 *Freeman's Journal* (FJ), 7 September 1797.

36 Cullen, "The Political Structures of the Defenders," 129–30.

37 Curtin, *United Irishmen: Popular Politics*, 127–34; 1 May and 1 November 1797, Minutes of the Forkhill Trustees, vol. 1.

38 Curtin, *United Irishmen: Popular Politics*, 69.

39 Ibid.

40 James Dawson to Dublin Castle, 10 January 1797, Reb Papers, 620/28/80, NAI.

41 Walter Synnot to Edward Cooke, 20 February 1797, Reb Papers, 620/28/13, NAI.

42 G. Atkinson to Edward Cooke, 5 March 1797, Reb Papers, 620/29/24, NAI.

43 John Reed to Dublin Castle, 28 February 1797, Reb Papers, 620/28/281, NAI.

44 Goddard, Anderson, and Beath to Dublin Castle, 4 March 1797, Reb Papers, 620/29/26a, NAI; C.M. Warburton to Dublin Castle, 13 March 1797, Reb Papers, 620/29/76, NAI; G. Atkinson to Edward Cooke, 5 March 1797, Reb Papers, 620/29/24, NAI; Walter Synnot to Dublin Castle, 20 February 1797, Reb Papers, 620/28/13, NAI.

45 *Belfast News-letter* (BNL), 13 March 1797.

46 This passage appears in the original article in the *Hibernian Journal* (HJ), 17 April 1797.

47 Carleton to Ross, 12 April 1797, Reb Papers, 620/29/27, NAI.

48 General Knox to Thomas Pelham, 4 April 1797, Reb Papers, 620/29/177, NAI.

49 Diary of Alexander Hamilton, vol. 1 (1793–97), 12 and 15 April 1797, Armagh Public Library.

50 Samuel Turner was a leading United Irishman from Newry. He became an informer later in 1797 and provided Dublin Castle with information about the intended rising in Armagh and south Down. In a rebellion that was partly fuelled by millennial aspirations, it is worth noting that the day appointed for the insurrection was Good Friday.

51 Colonel Ogle to Dublin Castle, 14 November 1796, Reb Papers, 620/26/50, NAI. A military barracks, known as Belmont Barracks, had

been established in the parish in 1795. It was financed partly by Susanna Barton, sister of Richard Jackson and mother-in-law of Colonel Ogle (*BNL*, 25 May 1795).

52 Colonel Ogle to Dublin Castle, 10 March 1797, Reb Papers, 620/29/50, NAI.

53 Colonel Ogle to Dublin Castle, 4 May 1797, Reb Papers, 620/30/15, NAI.

54 MS 1755/89, Irish Folklore Commission, Department of Irish Folklore, University College, Dublin (hereafter cited as IFC). In Tipperary, cutting down trees was also a form of protest by Whiteboys, but it did not always carry that connotation. M.R. Beames notes that the destruction of woods was "a way of obtaining fuel supplies" (*Peasants and Power*, 78).

55 Typescript of the song "The Carrive Blacksmith," in private possession.

56 *FJ*, 16 May 1797; *BNL*, 26 May 1797; Thomas Gataker to Pelham, 14 May 1797, Reb Papers, 620/30/67, NAI; Thomas Gataker to Dublin Castle, 14 May 1797, Reb Papers, 620/30/68, NAI; letter to John Lees Esq., 14 May 1797, Reb Papers, 620/30/74, NAI.

57 General Lake to —, 14 May 1797, Lake MS 56, no. 73, National Library (NL).

58 Thomas Gataker to Dublin Castle, 14 May 1797, Reb Papers, 620/30/68, NAI.

59 Norman Steele to Dublin Castle, 8 June 1797, Reb Papers, 620/31/55, NAI; Lord Blayney to Dublin Castle, 10 June 1797, Reb Papers, 620/31/71, NAI; John Giffard to Edward Cooke, 5 June 1797, Reb Papers, 620/31/36, NAI.

60 General Knox to Thomas Pelham, 16 June 1797, Pelham Transcripts, T/755/5, PRONI.

61 Bartlett, "Defence, Counter-Insurgency, and Rebellion," 270–1.

62 Colonel Ogle to Dublin Castle, 14 June 1797, Reb Papers, 620/31/93, NAI.

63 13 September 1797, Reb Papers, 620/32/121–2, NAI; Wolfe to Edward Cooke, 17 September 1797, Reb Papers, 620/32/132, NAI; Colonel Ogle to Edward Cooke, September-October 1797, Reb Papers, 620/32/195, NAI.

64 Elliott, *Catholics of Ulster*, 238.

65 Keogh, *Patriot Priest*, 19–21, 73–6.

66 Information of John Conellan, 10 June 1798, Reb Papers, 620/3/32/8, NAI.

67 Conellan's information confirmed that both communities were represented in the radical leadership until 1798. He named a diverse local executive, which included Pat Byrne, Valentine Derry, the cousin

of James Coigly, and James Kelly (all Catholics), and William Donaldson, Robert Campbell, and the Teeling brothers (all Protestants). Conellan later was a surgeon aboard a convict ship. Out at sea, the convicts rose, "literally cut Conellan to pieces and threw the fragments of his body into the sea" (Young, *Ulster in '98*, 18).

68 General Nugent to Knox, 11 June 1798, Lake MS 56, no. 190, NL.

69 Verses 3, 5, 6, 7, 10, 11, reprinted in Sherry, ed., *Along the Black Pig's Dyke.*

70 Patrickson to Downshire, 26 June 1798, Downshire Papers, D/607/F/276, PRONI; William Hartigan to Downshire, 29 June 1798, Downshire Papers, D/607/F/291, PRONI.

71 *Dundalk Democrat* (DD), 29 January 1898.

72 Whelan, *Tree of Liberty*, 129.

73 General Knox to Thomas Pelham, 19 April 1797, Pelham Transcripts T/755/4B, PRONI; 17–28 May 1797, Pelham Transcripts, T/755/5, PRONI.

74 Keogh, *Patriot Priest*, 12–13, 23.

75 Edward Hudson to Charlemont, 9 May 1797, Charlemont MS 12 R19, no. 52, RIA. Hudson made the connection in a later letter to Charlemont, remarking on the recent arrest and trial of Coigly (Hudson to Charlemont, 8 April 1798, Charlemont MS 12 R20, RIA).

76 Edward Hudson to Charlemont, 18 December 1794, Charlemont MS 12 R18, no. 48, RIA.

77 See, for example, Curtin, *United Irishmen: Popular Politics.*

78 Smyth, *Men of No Property*, 112–20, and passim.

79 *FJ*, 16 May 1797; *BNL*, 26 May 1797.

80 Armagh Assize Indictments (1737–97), Spring 1795; *Northern Star*, 23 November 1795. Seventy-six peaceful inhabitants of Armagh "were dragged from their beds by a party of Orangemen headed by two of Colonel Ogle's crimp sergeants, falsely charged with desertion and released at the eleventh hour by an unnamed magistrate." At the spring assizes in 1796, Ogle was required to pay damages for offences committed by his recruiting officers the previous December (Senior, *Orangeism in Ireland and Britain*, 32–6).

81 O'Muiri, "Rural Deanery of Creggan," 62.

82 Smyth, *Men of No Property*, 104.

83 *BNL*, 25 May 1795.

84 Magennis, "A 'Presbyterian Insurrection'?" 168.

85 *BNL*, 15 July 1763; Magennis, "A 'Presbyterian Insurrection'?" 168. Jackson's willingness to mediate with the protestors undoubtedly contributed to his reputation as a fair and generous landlord, a memory that has endured.

86 Numerous versions of this song have been recorded, with slightly different lyrics and even different verses. It remains a popular traditional song in south Armagh.

87 *BNL*, 29 June 1787.

CHAPTER FOUR

1 Lee, "On the Accuracy of the Pre-Famine Irish Censuses," passim.

2 Ibid.

3 *Abstract of Answers and Returns, Pursuant to Act 55 Geo. 3, for Taking an Account of the Population of Ireland in 1821*, HC 1824 (577) (hereafter cited as Census of Ireland, 1821, Abstract), 22:411.

4 Census of Ireland, 1821, Abstract, 22:411.

5 Ibid., 22:421.

6 The census instructions included a provision for strolling beggars whom the enumerator met on the roadside. Either they were to be included in the return for the house in which they had last lodged, or were to be added at the end of the list of the townland in which they were encountered.

7 This information is recorded in the manuscript-bound volume of the census.

8 Joseph Lee has raised some doubts about the accuracy of the enumeration because of an insufficient bank of information on the layout of the country and because of the inexperience of its chief administrator, William Shaw Mason (Lee, "On the Accuracy of the Pre-Famine Irish Censuses," 39–43).

9 Glass and Taylor, "Commentary: The Census, Great Britain and Ireland, 1801–91," in their *Population and Emigration*; Lee, "On the Accuracy of the Pre-Famine Irish Censuses."

10 Census of Ireland, 1821, Abstract. The collection of this information was mandatory, though the enumerators were encouraged to collect as much additional detail as practically possible.

11 A royal commission inquired into the state of "religious and other instruction" in Ireland in 1834. The commissioners sent the 1831 census returns to the original enumerators and requested them to provide an indication of the religious affiliation of each person who had been enumerated in 1831 (Akenson, *Small Differences*, 6).

12 Identification was made first on the basis of surname; if the result was uncertain, the Christian name of the individual was considered. For discussion, see Akenson, "The Population of the United States, 1790," 127–9.

13 The 1821 census enumerated 6,328 people by name, recording information about each individual. For eight houses in the townland of

Carrickaldreen, however, only the head of the household was identified; in the column of Observations the enumerator merely recorded the number of additional inhabitants in the house. No reason is given for this departure from the normal procedure. A total of 33 persons were enumerated in this way, giving us no information about their sex, age, occupation, or relationship to the head of the household. Five of the households were headed by Protestants (containing 22 additional inhabitants) and three were headed by Catholics (containing 11 additional inhabitants). When these inhabitants are included, the population of the parish rises from 6,328 to 6,361.

14 "Returns of Religious Denominations in the Several Parishes of the County of Armagh in 1834," Tenison Groves MS, T/808/14943, Public Record Office of Northern Ireland (PRONI); O'Kane, "A Statistical Return of Armagh Diocese in 1836," 181–9. See also the visitation reports for Forkhill in the Armagh Diocesan Registry Papers, DIO/4/9/8/1–33, PRONI.

15 Gamble, *Sketches of History, Politics, and Manners.*

16 The impressionistic evidence is reviewed in Clarkson, "Irish Population Revisited, 1687–1821," 19–20.

17 Hammel and Laslett, "Comparing Household Structure over Time and Between Cultures," 80–103. Their family classification system is explained in Guinnane, *The Vanishing Irish*, 133–46. The sample is slightly reduced because eight households in the townland of Carrickaldreen were recorded only by the name of the head of the household and the total number of inhabitants; thus, the relationships of the inhabitants to the household head is unknown.

18 This tendency helps to account for (a) the relatively high proportion of dependent men over the age of twenty and (b) the concentration of small farms in the parish.

19 Lee Soltow's study of the relationship between age and economic achievement in a barony in King's County offers a point of comparison. He analysed a sample of 390 males over the age of fifteen to determine the likelihood of land possession, at what age an adult male would be likely to take possession, and what size of farm he might expect to occupy. Most of the young men in the barony sampled became head of the household between the ages of 25 and 29; 38% of the men in this age group possessed land, compared with only 9% of men aged 20–24, and these figures approximate the situation in Forkhill. The odds of holding land rose steadily for several decades up to ages 55–59, an age group in which 62% of men were landholders. After the age of sixty, the odds of holding land decreased as farms were divided or turned over to a younger generation (Soltow, "Age and Economic Achievement in an Irish Barony in 1821," 389–98).

20 Laslett and Hammel's research into the history of household and family size was motivated in part by their suspicion that European families in the nineteenth century were smaller and less complicated than is historically assumed; the distribution of household types in Forkhill bears out their hypothesis (Guinnane, *The Vanishing Irish*, 135–6). A study of family structure in Armagh City in the late eighteenth century demonstrated that the nuclear family was common (Clarkson, "Household and Family Structure in Armagh City, 1770," 20–3).

21 Carney, "Aspects of Pre-Famine Irish Household Size," 32–46.

22 Carney used the term "houseful" in reference to the total number of inhabitants and used "household" to indicate a further shared activity criteria among the residents that excluded lodgers and boarders ("Aspects of Pre-Famine Irish Household Size," 34–5).

23 The sample size was 112 families.

24 In other words, Protestants were more likely to have servants than Catholics, and they were more likely to have *more* servants. Among Protestant households with domestic help, more than 50% had two or more servants; in Catholic households, the figure was closer to 23%.

25 Many of the other 325 households probably contained conjugal family units, but excluding extended and multiple-families from this analysis reduced complexity.

26 No return was made of lands amounting to less than one-quarter of an acre; in these cases the column was left blank.

27 Tithe Composition Book for the Parish of Forkhill (1828), FIN/5A/143, PRONI.

28 In the census there were 224 farms that were returned as "0" acres, suggesting that the household consisted of a single cabin with a scratch of garden around the perimeter.

29 The census showed that 20.6% of Catholic farms were under one acre.

30 Miller, "The Armagh Troubles," 155–89; Miller, "Politicisation in Revolutionary Ireland," 1–23.

31 Crawford, *The Handloom Weavers and the Ulster Linen Industry*, 26.

32 For farmers, I included those individuals who were classified as farmers only, since farmers engaged in secondary occupations were not strictly dependent on agricultural pursuits for income. Weavers of all types, including farmer/weavers and labourer/weavers, were included in the sample.

33 Within the weaving community, however, there was no real difference between the farm sizes of Catholics and Protestants; the average farm of a Protestant weaver was 2.6 acres and that of a Catholic weaver was 2.4 acres.

34 Hollingsworth, *Historical Demography*, 15–20, 98–102; Study Committee of the Office of the Foreign Secretary, *Rapid Population Growth*, 114–17.

35 Study Committee of the Office of the Foreign Secretary, *Rapid Population*, 116.

36 The age tables for Forkhill are comparable with figures in the rest of Ireland, except for one anomaly: the proportion of the Forkhill population in the 15–29 age group is smaller than the regional figures for Armagh, Ulster, and Ireland. Since the men and women in this age group were born roughly between 1790 and 1805, a period of upheaval in the parish, I wonder if there is any relationship between the outrage and rebellion in Forkhill during the 1790s and the apparently fewer number of births during this period. In times of acute crisis, there will be a lower birth rate; the possible relationship between epidemic, war, unrest, and age structure is discussed in Hollingsworth, *Historical Demography*, 99–100.

37 1,776 males and 1,023 females.

38 I sorted the occupations recorded in the census into nine categories, following (with minor modifications) the occupational classification system devised by Gordon Darroch and Michael Ornstein in their study of ethnicity and occupation structure in Canada based on the census of 1871 ("Ethnicity and Occupational Structure in Canada in 1871, 305–33). In cases where individuals (most often heads of households) were assigned more than one occupation by the enumerator, such as "farmer & blacksmith" or "farmer & weaver," I assigned these individuals to their secondary occupations. This allows a more complete picture of the trades and industries that were represented in the parish (and by whom), without artificially inflating the size of the working population. Dual occupations account for 152 of the total, including 121 "farmer & other" and 28 "labourer & other." In the sections where I examine farm size and the absolute number of agricultural workers in the population, I included these 149 farmers and labourers. The "other" category includes pensioners, a poor scholar, two fiddlers, and a pipeplayer. Both the fiddlers (one Protestant and the other Catholic) were blind.

39 The trustees stipulated that diligent boys would be admitted to weaving apprenticeships as long as they were bound by a Protestant master. At the end of the apprenticeship, each would be given a loom or the value of a loom (although they would forfeit the loom if they left the estate.) Both Protestant and Catholic pupils received looms from the Jackson trust. In the summer of 1807, looms were given to Michael Hearty, Michael Bennett, John Murphy, James Brown, and

Francis Campbell (1 August 1807, Minutes of the Forkhill Trustees, vol. 1).

40 Gray, “Rural Industry and Uneven Development,” 590–611.

41 Even lower rates of illegitimacy were reported from Forkhill in 1835. Father Daniel O’Rafferty knew of only three cases of illegitimacy in the parish, Major Arthur Bernard knew of only one, and the Reverend William Smith did not know of any. *First Report of Inquiry into the Condition of the Poorer Classes in Ireland, with Appendix (A.) and Supplement*, [369], HC 1835, 32:305.

42 Brozyna, “Female Virtue and Chastity in Pre-Famine Ireland,” 117–26, reviews the pitfalls of fixing actual levels of illegitimacy in nineteenth-century Ireland. See also Connolly, *Priests and People in Pre-Famine Ireland*, 187–91.

43 The remainder included housekeepers and other domestic staff in the larger households such as cooks, kitchen maids, grooms, and butlers.

44 There was a slightly higher percentage of female servants between the ages of 30 and 34, but their numbers dwindled as they married or left the area.

45 Hollingsworth, *Historical Demography*, 346.

46 Although the proportion of tradespeople in the Protestant community was nearly twice the Catholic proportion, seventy-two out of eighty-four tradespeople were Catholic. There was only one woman represented in the trades, a Catholic seamstress named Mary McNeill.

47 Protestants had their own pub, however. One of the five public houses in the parish, in Shean, was owned by a Protestant, James Fenton.

48 *First Report of Inquiry into the Condition of the Poorer Classes in Ireland, Appendix (B.) and Supplement*, [369] HC (1835), vol. 32, part 2, appendix B, 209–11, and supplement [1].

49 There were five schoolmasters and three sewing mistresses.

50 James Dawson, seventy years of age in 1821, lived in the townland of Carrickasticken with his much younger wife (she was only forty) and their five children. He lived on a 42 acre farm, and the estate boasted a full household staff that included a butler, a groom, a steward, and a lady’s maid.

51 James Campbell was educated at Trinity College, Dublin. He earned his BA in 1799 and an LL D in 1818. He never married and died in 1858 at the age of eighty-one, shortly after resigning his post at Forkhill (Leslie, *Armagh Clergy and Parishes*, 303).

52 The housekeeper was Bridget Hughes, a twenty-four-year-old woman who had two children: Bernard, aged four years, and Nicholas, an infant.

53 On his tour of Forkhill in 1837, Samuel Lewis remarked that “the linen and cotton manufactures are carried on to a limited extent” (*Topographical Dictionary of Ireland*, 633).

CHAPTER FIVE

1 Application for grant-in-aid from the Board of Commissioners for National Education and related correspondence, ED/1/11/22, Public Record Office of Northern Ireland (PRONI).
2 Quoted in Akenson, *Irish Education Experiment*, 21–2.
3 McManus, *Irish Hedge School*, 15–25.
4 Ibid., 15–106.
5 Dowling, *Hedge Schools of Ireland*, passim; Akenson, *Irish Education Experiment*, 45–8.
6 de Ris, *Peadar O'Doirnin*, 58; Hughes, "Anecdotes Relating to Peadar O Doirnin and Cormac na gCeann,"128–37; Hughes, "Gaelic Poets and Scribes," 513–16.
7 de Ris, *Peadar O'Doirnin*, 56–88.
8 The major events in his life have been confirmed in separate biographies by Sean de Ris and Breandan O Buachalla.
9 McManus, *Irish Hedge School*, 57.
10 *Royal Commission on Irish Education: Second Report, Appendix (Parochial Abstracts)*, HC 1824–27 (hereafter Report of the Irish Education Inquiry, 1824–27), vol. 12, app. 12 and 22.
11 There were only five "free" schools sponsored by the Jackson trust, and there were three others connected with the Society for Promoting the Education of the Poor in Ireland, also known as the Kildare Place Society.
12 The Trustees of Forkhill Charities; copies of petition order and report approving of further scheme, Armagh Diocesan Registry Papers, DIO/4/9/8/11, PRONI.
13 2 August 1790, Minutes of the Proceedings of the Trustees of the Charitable Donations of Richard Jackson of Forkhill, Esq. (hereafter Minutes of the Forkhill Trustees), vol. 1, (1789–1830).
14 Ibid.
15 See chapter 2, above.
16 1 February 1791, Minutes of the Forkhill Trustees, vol. 1. "Resolved. That in consideration of the late very shocking outrages committed on the person of one of the schoolmasters on this estate and on his family render it impracticable at present to protect Protestant schoolmasters in the execution of their duty and that we therefore recommend it to the general board to suspend every operation of the charity until the country be restored to a state of tranquillity" (2 August 1791, ibid.).
17 Edward Hudson to Francis Dobbs, 29 January 1791, Charlemont MS 12 R16, no. 51, Royal Irish Academy (RIA).
18 1 May 1795, Minutes of the Forkhill Trustees, vol. 2.

19 Miscellaneous documents, Forkhill Parish, Armagh Diocesan Registry Papers, DIO/4/9/8/4, PRONI.
20 Ibid., DIO/4/9/8/1–33, PRONI.
21 1 May and 1 November 1797, Minutes of the Forkhill Trustees, vol. 1.
22 2 November 1795, Minutes of the Forkhill Trustees, vol. 1.
23 Miscellaneous documents, Forkhill Parish, Armagh Diocesan Registry Papers, DIO/4/9/8/1–33, PRONI.
24 Minutes of the Forkhill Trustees, vol. 1.
25 1 November 1807 and 1 November 1811, Minutes of the Forkhill Trustees, vol. 1.
26 Akenson, *Irish Education Experiment*, 76–9.
27 *Report from the Commissioners of the Board of Education in Ireland, 1809–1812. Thirteenth Report: English Schools of Private Foundation*, HC 1813–14 (47) (hereafter Report of the Irish Education Inquiry, 1809–12), 1:289–90.
28 1 May 1792, Minutes of the Forkhill Trustees, vol. 1.
29 1 February 1794, Minutes of the Forkhill Trustees, vol. 1.
30 Ibid.
31 Top honours went to Protestant pupils, but honorable mentions included Francis Murphy, Cornelius Rafferty, and the McCoy brothers (1 February 1794, Minutes of the Forkhill Trustees, vol. 1 and passim).
32 Akenson, *Irish Education Experiment*, 93–5.
33 During this period, the Forkhill schools were reportedly operating according to the guidelines of the Society for Promoting the Education of the Poor in Ireland, more commonly known as the Kildare Place Society.
34 Report of the Irish Education Inquiry, 1824–27, 1:294–5.
35 Ibid., 1:280–97.
36 Separate attendance reports were provided by both Catholic and Church of Ireland clergy, and both are included in the return. As a result, there is some mild disagreement on the number of pupils enrolled.
37 Report of Irish Education Inquiry, 1824–27; Beresford Correspondence, 3:203, Armagh Public Library (APL); 1 August 1821, Minutes of the Forkhill Trustees, vol. 1.
38 The higher figure is actually from the Protestant return.
39 2 May 1825, Minutes of the Forkhill Trustees, vol. 1.
40 Quoted in McManus, *Irish Hedge School*, 43.
41 Its annual grant climbed steadily, reaching a peak of £30,000 before ceasing in 1831 (Akenson, *Irish Education Experiment*, 86–98).
42 Ibid.

43 H.E. Bell, "Notes of Three Tours in Ireland in 1824 and 1826," T/2466/4, PRONI.

44 The Douay Version was an English translation of the Bible from the Latin Vulgate completed by Roman Catholic scholars at Douai in 1610. The Authorized Version, preferred by the Church of England, was an English translation of the Bible published in 1611 under James I.

45 Akenson, *Irish Education Experiment*, 89.

46 Connolly, *Priests and People in Pre-Famine Ireland*, passim.

47 Catholic Emancipation was achieved in 1829. Under the new law, Catholics had the right to sit in Parliament, belong to corporations, and hold high military and civic office.

48 In September 1828, Daniel O'Connell's deputy, John Lawless, embarked on an "invasion of Ulster," intending to make common cause with Catholics in the north. Lawless was greeted by great crowds as he travelled through Meath and Louth but was forced to retreat when Orangemen threatened to prevent his visit to the Protestant stronghold of Ballybay in County Monaghan (Elliott, *Catholics of Ulster*, 272; Wright, *Two Lands on One Soil*, 187).

49 Protestant fears were inflamed by the circulation of the prophecies of Pastorini in 1821–24, which forecast the destruction of the Protestant Church in the year 1825 and inspired a wave of anti-Protestant sentiment among Catholics in Munster and Leinster. The millenarianism was not so virulent in Ulster, but the tenor of the movement fed Protestant anxieties nonetheless. Pastorini was the pseudonym of an English Catholic bishop, Charles Walmesley (Donnelly, "Pastorini and Captain Rock," 102–42).

50 Signatories to the 1825 letter included a number of the major landowners from Killeavy and Forkhill, including H.W. Chambré, Jonathan Seaver, Arthur Bernard, and Powell Foxall (D/801/2B, PRONI).

51 Foster, *Modern Ireland*, 304.

52 *Newry Telegraph* (*NT*), 27 January 1829.

53 *NT*, 12 June 1829.

54 *NT*, 3 January 1832.

55 Ibid.

56 *NT*, 17 January 1832.

57 1 May and 1 November 1825, Minutes of the Forkhill Trustees, vol. 1.

58 1 August 1831 and 1 August 1832, Minutes of the Forkhill Trustees, vol. 2.

59 H.E. Bell had been struck by the commanding influence enjoyed by the Catholic priests over their parishioners. When a mixed school in

Drumcar was denounced by the local priest in 1824, all the Catholic children but three were withdrawn. At an Erasmus Smith school, where sixty-six of the seventy pupils were Catholic, the priest came and himself "turned out" all the Catholic children (Bell, "Notes of Three Tours in Ireland in 1824 and 1826," T/2466/4, PRONI).

60 Father Daniel O'Rafferty died in 1837 at the age of forty-eight. He was succeeded by Father Hugh Mulligan, nephew of the former parish priest, Father Nicholas McIvor (O'Fiaich, "Parish Priests of Mullaghbawn," passim).

61 Reverend Daniel O'Rafferty to Reverend Dr James Campbell, 12 July 1834, ED/1/11/22, PRONI.

62 Reverend Dr James Campbell to Reverend Daniel O'Rafferty, 12 July 1834, ED/1/11/22, PRONI.

63 Application for grant from the Board of Commissioners for National Education, and related correspondence, ED/1/11/22, PRONI.

64 Ibid.

65 County Armagh National School Register, vol. 1, ED/6/1/2/1/ folio 29, National Archives of Ireland (NAI).

66 Reverend Dr Campbell to J.G. Beresford, 4 February 1839, Beresford Correspondence, 9:10, APL.

67 Application for grant-in-aid from the Board of Commissioners for National Education and related correspondence, ED/1/11/22, PRONI.

68 Reverend William Smith to J.G. Beresford, 4 February 1839, Beresford Correspondence, 9:10, APL.

69 National Board of Education correspondence, ED/1/11/34, PRONI. In 1839 there were 136 boys and 63 girls at Maphoner; 58 boys and 66 girls at Aughanduff (*Sixth Report of the Commissioners of National Education in Ireland, for the Year 1839*, [246], HC 1840, 28:47).

70 *Reports from the Select Committees on Foundation Schools and Education in Ireland, Part I*, HC 1836 (630), 13:535.

71 1 August 1836, Minutes of the Forkhill Trustees, vol. 2.

72 2 May 1842, Minutes of the Forkhill Trustees, vol. 2.

73 Reverend Dr James Campbell to J.G. Beresford, 1 February 1853, Beresford Correspondence, 9:12–13, APL.

74 National Board of Education Papers, ED/1/12/26, PRONI.

75 Ibid.

76 Reverend Alexander Irwin to J.G. Beresford, 13 October 1857, Beresford Correspondence, 3:46–7, APL.

77 14 May 1858, Minutes of the Forkhill Trustees, vol. 3.

78 Recent historiography argues for a distinction between schooling and the acquisition of literacy. The ability to read or to read and write

could exist independent of schooling and predates educational systems in some countries. The experience of Ireland does not appear to fit this category, however, and the increase in national literacy levels corresponds closely to the march of the national schools system after 1831 (O'Ciosain, *Print and Popular Culture*, 31–9).

79 There were three classifications of literacy: the ability to read and write, the ability to read only, and the ability to do neither (illiteracy). For discussion, see O'Ciosain, *Print and Popular Culture in Ireland*, 31–9.

80 Ibid., 32.

81 J. Logan, "Schooling and the Promotion of Literacy in Nineteenth Century Ireland," PH D dissertation, University College, Cork, 1997, cited in O'Ciosain, *Print and Popular Culture*, 32.

82 In 1792 J. Byrne had remarked on the "very illiterate" population in Forkhill and neighbourhood, a situation that should have been improved by the introduction of the charity schools (Byrne, "Impartial Account," 105).

83 *Report of the Commissioners Appointed to Take the Census of Ireland for the Year 1841*, [504] HC 1843, vol. 24, 1.

84 Ibid.

85 Literacy levels for individual parishes were sorted according to age in the published census returns beginning in 1861. Men and women who were forty years and over in 1861 were fifteen years or older when the first school opened in 1836 and did not have the opportunity to attend the national schools (*Census of Ireland for the Year 1861, Part IV, Report of Tables Relating to the Religious Professions, Education, and Occupations of the People.* [3204-III] HC 1863, vol. 60).

86 Ibid.

87 Ibid.

88 *Census of Ireland for the Year 1901, Part I, Area, Houses, and Population, also the Ages ...* [etc.,] *Volume III, Province of Ulster*, [Cd 1123], HC 1902, vol. 126, 1.

89 O'Cuiv, "Irish Language and Literature, 1845–1921," 395–6, 401–8.

90 Mason, *Statistical Account of Ireland*, 2:208–9.

91 Ibid.

92 O'Cuiv, "Irish Language and Literature, 1845–1921," 391–5. For attitudes to the Irish language in rural Ulster during this period, see Elliott, *The Catholics of Ulster*, 181, 191.

93 *Census of Ireland for 1851, Part VI, General Report* [2134], HC 1856, 31:1.

94 There were 41 living in the barony of Upper Fews and 107 in the barony of Upper Orior.

CHAPTER SIX

1 Private monthly report of Brigadier Major Hassard's District, January 1807, State of the Country Papers (hereafter cited as SOC), 1121/30, National Archives of Ireland (NAI). In April 1803 twelve men were appointed by the Church of Ireland vestry in Forkhill to "superintend the police of this parish ... [and] exert themselves to suppress all illegal meetings," which suggests that the business of the Defenders persisted (12 April 1803, Forkhill Vestry Minute Book, 1793–1846, in private collection).

2 Jonathan Seaver to —, 21 August 1807, SOC, 1120/7, NAI. When the Regenerated Defenders emerged after the collapse of the rebellion, it was clear that "their leaders had been United Irishmen in the rebellion year" (Elliott, *Catholics of Ulster*, 254).

3 Jonathan Seaver to —, 21 August 1807, SOC, 1120/7, NAI.

4 Ibid.

5 James Dawson to —, 8 January 1812, SOC, 1537/11, NAI.

6 Ibid.

7 Ibid.

8 John Hill to CSO, 7 June 1814, SOC, 1560/45, NAI.

9 Forkhill was less disturbed, perhaps owing to the militia presence: "The troops in the Barrick of Forkhill keep the county in awe" (James Dawson to Robert Peel, 2 November 1814, SOC 1565/25, NAI).

10 William Barker to —, 31 October 1814, SOC, 1565/25, NAI.

11 William Richardson to Earl of Gosford, 3 January 1815, Gosford Papers, D/1606/1/1/245, Public Record Office of Northern Ireland (PRONI).

12 Reverend Henry Stewart to —, 15 December 1815, SOC, 1711/24, NAI.

13 James Dawson to William Gregory, 24 March 1816, SOC, 1765/17, NAI; James Dawson to William Gregory, 1 July 1816, SOC, 1765/21, NAI; — to —, 2 July 1816, SOC, 1765/22, NAI. Only three men in Forkhill were licensed to keep guns in 1816: Stephen Grant in Mullaghbawn, Phelemy McCoy in Aughadanove and John O'Here in Longfield.

14 James Dawson to William Gregory, 22 March 1816, SOC, 1765/16, NAI; Dawson to Gregory, 24 March 1816, SOC, 1765/17, NAI; Dawson to Gregory, 7 April 1816, SOC, 1765/18, NAI.

15 James Dawson to William Gregory, 7 April 1816, SOC, 1765/18, NAI.

16 James Dawson to William Gregory, 24 March 1816, SOC, 1765/17, NAI.

17 "Through the last spring & winter, a system of Robbery & depredations has been establish'd in this neighbourhood that is truly

alarming; and most extraordinary it is, that hitherto the attacks at night have been confined to the Habitations of Roman Catholics, & what is still more extraordinary, the Persons whose Houses have been attack'd, whose Property has been carried off, in general cannot be prevail'd upon to stand forward & prosecute" (James Dawson to William Gregory , 1 July 1816, SOC, 1765/21, NAI).

18 Henry Stewart to —, 15 December 1815, SOC, 1711/24, NAI.

19 Affidavit sworn before Hunt Walsh Chambré, 22 June 1832, Chief Secretary's Office Registered Papers (hereafter cited as CSORP), 1832/1124 (Private Index), NAI.

20 Chambré had learned from the head constable at Forkhill that "nightly armed meetings of the country people" were "frequent" (Chambré to CSO, 22 June 1832, CSORP, 1832/1124 (no.1 Private Index), NAI.

21 Ibid., copy of reply attached.

22 Deposition of Hugh McGill and Peter McGill of Tivecrom [Tiffcrum], 14 January 1837, Outrage Papers (Armagh, 1837), 2/85, NAI; John Foxall to CSO, 15 January 1837, Outrage Papers (Armagh, 1837), 2/85, NAI. Additional testimony from the McGill brothers (including a list of alleged ribbonmen in the parish) is attached to an outrage report filed in December 1837, although the content of the report suggests that it was provided during the original deposition in January 1837; see 10 December 1837, Outrage Papers (Armagh, 1837), 2/138, NAI.

23 Ibid.

24 Ibid.

25 For the historiography of ribbonism, see Beames, "The Ribbon Societies"; Garvin, "Defenders, Ribbonmen, and Others"; Lee, "The Ribbonmen"; and Murray, "Agrarian Violence and Nationalism in Nineteenth-Century Ireland." For contemporary accounts, see Lewis, *On Local Disturbances*; Carleton, *Autobiography*; Trench, *Realities of Irish Life*; and Sullivan, *New Ireland.*

26 Sullivan, *New Ireland*, passim.

27 In a study of ribbonism in Liverpool, John Belchem found that the society's networks gave Irish migrants political sanctuary and a range of welfare benefits ("Freedom and Friendship to Ireland," 33–56). For the development of similar benevolent societies in Canada, see Clarke, *Piety and Nationalism*, 168–98 and passim.

28 Statement of Informer, 25 July 1839, CO/904/1/271–2, PRONI; cited in Garvin, "Defenders, Ribbonmen, and Others," 234.

29 Garvin, "Defenders, Ribbonmen, and Others," 232n23. The first reference to the movement in Armagh that I have come across concerned a murder that was committed in June 1814 near the village of Richhill "by a party called Ribbon Men" (— to —, 9 June 1814, SOC, 1565/25, NAI).

30 Garvin, "Defenders, Ribbonmen, and Others," 234.
31 Beames, "The Ribbon Societies," 247.
32 Ibid.
33 Garvin, "Defenders, Ribbonmen, and Others," 235.
34 According to both Tom Garvin and Michael Beames, who have made a close study of the society in its early stage and during this interim period, the society never recovered its original political momentum (Garvin, "Defenders, Ribbonmen, and Others," 237; Beames, "The Ribbon Societies," 251, 258–61).
35 Beames, "The Ribbon Societies," 247.
36 The society's greatest weakness was its factionalism; beset by infighting, the ribbonmen never posed a credible revolutionary threat (Beames, "The Ribbon Societies," 250–2, 260–1; Garvin, "Defenders, Ribbonmen, and Others," 238–41).
37 Some of the disturbances in Forkhill in the 1830s bore a resemblance to Whiteboyism in style and substance, but the historian of Whiteboyism, M.R. Beames, does not associate the movement with Ulster. He describes Ulster between 1800 and 1848 as a "quiescent area" in which there were no serious outbreaks of agrarian violence – though in the context of the unrest in south Armagh, this is arguable (Beames, *Peasants and Power*, 24–6, 42–3, 144).
38 Lewis, *On Local Disturbances*, 157.
39 Ibid., 157–8.
40 Ibid., 155.
41 Ibid., 163–73. On the other hand, the ribbon societies of the 1820s disclaimed association with the Rockite campaign in the south of Ireland, and the ribbon masters "were reportedly actually embarrassed by the southern agrarian agitation" (Garvin, "Defenders, Ribbonmen, and Others," 235).
42 *Belfast News-letter* (BNL), 4 August 1815
43 Ibid.
44 Ibid.
45 Deposition of Hugh McGill and Peter McGill of Tivecrom [Tiffcrum], 14 January 1837, Outrage Papers (Armagh, 1837), 2/85, NAI.
46 The tithe was a tax levied on agricultural produce, mainly wheat, barley, and oats but also on hay and flax, eggs, dairy produce, and (in some areas) potatoes. The tithe on grain was from four to eight shillings per acre, though it varied widely across the country. It was generally collected biannually by proctors appointed by the Church of Ireland clergymen in each parish (Akenson, *The Church of Ireland*, 87–95, 148).
47 MacDonagh, "Economy and Society, 1830–45," 222–5.

48 Beames, *Peasants and Power*, 9–10, 28–9, 114–18; O'Hanrahan, "The Tithe War in County Kilkenny," 482.
49 Lewis, *On Local Disturbances*; O'Hanrahan, "The Tithe War in County Kilkenny," 482.
50 For background to the tithe agitation, see O'Hanrahan, "The Tithe War in County Kilkenny," 481–505; MacDonagh, "Economy and Society, 1830–45," 222–5.
51 By mid-1832, less than half of the tithe in Ireland had been collected, and the casualties among peasantry and the constabulary were rising. The government wrestled with the issue, at first passing legislation to permit the collection of the tithe by force and later modifying the Tithe Composition Act to relieve the burden from the poorest tenants; overall, it was a legislative mess and an administrative nightmare (MacDonagh, "Economy and Society, 1830–45," 222–5).
52 MacDonagh, "Economy and Society, 1830–45," 222–3.
53 O'Hanrahan, "The Tithe War in County Kilkenny," 482.
54 Hunt Walsh Chambré and Major A.A. Bernard, 23 February 1832, CSORP, 1832/426 (Private Index), NAI.
55 Affidavit sworn before Hunt Walsh Chambré, 22 June 1832, CSORP, 1832/1124 (Private Index), NAI.
56 *Newry Telegraph* (*NT*), 27 July 1832.
57 Arthur Johnston was the same man who had donated the site for the first national school in Forkhill in 1834. He was also the only resident Protestant to support the school application. Several parties of police had been alerted about the meeting, and they assembled near the chapel, but the resident magistrate, Major Bernard, did not allow them to attend the meeting (*NT*, 27 July 1832).
58 Reverend Dr James Campbell to CSO, 21 August 1832, CSORP, 1832/1631 (no. 1 Private Index), NAI.
59 Affidavit of Archibald Murdock, "tythe proctor for Forkhill," August 1832, CSORP, 1832/1631 (no. 1 Private Index), NAI. The tithe had been withheld in the townland of Aughanduff in 1830 (2 May 1831, Forkhill Vestry Minute Book, 1793–1846, in private collection).
60 Ibid.
61 12 September 1832, CSORP, 1832/1631 (no.1 Private Index), NAI.
62 Ibid.
63 *NT*, 9 October 1832.
64 28 November 1832, Minutes of the Forkhill Trustees, vol. 2; Forkhill Parish, Certificate and Declaration relative to the Tithes on the Estate of the Trustees of Jackson's Charity, 19 December 1832, Ecclesiastical Deeds, box 1, NAI.
65 Earl of Gosford to CSO, 10 January 1833, CSORP, 1833/143, NAI.

66 Chief Constable at Ballybot to Lord Lieutenant, 17 January 1833, CSORP, Official Papers, NAI.

67 Examinations of James Tuft of Shanroe in the parish of Forkhill, 16 January 1833, examinations of Owen Macan of Shanroe in the parish of Forkhill, 16 January 1833, and Chief Constable at Ballybot to Lord Lieutenant, 17 January 1833, CSORP, Official Papers, unnumbered. All three are copies in the possession of the Creggan Historical Society, made in the 1970s from originals in the National Archives of Ireland.

68 Examinations of James Tuft of Shanroe in the parish of Forkhill, 16 January 1833, CSORP, Official Papers, unnumbered (copy in private collection).

69 Examinations of Thomas Gracey of Shanroe in the parish of Forkhill, 16 January 1833, CSORP, Official Papers, unnumbered (copy in private collection).

70 Ibid.

71 Examinations of Catherine Macan of Shanroe in the parish of Forkhill, 17 January 1833, CSORP, Official Papers, unnumbered (copy in private collection).

72 Examinations of Owen Macan of Shanroe in the parish of Forkhill, 16 January 1833, CSORP, Official Papers, unnumbered (copy in private collection).

73 Examinations of Philip Trainor of [word obscured] in the parish of Dundalk, 16 January 1833, CSORP, Official Papers, unnumbered (copy in private collection).

74 Examinations of James Trainor of Tullydonnell in the parish of Creggan, 16 January 1833, CSORP, Official Papers, unnumbered (copy in private collection).

75 Chief Constable at Ballybot to Lord Lieutenant, 17 January 1833, CSORP, Official Papers, unnumbered (copy in private collection).

76 Examinations of Catherine Macan of Shanroe in the parish of Forkhill, 17 January 1833, CSORP, Official Papers, unnumbered (copy in private collection).

77 Examinations of Owen Macan of Shanroe in the parish of Forkhill, 17 January 1833, CSORP, Official Papers, unnumbered (copy in private collection).

78 Ibid.; Examinations of James Tuft of Shanroe in the parish of Forkhill, 16 January 1833, CSORP, Official Papers, unnumbered (copy in private collection).

79 Chief Constable at Ballybot to Lord Lieutenant, 17 January 1833, CSORP, Official Papers, unnumbered (copy in private collection).

80 Examinations of several unnamed persons taken before H.W. Chambré and Reverend Campbell, 23 February 1833, Official Papers (series 2),

1833/289, NAI; Chief Constable at Ballybot to Lord Lieutenant, 23 February 1833, CSORP, Official Papers, unnumbered (copy in private collection).

81 Ibid. In his study of Whiteboyism, M.R. Beames argues that the Whiteboys, "objected to the police less as the representatives of an oppressive colonial order but rather as interlopers and disrupters of the Whiteboy pursuit of justice. They were willing to accept the constabulary provided it left them alone" (*Peasants and Power*, 87–91).

82 *Copy of the Proceedings of an Investigation held at Armagh, of the Transaction ... between the Police and Country People, on collecting an arrear of Tithe*, HC 1835 (179), 47:99–130.

83 The leader was likely a ribbonman. See 20 November 1835, Outrage Papers (Armagh, 1835), 2/50, NAI.

84 *NT*, 18 and 25 December 1835.

85 January 1837, Outrage Papers (Armagh, 1836), 2/19, NAI.

86 Report from the *Newry Telegraph* quoted in McMahon, "Agrarian Disturbances around Crossmaglen," 302–32.

87 Ibid.

88 29 December 1836, Outrage Papers (Armagh, 1836), NAI.

89 Deposition of Hugh McGill and Peter McGill of Tivecrom [Tiffcrum], 14 January 1837, Outrage Papers (Armagh, 1837), 2/85, NAI.

90 Lecky, *A History of Ireland in the Eighteenth Century*, 2:31. The tithe proctor received a commission for collecting the tithe (valued at between 1s and 2s 6d in the pound), which gave him a vested interest in overvaluing the crop (O'Hanrahan, "The Tithe War in County Kilkenny," 482).

91 Examinations of Thomas Gracey of Shanroe in the parish of Forkhill, 16 January 1833, CSORP, Official Papers, unnumbered (copy in private collection).

92 Lewis, *On Local Disturbances*, 102; Beames, *Peasants and Power*, 75–6.

93 Trench, *Realities of Irish Life*, 115–19.

94 Ibid., 125–7.

95 Report from the *Newry Telegraph* quoted in McMahon, "Agrarian Disturbances around Crossmaglen," 302–32.

96 Examinations of Owen Macan of Shanroe in the parish of Forkhill, 16 January 1833, CSORP, Official Papers, unnumbered (copy in private collection).

97 Statement of Informer, 25 July 1839, CO/904/1/217–2, PRONI.

98 Byrne, "Impartial Account," 83.

99 James Dawson to —, 8 January 1812, SOC, 1537/11, NAI.

100 Simon Langley to CSO, 10 January 1814, SOC, 1565/21, NAI.

101 MS 1755/53, Irish Folklore Commission, Department of Irish Folklore, University College, Dublin (hereafter cited as IFC).

102 *NT*, 18 and 25 December 1835.

103 O'Hanrahan, "The Tithe War in County Kilkenny," 498. In 1793, at the height of the militia disturbances, a band of rioters in Sligo were reported to have carried "a white flag emblematic of peace and a red one of loyalty to King and country" (quoted in Bartlett, "An End to Moral Economy," 208–9).

104 Danaher, *The Year in Ireland*, 90–5.

105 Description from the *Ulster Journal of Archaeology*, 1855, quoted in Danaher, *The Year in Ireland*, 97.

106 William Shaw Mason, writing in 1816, quoted in Danaher, *The Year in Ireland*, 97.

107 Description from the *Journal of the Cork Historical and Archaeological Society*, 1895, quoted in Danaher, *The Year in Ireland*, 31–2.

108 Ibid., 33.

109 Ibid., 32–3.

110 Beames, *Peasants and Power*, 23.

111 Examinations of James Tuft of Shanroe in the parish of Forkhill, 16 January 1833, CSORP, Official Papers, unnumbered (copy in private collection).

112 5 February 1833, Lord Gosford to CSO, CSORP, 1833/87 (Private Index), NAI.

113 31 May 1835, Outrage Papers (Armagh, 1835), 2/18, NAI.

114 For further discussion, see the article by A.C. Murray on ribbonism in Westmeath in 1869–71.Reading the hundreds of threatening notices that were sent to unpopular landlords and magistrates during those years, Murray noticed that nowhere was there any mention of "ribbonism," "the ribbon society," or "ribbonmen." Despite this, the terms recur as motives for outrages throughout police reports for this period. Murray believes that Ribbonism was a "catch-all phrase" for crimes the police could not solve: "The phenomenon of Ribbonism ... was an illusion created by their failure to maintain law and order in the countryside" (Murray, "Agrarian Violence in Nineteenth-Century Ireland: The Myth of Ribbonism," 71–2).

115 Lewis, *On Local Disturbances*, 170–1.

116 Carleton, *Autobiography*, 77–80.

117 Ibid.

118 The voluntary confession of John Kerr, 3 December 1815, SOC, 1765/17, NAI.

119 — to —, 25 March 1859, Official Papers (series 2), 1859/12, NAI.

120 *NT*, 7 February 1832.

121 *NT*, 27 July 1832.

122 17 November 1835, Outrage Papers (Armagh, 1835), 2/49, NAI.

123 The petition, printed in the *Newry Telegraph* on 7 November 1834, is contained in a sheaf of documents, along with Brownlow's reply and a letter from the Earl of Gosford to Chambré on 27 October 1834. Gosford also advised Chambré against holding such a meeting; he felt it would be provocative (Earl of Gosford to H.W. Chambré, 27 October 1834, Chambré Papers, MS 7035/14/27, NAI). Chambré replied that he would like to see such a meeting take place so that he could gather opinion from the Armagh gentry on the "many changes that are taking place and contemplated in the Protestant Establishments of this Country" (H.W. Chambré to Gosford, 30 October 1834, Chambré Papers, MS 7035/27A, NAI).

124 *NT*, 7 November 1834.

125 Ibid. In defiance, they vowed to meet later that week in Armagh town to hear the sheriff's answer read aloud and to "make the necessary arrangements." In August 1835, Colonel Verner presented a number of petitions to the House of Commons protesting against the Church Spoilation Bill; one of the petitions originated in the parish of Forkhill (*NT*, 18 August 1835).

126 Conley, *Melancholy Accidents*, 17–50.

127 As one witness explained, factions often consisted of "extensive families united to each other by consanguinity and relations of different kinds" (Lewis, *On Local Disturbances*, 287).

128 Conley, *Melancholy Accidents*, 20–1; Lewis, *On Local Disturbances*, 287–9.

129 Roberts, "Caravats and Shanavests," 68–9.

130 Statement of Major Willcocks quoted in Lewis, *On Local Disturbances*, 282.

131 Lewis, *On Local Disturbances*, 279–95.

132 29 June 1835, Outrage Papers (Armagh, 1835), 2/22, NAI; 1 and 4 July, Outrage Papers (Armagh, 1835), 2/23, NAI.

133 The 1835 fight in Forkhill made the front page of the *Times* of London: "FACTION FIGHT AND LOSS OF LIFE: We regret to state that between the night of Sunday last and the following morning a very serious engagement took place between two armed bodies of the peasantry in the parish of Forkhill towards the border of Killeavy. The dispute originated in an attempt by one faction to extinguish the bonfire kindled by the other. They had recourse to firearms, and one man, named Hanlon, was killed; his body was shockingly mutilated. Several persons are lying in a hopeless state from the effects of the affray. The parties were all Roman Catholics" (6 July 1835).

134 Information of Charles Hayden, Chief Constable of Forkhill, 4 July 1835, Outrage Papers (Armagh, 1835), 2/23, NAI. According to reports, not a shot was fired during the incident, and police estimated

that there were no more than six or seven guns involved, and a few pistols. The cuts on the heads of victims had been made with a sword.

135 Ibid.

136 Ibid. An account of Daniel O'Connell's visit to Ulster in 1841 expressed concern about an ambush by "the 'Redshanks' from the classic regions of Killeavy and Forkhill; the latter, consecrated in story by deeds of darkness and blood" (quoted in *Repealer Repulsed!* 26).

137 5 March 1837, Outrage Papers (Armagh, 1837), 2/34, NAI.

138 *NT*, 28 March 1828.

139 Lewis, *On Local Disturbances*, 279–95.

140 Ibid., 287.

141 Conley, *Melancholy Accidents*, 17–50.

142 Ibid. Conley emphasizes the "recreational" aspect of faction fighting and its resemblance to organized sport, and the fact that the outbreak of a faction fight "did not always require a grievance" (24–7).

143 Roberts, "Caravats and Shanavests," passim; Beames, *Peasants and Power*, 71.

144 5 March 1837, Outrage Papers (Armagh, 1837), 2/34, NAI.

145 The meeting was scheduled to follow the fair day in Forkhill (CO/904/1/444–5, PRONI). In 1836 Bernard Smith was one of seven men in Forkhill who were licensed to carry arms. Smith had registered two guns, two pistols, and one sword. (The others were Felix Hanratty of Shean, the local schoolmaster; John McNamee, Michael Stanley, and Thomas Murphy of Shean; John McNeill of Carrickasticken; and Patrick Conyngam of Tiffcrum.) See *A Return of the Name and Residence of Each Person in Ireland, to whom Licenses Have Been Granted to Keep Arms, by the Magistrates at Quarter Sessions ... since 1st August 1832*, HC 1836 (255), 47:420–1.

146 5 March 1837, Outage Papers (Armagh, 1837), NAI.

147 Examinations of Owen Macan of Shanroe in the parish of Forkhill, 16 January 1833, CSORP, Official Papers, unnumbered (copy in private collection).

148 The feud continued for some years. In 1854 Macan (McCann) charged a number of men from Forkhill with waylaying and violently assaulting him on the public road as he returned home from the fair at Crossmaglen (12 December 1854, Forkhill Petty Sessions Order Book, October 1854 – March 1856, HAI/52/A/3, PRONI). In 1857 he charged Bernard Smith and Charles Magee with entering his lands "and making use of threats towards him" (25 March 1857, Forkhill Petty Sessions Order Book, April 1856 – September 1857, HAI/52/A/4, PRONI).

149 19 March 1837, Outrage Papers (Armagh, 1837), 2/36, NAI.

150 Deposition of Hugh McGill and Peter McGill of Tivecrom [Tiffcrum], 14 January 1837, Outrage Papers (Armagh, 1837), 2/85, NAI

151 3 April 1837, Outrage Papers (Armagh, 1837), 2/87, NAI.

152 1 May 1839, Outrage Papers (Armagh, 1839), 2/3277, NAI.

153 See the correspondence of Richard Jones, Dublin-based secretary of the society, for the 1838–39 period: "Transcript of the Books Written in Short Hand Found on the Person of Richard Jones on the 1st October, 1839," Frazer MSS no. 43, NAI.

154 Ibid.; Garvin, "Defenders, Ribbonmen, and Others," 238; Mac Giolla Choille, "Fenians, Rice, and Ribbonmen in County Monaghan," 221–52.

155 MS 1755/53 and MS 1807/116, IFC.

156 List of Fenian activities reported in Armagh between 1 January 1872 and 27 March 1877, CSORP, 1877/12827, NAI.

157 *Report of the Commissioners Appointed to take the Census of Ireland for the Year 1841*, HC 1843 (504), 24:13.

158 Between March 1830 and March 1832, the rent had been withheld from the trustees by the new beneficial tenant and nominal landlord, Sir George Jackson, who had come into his inheritance upon the death of Julia Ogle. Whether or not the rent had been collected from the tenants by Jackson's agents is difficult to know, but the suspension of payment disabled the operation of the Forkhill charities, and the trustees were forced to sell off stock to meet their obligations as superintendents of the trust fund. In order to recover their losses, the trustees had served ejectment notices on some of the tenants, which had inspired the case before the court. One of the witnesses was Thomas Henry, the agent for the trustees, who admitted that he had distrained several tenants since May 1830 and had levied close to £400. Counsel for the plaintiffs argued that the trustees were not in a landlord-tenant relationship with the tenants on the estate, and had no right to eject tenants. The court decided in favour of the plaintiffs, rendering the ejectments null, and directed Sir George to pay £1,304 due in arrears. The history of the estate is summarized in the *Newry Telegraph* in a report on the case then before the Record Court. See *NT*, 19 March 1832.

159 Reverend James Campbell to Nathaniel Alexander, 24 April 1838, Chambré Papers, D/294/146, PRONI.

160 Ibid. The minute books of the trustees indicate that there was some difficulty collecting the estate rental during this period (1 February 1838 and 1 February 1839, Minutes of the Forkhill Trustees, vol. 2; copy of letter dated 29 December 1838 from the Receiver, who was "unable to collect" the rent for 1838, Minutes of the Forkhll Trustees, vol. 2).

161 There is a small bundle of these proposals among the estate papers in the Chambré Papers, D/294/146, PRONI.

162 Shevlun also sketched a crude map of his property, showing the rocky, rugged patches which were impossible to reclaim.

163 Patrick Shevlun, April 1840, Chambré Papers, D/294/146, PRONI.

164 Evidence of Richard Thomas James Dawson, cited in *Report from Her Majesty's Commissioners of Inquiry into the State of the Law and Practice in Respect to the Occupation of Land in Ireland, Minutes of Evidence, Part I*, [606] HC 1845 (hereafter cited as Report of the Devon Commission), 19:428.

165 MacDonagh, "Politics, 1830–45," 188.

166 Report of the Devon Commission, 19:57.

167 Father Lennon's testimony is the most extensive and the most useful, since he claimed to know the parishes of Forkhill and Killeavy "pretty intimately," and a good part of his evidence applied to this wider area.

168 Evidence of the Reverend Michael Lennon, Report of the Devon Commission, 19:430. Occasionally these farms consisted of a collection of plots or strips of land that were intermixed and shared among several families. This helped to compensate for the unpredictable or varying quality of the land by ensuring that everyone shared in both the good land and the bad. This was similar to the rundale system, though the lands were not held under a joint tenancy. Although the intermixing of fields was favoured by tenants, landlords found it messy, and they occasionally interfered with the system by rearranging the holdings into neat units. This practice, known as "drawing straight lines," was resented by tenants and opposed by the ribbonmen, who frequently threatened landlords and agents who engaged in the practice.

169 Evidence of Thomas Seaver, ibid., 19:483.

170 Evidence of the Reverend Michael Lennon, ibid., 19:428.

171 Evidence of Walter James Dawson, ibid., 19:922–7.

172 Evidence of the Reverend Michael Lennon, ibid., 19:427.

173 Evidence of the Reverend Michael Lennon, ibid., 19:430; Evidence of Walter James Dawson, ibid., 19:927.

174 In 1845 the Devon Commission produced a multivolume report on the system of land tenure in Ireland, including recommendations for reform in land legislation. A compendium of this report was published in 1847, and the extracts are from this two-part digest: *Digest of Evidence Taken before Her Majesty's Commissioners of Inquiry into the State of the Law and Practice in Respect of the Occupation of Land in Ireland* (hereafter cited as Devon Commission Digest), 1:333–62.

175 Ibid.

176 The Outrage Papers formed a subsidiary set of the Chief Secretary Office's Registered Papers for the 1835–52 period; they were sorted by county and year (Quinlan, "The Registered Papers of the Chief Secretary's Office," 5–21).

177 6 February 1836, Outrage Papers (Armagh, 1836), NAI.
178 Ibid.
179 1 July 1836, Outrage Papers (Armagh, 1836), NAI.
180 7 August 1836, Outrage Papers (Armagh,1836), NAI.
181 18 August 1836, Outrage Papers (Armagh, 1836), NAI.
182 9 March 1837, Outrage Papers (Armagh, 1837), NAI.
183 24 September 1837, Outrage Papers (Armagh, 1837), 2/92, NAI.
184 20 February 1838, Outrage Papers (Armagh, 1838), 2/19, NAI.
185 The outrage reports for County Armagh c.1835–52 are most numerous and most detailed for the first six years of this period. During those years, the religious affiliations of both the victims and the suspected attackers were carefully recorded, along with the possible motivation for the attack and lengthy descriptions. Beginning in 1841, this information was less likely to be recorded, and the detailed reports gave way to abstracts and short summaries of incidents.
186 In eleven cases (7.8%), the religion of the parties was not stated, and it is impossible to determine it satisfactorily.
187 Devon Commission Digest, 1:333–62.
188 In 1840 Dublin Castle received information concerning the activities of a "Ribbon man living in Newry," a town less than ten miles from Forkhill. According to the informer, John McDonnell of Market Square served as a clerk to a fellow ribbonman named Edward Moore, who at the time was on trial in Downpatrick. McDonnell had stowed "all of Moore's party colours": "He has 6 cloaks of green, 12 suits of different colours, 40 sashes of green and white books, letters, pass signs etc. all of which he has in his father's cellar getting them ready to bring to England on Wednesday … I am a Prodestant [sic] Bread [sic] and Born and I will Die to have him punished perhaps you might think this all fun or Devilment on account of me not going in person but Sir I would not wish to have my name mentioned … Delay not and you will get all and if this is a lie I shall go forward and prove I have seen them. William Wright, shoemaker" (August 1840, Outrage Papers [Armagh, 1840], 2/14995, NAI).
189 December 1837, Outrage Papers (Armagh, 1837), 2/138, NAI.
190 Examinations of Philip Trainor of [word obscured] in the parish of Dundalk, 16 January 1833, CSORP, Official Papers, unnumbered (copy in private collection).
191 *Report from the Select Committee on Outrages (Ireland)*, HC 1852 (438) (hereafter cited as Report on Outrages, 1852), 14:126, no. 1295.
192 Evidence of Captain B. Warburton, Report on Outrages, 1852, 14:11, no. 90.
193 Evidence of Edward Golding, ibid., 14:86, nos. 914–17.
194 Ibid., no. 918.

195 Trench, *Realities of Irish Life*, 48. Trench served as land agent on the Shirley Estate in County Monaghan in 1843 and on the neighbouring Bath Estate in 1851.

196 10 December 1837, Outrage Papers (Armagh, 1837), 2/138, NAI; Deposition of Hugh McGill and Peter McGill of Tivecrom [Tifferum], 14 January 1837, Outrage Papers (Armagh, 1837), 2/85, NAI: "James Begley is a head committee man and has the District of Tivecrum and upper Carrickasticken. Michael Stanley is a Committee man and has District of Shean. Archibald McNeal is a member and acts as writing clerk or secretary. Thomas Hearty of Tivecrum is a member." Other members included Peter Cahy, William Crilly, John Murphy, Terence Tole, Hugh Dunn, Thomas Murphy, Edward Kelly, Thomas Henry, Andrew Begley, Michael Loughran, Thomas McElroy, Owen McElroy, and Laurence McElroy, all from Tiffcrum; Michael McElroy Jr, Michael Houghy, Michael McNamee, Peter McGill, and P. Murphy, all from Carrickasticken; and Owen McNamee of Cloghinny "and several others whom they cannot recollect."

197 Identification was made possible on the basis of the individual's full name and townland of residence. In a few instances, duplicate names appeared, in which case identification was made on the basis of age. Six men identified by Hugh and Peter McGill could not be traced in the census; they were not quite twenty years of age in 1821 and were possibly working as migrant labourers.

198 M.R. Beames has made a similiar correlation between socio-economic prospects and the tendency to be involved in Whiteboyism, arguing that Whiteboy activity was the "mode of protest for a specific 'class' within the rural social structure and not ... the typical vehicle of protest for the Catholic rural community as a whole" (*Peasants and Power*, 55).

199 April 1851, Outrage Papers (Armagh, 1851), 2/265, NAI.

200 6 August 1851, Outrage Papers (Armagh, 1851), NAI.

201 3 January 1852, Outrage Papers (Armagh, 1852), 2/93, NAI; 2 January 1852, Outrage Papers (Armagh, 1852), 2/12, NAI; *A Return of the Number of Murders, Waylayings, Assaults ... or other Crimes ... within the Counties of Louth, Armagh, and Monaghan, since the 1st Day of January 1849*, HC 1852 (448), 47:465–74.

202 Ibid.

203 *Copies of the Depositions Taken by the Coroner of Armagh County at the Inquest Held on the Body of the Late Mr Mauleverer*, HC 1850 (566), 51:518–21.

204 In a series of articles published in *Seanchas Ardmhacha*, Kevin McMahon compiled a large number of reports on outrages in the region around Crossmaglen between 1835 and 1855. During this

period, at least twenty-five murders were committed within ten miles of Crossmaglen, in south Armagh, north Louth, and north Monaghan. "Literally hundreds" of less serious outrages took place during the same period: beatings, shootings, property damage, burnings, and threats ("Agrarian Disturbances around Crossmaglen," 302–32). See also Report on Outrages, 1852, passim.

205 Threatening notice dated 12 December 1851, printed in Report on Outrages, 1852, 14:184–5.

206 For contemporary accounts of the attack on Meredith Chambré, see reports in the *Newry Telegraph* and the *Dundalk Democrat* for 1852. There is detailed coverage in the Report on Outrages, 1852, and the case has also been described in McKeown, "The Wounding of Meredith Chambré." Carlo Gebler borrowed many details of the attack and the trial in his historical fiction of the ribbonmen, *How to Murder a Man*.

207 The *Newry Telegraph* suggested that Father Michael Lennon, parish priest of Creggan, had denounced Chambré by name at Sunday Mass, his gestures "as violent and of as deep meaning as his words were charged with malevolence." The newspaper drew a parallel between the remarks allegedly made by the priest and Henry II's exasperation over Thomas Becket: "Have I no friends to rid me of this torment?" Lennon vehemently denied the charge both in the pages of the *Dundalk Democrat* and before the Select Committee on Outrages in 1852.

208 NT, 22 January 1852.

209 The Chambré name had had unpopular associations in the countryside for many years. Remarking on a period of upheaval in 1815, William Richardson informed the Earl of Gosford that the unrest apparently proceeded "entirely from the exorbitant rents exacted by a Mr Chambré in one of the baronies," though he could not confirm the truth of the rumour (William Richardson to Earl of Gosford, 3 January 1815, Gosford Papers, D/1606/1/1/245, PRONI).

210 MSS 1753/45, 1783/285, and 1072, IFC, University College, Dublin. The same story circulated about the Killeavy landlord Jonathan Seaver. In this case, the geese were ducks, known as "duty ducks" (O'Kane, *Lower Killevy, Ireland*, 36).

211 A blunderbuss full of shot had been recovered at the scene, along with several percussion caps wrapped in newspaper and some oaten bread and carrots (McKeown, "The Wounding of Meredith Chambré").

212 Berry's confession was printed in the *Newry Telegraph* on 10 August 1852, shortly after his execution.

213 A poignant article in the *Newry Telegraph* on 10 August 1852 described Berry's execution and how he spent his last hours.

214 *NT*, 10 August 1852.

215 Handwritten extract from the Speech from the Throne, 3 February 1852, facing the title page of the Report on Outrages, 1852.

216 Evidence of Captain B. Warburton, Report on Outrages, 1852, 14:2, no. 20.

217 Evidence of Captain G. Fitzmaurice, ibid., 14:32, no. 278.

218 Evidence of H.J. Brownrigg, ibid., 14:138, no. 1390.

219 Lindsay Mauleverer (land agent, murdered May 1850), Thomas Bateson (land agent and magistrate, murdered December 1851), James Eastwood (landlord, attempted murder, December 1851), Meredith Chambré (landlord and magistrate, attempted murder, January 1852).

220 Evidence of Captain B. Warburton, Report on Outrages, 1852, 14:17, no. 140.

221 Evidence of Edward Golding, ibid., 14:103, nos. 1093–4.

222 Evidence of Captain G. Fitzmaurice, ibid., 14:47, nos. 481–3.

223 Evidence of Captain G. Fitzmaurice, ibid., 14:38, no. 367. See Trench, *Realities of Irish Life*, for the story of Joe McKey, a Presbyterian in the district who was famed for his resistance to land agents.

224 Evidence of James O'Callaghan, Report on Outrages, 1852, 14:511, no. 5023.

225 The ribbonmen sought a way around this. To avoid lying in confession, some ribbonmen would recant their oaths quarterly, confess their sins, receive the sacraments, and promptly swear a new oath of membership. It was cynically suggested that this is one of the reasons that the society changed its passwords quarterly. As well, many printed versions of ribbon oaths contained a pledge of allegiance to the king (or queen), so that the society could not be accused of treasonable intentions. The pledge was said to be a blind, however, and was recanted at the end of the oath (evidence of informer, 30 June 1839, CO/904/reel 1, 269, PRONI).

226 Larkin and Freudenberger, eds., *A Redemptorist Missionary in Ireland*, 64.

227 The Reverend Nicholas J. Hughes to the Reverend Joseph Dixon, 28 November 1853, Papers of Most Reverend Joseph Dixon, 1852–1856, folder no. 7, Cardinal Tomas O'Fiaich Memorial Library.

228 The Reverend James Malone to the Reverend Joseph Dixon, 22 July 1864, Papers of Most Reverend Joseph Dixon, ibid.

229 Ibid. The stubborn parish master was, I suspect, Redmond O'Hanlon, who lived in the region of Tullymacreeve and Mullaghbawn (Reverend James Malone to the Reverend Joseph Dixon, 6 September 1864, ibid.).

230 The rehabilitation of protest in history began with the work of E.P. Thompson and George Rudé on the "crowd," and Eric Hobsbawm on rural vendetta societies, and much of the argument in

subsequent historiography has been based on these interpretations. See George Rudé, *The Crowd in History* (London: Wiley, 1964); Eric Hobsbawm and George Rudé, *Captain Swing* (New York: Pantheon Books, 1968); Eric Hobsbawm, *Primitive Rebels* (Manchester: Manchester University Press, 1971); Douglas Hay et al., *Albion's Fatal Tree: Crime and Society in Eighteenth-Century England* (New York: Pantheon Books, 1975); E.P. Thompson, "The Moral Economy of the English Crowd in the Eighteenth Century," *Past and Present* 50 (1971): 76–136; E.P. Thompson; *Whigs and Hunters* (New York: Pantheon Books, 1975); Eric Hobsbawm, *Bandits* (Middlesex: Penguin Books, 1985); Mick Reed and Roger Wells, *Class, Conflict, and Protest in the English Countryside, 1700–1800* (London: Frank Cass, 1990); E.P. Thompson, "Moral Economy Reviewed," in Thompson, ed., *Customs in Common* (London: Merlin, 1991).

231 Musgrave's *Memoirs of the Different Rebellions in Ireland* is the classic example of Protestant alarmism. Lewis's *On Local Disturbances* is noteworthy for its objectivity, particularly given the atmosphere of the 1830s.

232 The literature is represented in the following works. Williams, ed., *Secret Societies in Ireland*; Beames, *Peasants and Power* and "The Ribbon Societies"; Clark and Donnelly, Jr, eds., *Irish Peasants: Violence and Political Unrest*; Garvin, "Defenders, Ribbonmen, and Others"; Smyth, *The Men of No Property*; Farrell, *Rituals and Riots*.

233 The sectarianism of membership was not foolproof. According to Beames, the informers who had infiltrated the ribbon society in Dublin and subsequently testified at the trial of Michael Keenan in 1822 were not Catholics ("The Ribbon Societies," 252).

234 See, for example, Beames, *Peasants and Power*, 24–6, 42; Farrell, *Rituals and Riots*, 5–9, 21–5, and passim; Hirst, *Religion, Politics, and Violence in Nineteenth-Century Belfast*, 19, 189, and passim; Curtin, *The United Irishmen: Popular Politics*, 284–8. In the context of the 1798 rebellion, "it was inevitable that the Catholic peasantry would regard their burden in sectarian and nationalist terms" (Curtin, *The United Irishmen: Popular Politics*, 285).

235 Connolly, *Priests and People*, 243–52.

236 20 February 1842, Outrage Papers (Armagh, 1842), 2/3425, NAI.

237 15 January 1838, Outrage Papers (Armagh, 1838), 2/4, NAI.

238 The ribbonmen reportedly did not interfere in mixed marriages but only in unions between "their own people" (evidence of Captain G. Fitzmaurice, Report on Outrages, 1852, 14:52, no. 548–50).

239 See the ribbon oath and rules of membership c.1835 in the appendix.

240 Lewis, *On Local Disturbances*, 219–23; Beames, *Peasants and Power*, 89–90; threatening notice, 1840, Outrage Papers (Armagh, 1840), 2/10583, NAI.

241 For each case, the Forkhill Petty Sessions Order Books recorded the name, townland, and occupation of the complainant and defendant, a description of the alleged offence, the decision of the court, and the penalty, if one was awarded.
242 20 March 1855, Forkhill Petty Sessions Order Book, October 1854 – March 1856, HAI/52/A/3, PRONI.
243 7 August 1855, Ibid.
244 The series of petty sessions books for Forkhill in PRONI begins in November 1851, though the court may have been in existence prior to 1851 (Forkhill Petty Sessions Order Books, November 1851 – June 1873, HAI/52/A/1–12, PRONI).
245 *First Report of Inquiry into the Condition of the Poorer Classes in Ireland*, supplement 2 to appendices D, E, and F, HC 1836, 34:50.
246 26 October 1852, Forkhill Petty Sessions Order Book, November 1851 – May 1853, HAI/52/A/1, PRONI.
247 2 November 1853, Forkhill Petty Sessions Order Book, May 1853 – October 1854, HAI/52/A/2, PRONI.
248 Hoppen, *Election, Politics, and Society in Ireland*, 17–18.
249 Deposition of Hugh McGill and Peter McGill of Tivecrom [Tiffcrum], 14 January 1837, Outrage Papers (Armagh, 1837), 2/85, NAI.
250 Memorial of Peter McGill, May 1846, Outrage Papers (Armagh, 1846), 2/11109, NAI.
251 *Armagh Guardian*, 10 March 1846.
252 Memorial of Peter McGill, May 1846, Outrage Papers (Armagh, 1846), 2/11109, NAI.

CHAPTER SEVEN

1 Story told to Michael J. Murphy, a resident of south Armagh and collector for the Irish Folklore Commission. See MS 1072/312–67, Irish Folklore Commission, Department of Irish Folklore, University College, Dublin (hereafter cited as IFC).
2 Donnelly, "Excess Mortality and Emigration," 350–1; Kennedy et al., *Mapping the Great Irish Famine*.
3 For the famine in Ulster, see the edited collection by Christine Keneally and Trevor Parkhill, *The Famine in Ulster*, and MacAtasney, *This Dreadful Visitation*.
4 *Census of Ireland for 1851, Part I. Province of Ulster. County of Armagh*, [1547] HC 1852–53 (hereafter cited as Census of Ireland for 1851, Armagh), 92:45–68; *Census of Ireland for 1851. Part VI. General Report*, [2134] HC 1856 (hereafter cited as Census of Ireland for 1851), 31:1.
5 Census of Ireland for 1851, Armagh, 92:45–68.

6 Bourke, *The Visitation of God?* 11–25, 53–4.
7 Connell, *Population of Ireland*, 151–6.
8 Nicholas and Steckel, "Tall but Poor," 105–34.
9 Bourke, *The Visitation of God?* 52–5, 91–4. Bourke uses the more conservative estimate of 12 lb per day for an adult male. The consumption of an adult woman and of children between the ages of 11 and 15 years is taken to be 80 per cent of a man's daily take. A value of 35 per cent is used for children under 11 years.
10 Anonymous contributor to the *Edinburgh Review*, 1822, quoted in Bourke, *The Visitation of God?* 54–5.
11 Ibid., 67 and passim.
12 *Report of the Commissioners Appointed to take the Census of Ireland for the Year 1841*, HC (504), 1843, 24:13.
13 *First Report of Inquiry into the Condition of the Poorer Classes in Ireland, with Appendix (A) and Supplement*, [369], HC 1835 (hereafter cited as Poor Inquiry, appendix A), 32:1. For discussion of the introduction of the poor law system, see Burke, *The People and the Poor Law in Nineteenth-Century Ireland*.
14 *Poor Inquiry (Ireland); Appendix (D) and Supplement*, [36] HC 1836 (hereafter cited as Poor Inquiry, appendix D), 31:290–1; *Poor Inquiry (Ireland); Appendix (E) and Supplement*, [37] HC 1836 (hereafter cited as Poor Inquiry, appendix E), 32:290–1.
15 Poor Inquiry, appendix A (supplement), 32:305.
16 Poor Inquiry, appendix D (supplement), 31:290–1.
17 Ibid.
18 Ibid., 283.
19 Ibid., 280–92.
20 *Poor Inquiry (Ireland); Appendix (B) and Supplement*, [369] HC 1835, (hereafter cited as Poor Inquiry, appendix B), 32 (pt 2):209–11; ibid., appendix B (supplement), 104–5, 227.
21 Quarterly Report of the Forkhill Dispensary (February–May 1842), 1 May 1842, Minutes of the Proceedings of the Trustees of the Charitable Donations of Richard Jackson of Forkill, Esq. (hereafter Minutes of the Forkhill Trustees), vol. 2.
22 Crawford, "Dietary Considerations in Pre-Famine Louth and Its Environs," 116.
23 Ibid., 127.
24 In his will, made in 1776, Richard Jackson awarded the sum of £100 to the infirmary in Dundalk and instructed that the sum of three guineas be paid annually to the infirmaries in both Armagh and Dundalk. He further requested that the resident clergyman of Forkhill should be a governor of each hospital "for the advice of my poor fellow-creatures, who are destroyed by the advice of quack doctors" (Will of

Richard Jackson, 1776, printed in Miller, ed., *Peep O'Day Boys and Defenders*, 91–3).

25 Poor Inquiry, appendix B, 32 (pt 2):209–11. A motion to build a dispensary was passed by the trustees in 1818 (1 August 1818, Minutes of the Forkhill Trustees, vol. 1).

26 Ibid.; 1 May 1823, Minutes of the Forkhill Trustees, vol. 1.

27 Poor Inquiry, appendix B, 32 (pt 2):209–11; ibid., supplement, 104.

28 Poor Inquiry, appendix B, 32 (pt 2):209–11.

29 Ibid.

30 Poor Inquiry, appendix D (supplement), 31:284, 290–1.

31 *Papers Relating to Proceedings for the Relief of the Distress, and State of Unions and Workhouses in Ireland; Eighth Series, 1849*, [1042] HC 1849, 48:221.

32 Poor Inquiry, appendix E (supplement), 32:290.

33 Ibid.

34 Ibid., 280–92.

35 Ibid., 290.

36 *Poor Inquiry (Ireland), Appendix (F) and Supplement*, HC 1836 (hereafter cited as Poor Inquiry, appendix F), 32:290–1.

37 Poor Inquiry, appendix F (supplement), 290–1.

38 Ibid. In the early 1850s, two brothers from the townland of Shean emigrated from Forkhill; James Carlisle sailed to America, and William Carlisle to Australia. Their letters home between 1851 and 1892 are preserved in the collection of emigrant correspondence in the Public Record Office in Belfast (correspondence of James Carlisle and his wife Kate Carlisle, to his mother and family in Forkhill, Co. Armagh and Newry, Co. Down, 1851–92, MIC/143, Public Record Office of Northern Ireland (PRONI)).

39 Poor Inquiry (appendix E), 32:290–1.

40 Ibid.

41 Bourke, *The Visitation of God?* 90.

42 11 October 1845, Minute Book of the Newry Union (September 1844 – March 1846), Records of Newry Board of Guardians, BG 24/A/3, PRONI.

43 Richard Pennefather to Relief Commission, 20 October 1845, Relief Commission Papers (RLFC), 2/Z14008, National Archives of Ireland (NAI).

44 Ibid.; Pennefather to Relief Commission, 28 October 1845, RLFC, 2/Z14556, NAI.

45 Constabulary Report for Crossmaglen, 11 November 1845, RLFC, 2/Z15796, NAI. The Lumper was also the least nutritious variety of potato. On the quality and distribution of the Lumper, see Bourke, *The Visitation of God?* 39–42.

46 Members included Major Bernard, John Foxall, the Reverend James Campbell, the Reverend Father Hugh Mulligan, the Reverend Father Matthew McParland, Robert Wray (land agent to the Forkhill estate), Dr Henry Stanley (supervisor of the Forkhill dispensary), Archibald Murdock, Michael Hughes, John Murdock, and Thomas Brooks (treasurer of the Forkhill Agricultural Society).

47 William Smith to Relief Commission, 30 May 1846, RLFC, 3/1/2717, NAI. The committee met first in December 1845 but was not formally instituted until May 1846.

48 William Smith to Relief Commission, 9 December 1845, RLFC, 2/Z17618, NAI.

49 Art Bennett to Robert MacAdam, 7 January 1846, quoted in O'Mordha, "Arthur Bennett's Correspondence," 369.

50 Art Bennett to Robert MacAdam, 15 February 1846, quoted in O'Mordha, "Arthur Bennett's Correspondence," 372.

51 1 May 1846, Minutes of the Forkhill Trustees, vol. 3.

52 William Smith to Relief Commission, 30 May 1846, RLFC, 3/2/2717, NAI.

53 MS 1072/312–67, IFC.

54 Oats had been sown on the rest of the land as an insurance against the collapse of the crop, but also because there was a shortage of seed after the failure of 1845 (Constabulary Report, Forkhill, 27 May 1846, RLFC, 4/2/38, NAI).

55 *Nation*, 20 August 1846.

56 Constabulary Report for Newtownhamilton, August 1846, RLFC 5/2/5.

57 Reverend Michael Lennon to CSO, 19 September 1846, CSORP, Distress Papers 1846/D5263, NAI.

58 Extracts from Journal of Lieutenant Griffith, RN, Inspecting Officer, 21 November 1846 and 28 November 1846, *Relief of the Distress in Ireland. Correspondence, from July 1846 to January 1847, Relating to the Measures Adopted for the Relief of the Distress in Ireland*, [764] HC 1847, 50:302–15.

59 Mr Stanley to Mr Hornsby, Commissariat Relief Office, 9 December 1846, *Relief of the Distress in Ireland. Correspondence, from July 1846 to January 1847, Relating to the Measures adopted for the Relief of the Distress in Ireland*, HC [761], 1847, 51:441–2.

60 Extracts from Journal of Lieutenant Griffith, RN, Inspecting Officer, 21 November 1846 and 28 November 1846, *Relief of the Distress in Ireland. Correspondence, from July 1846 to January 1847, Relating to the Measures Adopted for the Relief of the Distress in Ireland*, [764] HC 1847, 50:315.

61 26 September 1846, Minutes of the Forkhill Trustees, vol. 3.

62 Reverend Michael Lennon to CSO, 4 and 6 January 1847, CSORP, Distress Papers 1847/D562, NAI.

63 Extract from Report of Lieutenant Griffith, RN, Inspecting Officer (hereafter Weekly Report of Lieutenant Griffith), 16 January 1847, *Relief of the Distress in Ireland. Correspondence from January to March 1847, relating to the Measures Adopted for the Relief of the Distress in Ireland (Board of Works Series), Second Part*, [797] HC 1847, 52:98–250.

64 Weekly Report of Lieutenant Griffith, 23 January 1847.

65 26 November 1846, Minutes of the Forkhill Trustees, vol. 3.

66 Ibid.; 1 May 1847, Minutes of the Forkhill Trustees, vol. 3.

67 William Smith to Relief Commission, 30 May 1846, RLFC, 3/1/2717, NAI.

68 Ibid., 5 June 1846, RLFC, 3/1/2906, NAI.

69 Ibid., 15 June 1846, RLFC, 3/1/3266, NAI.

70 The commissioners appended an internal memo to Smith's last letter, stating that all applications had been refused and an explanation had been provided. See letters of William Smith to the Relief Commission, 22 June 1846, RLFC, 3/1/3567, 29 June 1846, RLFC, 3/1/3794, 8 August 1846, RLFC 3/1/5239, 24 October 1846, RLFC, 3/2/2/37, NAI. Gerard MacAtasney reported similar frustrations by the relief committees in Lurgan and Portadown (*This Dreadful Visitation*, 34).

71 William Smith to Relief Commission, 30 May 1846, RLFC, 3/1/2717, NAI.

72 Resolutions of Forkhill Relief Committee, 9 January 1847, RLFC, 3/2/2/37, NAI.

73 *Newry Examiner*, 16 January 1847.

74 Ibid. Similar stories of landlord indifference were reported in north Armagh (MacAtasney, *This Dreadful Visitation*, 34, 106–7).

75 Edwards and Williams, *The Great Famine*, 223–34; MS 1072/312–67, IFC.

76 Minute Book of the Newry Union (June 1839 – March 1843), Records of Newry Board of Guardians, BG 24/A/1, PRONI.

77 September 1846, Minute Book of the Newry Union (March 1846 – April 1847), Records of Newry Board of Guardians, BG/24/A/4, PRONI.

78 9 January 1847, ibid.

79 12 March 1847, ibid.

80 Food rations were not scheduled to begin until 15 March, and they began weeks later in many areas.

81 Resolutions of Forkhill Relief Committee, 15 January 1847, RLFC 3/2/2/37.

82 Resolutions of Forkhill Relief Committee, 29 January 1847, RLFC 3/2/2/37.

83 Ibid.

84 MS 1072/312–67, IFC, University College, Dublin.
85 Ibid.
86 *Armagh Guardian*, 13 October 1846.
87 George Robinson and others to J.R. Redington, Under-Secretary, 17 December 1846, Outrage Papers (Armagh, 1846), 2/unnumbered, NAI.
88 *Nation*, 23 January 1847.
89 December 1846, Outrage Papers (Armagh, 1847), 2/36775, NAI.
90 Ibid.
91 12 March 1846, Outrage Papers (Armagh, 1846), 2/5403; 28 July 1847, Outrage Papers, (Armagh, 1846), 2/268, NAI.
92 Extract from Journal of Lieutenant Griffith, RN, Inspecting Officer, 12 December 1846, *Relief of the Distress in Ireland. Correspondence, from July 1846 to January 1847, Relating to the Measures Adopted for the Relief of the Distress in Ireland*, [764] HC 1847, 50:412.
93 January 1847, Outrage Papers (Armagh, 1847), 2/22, NAI.
94 20 December 1846, Outrage Papers (Armagh, 1847), 2/1, NAI.
95 21 January 1847, Outrage Papers (Armagh, 1847), 2/42, NAI.
96 "A Register of Babtisms [sic] Celebrated in the Parish of Fork Hill, County and Archdiocese of Armagh from the 1st Jan. 1845, by H. Mulligan, P.P.," MIC/1D/38, PRONI.
97 Kelleher, *Feminization of Famine*, 24, 140–6.
98 Ela Sen, quoted in Kelleher, *Feminization of Famine*, 190.
99 "A Register of Marriages Celebrated in the Parish of Fork Hill, County and Archdiocese of Armagh from the 1st Jan. 1844, by H. Mulligan, P.P.," MIC/1D/38, PRONI.
100 The Church of Ireland marriage register for Forkhill shows similar low numbers: two marriages in 1845, two in 1846, one in 1847, three in 1848. Given the size of their population, however, the decline would not appear so dramatic ("Register of Marriages for the Parish of Forkhill, 1845–1932," private collection).
101 MS 1072/312–67, IFC.
102 1 May 1847, Minutes of the Forkhill Trustees, vol. 3. In the fall of 1850, the Forkhill tenantry sent a memorial to the trustees requesting a rent reduction but received a negative reply: "It [was] not in the power of the Trustees of this Charity to alter in any way the rent of the Estate." The matter was left to the landlord. A note in the minute books for 1854 mentioned that a reduction of between 5 and 10 per cent had been agreed in 1850 "on account of the depressed times" (1 November 1850, 1 May 1854, Minutes of the Forkhill Trustees, vol. 3).
103 See also McHugh, "The Famine in Irish Oral Tradition," 410–12.
104 MS 1072/312–67, IFC.

105 Ibid.

106 Ibid.

107 Ibid.

108 Ibid. Although the story of this theft and prosecution cannot be verified, there was such an incident in August 1855 when the landlord Hunt Walsh Chambré of Killeavy charged Anne Connely with trespassing on his property and stealing carrots (7 August 1855, Forkhill Petty Sessions Order Book, October 1854 – March 1856, HAI/52/A/3, PRONI).

109 Ibid.

110 The term "souper" was used in reference to both the suspected proselytizers who distributed the soup and the individuals who took it.

111 O Ciosain, "Famine Memory," 97–8.

112 Ibid., 98.

113 The Forkhill Relief Committee consisted entirely of members of the Protestant community, with the exception of the two Catholic priests.

114 MS 1072/312–67, IFC, University College, Dublin. A man named Johnny Robin, who lived in the townland of Cloghinny, told Michael J. Murphy that "there was none died around here with hunger during the famine, I heard them say that, though they said it was a holy terror over in Connaught."

115 *Census of Ireland for the Year 1851. Tables of Deaths, Part II*, [2087-I] HC 1856, 30:476–82 (hereafter cited as Tables of Deaths, 1851). The tables were based on the recollections of householders, and they underestimate the actual extent of disease and mortality during this decade – nor can we be absolutely sure of the accuracy of these lay diagnoses.

116 Tables of Deaths, 1851.

117 9 January 1847, Minute Book of the Newry Union (March 1846 – April 1847), Records of Newry Board of Guardians, BG/24/A/4, PRONI; Resolutions of the Forkhill Relief Committee, 29 January 1847, RLFC, 3/2/2/37, NAI.

118 20 January, 25 February, and 6 March 1847, Minute Book of the Newry Union (March 1846 – April 1847), Records of Newry Board of Guardians, BG/24/A/4, PRONI.

119 *Report on the Status of Disease in Ireland*, [1765] HC 1854, vol. 58 (hereafter cited as Report on the Status of Disease, 1851).

120 James Dick, the poor rate collector, died in April 1847. See 24 April 1847, Minute Book of the Newry Union (March 1846 to April 1847), Records of the Newry Board of Guardians, BG/24/A/4, PRONI.

121 MS 1072/312–67, IFC.

122 O'Grada, *Black '47 and Beyond*, 40.

123 Minute Books of the Newry Union (April 1847 – May 1849), Records of the Newry Board of Guardians, BG/24/A/5–7, PRONI.

124 Report on the Status of Disease, 1851.

125 MSS 1783/283 and 1072/312–67, IFC.
126 Bennett to MacAdam, 8 July 1849, quoted in O'Mordha, "Arthur Bennett's Correspondence," 378.
127 O Tuathail, "The Bennett Family of Forkhill, Co. Armagh," 32; Céitinn, *Art Bennett and His Poetry*; Keating, "Art Bennett and the Bible"; O'Mordha, "Arthur Bennett's Correspondence," 360–87; Hughes, "Gaelic Poets and Scribes," 521–5, 533–47, and *Robert Shipboy MacAdam*, 44–6. For commentary on Bennett's writing, see Elliott, *Catholics of Ulster*, 141, 273–4, 366–7.
128 Bennett to MacAdam, 24 February 1850, quoted in O'Mordha, "Arthur Bennett's Correspondence," 383–4.
129 Ibid., 384.
130 Bennett to MacAdam, 26 December 1846, quoted in O'Mordha, "Arthur Bennett's Correspondence," 376.
131 Bennett to MacAdam, 15 February 1846, quoted in O'Mordha, "Arthur Bennett's Correspondence," 372.
132 Céitinn, *Art Bennett and His Poetry*, 8; Hughes, *Robert Shipboy MacAdam*, 44–6.
133 This passage is printed in O'Mordha, "Arthur Bennett's Correspondence," 382–3.
134 *Newry Examiner*, 12 April 1848.
135 *Newry Examiner*, 31 January and 7 March 1846. The "O'Connell Tribute" was established as a source of financial assistance to Daniel O'Connell and was raised among his supporters. It was collected annually by the Catholic clergy in each parish.
136 For the life of Thomas Seaver, see Seaver, *History of the Seaver Family*, 93–103.
137 Hughes, *Robert Shipboy MacAdam*, 46. Bennett eventually completed the work under the patronage of a Newry stationer, Edward Augustus Maginnis. It was discovered in 1978 and has been edited and published by Reamonn O Muiri.

CHAPTER EIGHT

1 Bowen, *Souperism*, 67–149, and *Protestant Crusade in Ireland*, 195–256; Hempton and Hill, *Evangelical Protestantism in Ulster Society*, 46–61, 86–95; Brown, "The New Reformation Movement in the Church of Ireland,"180–208; Elliott, *Catholics of Ulster*, 269–90.
2 Julia Eliza Ogle, daughter of Susanna Barton and niece of Richard Jackson, also subscribed to the grammar book (O'Snodaigh, *Hidden Ulster*, 67–8).
3 Brown, "The New Reformation Movement in the Church of Ireland," 189.

4 2 May 1836, Minutes of the Forkhill Trustees, vol. 2.
5 Hempton and Hill, *Evangelical Protestantism in Ulster Society*, 93, 188–9. The revival did have some positive results, including its rejuvenating effect on Ulster Protestantism (ibid., 61).
6 Bowen, *Souperism*, 133.
7 Dallas, *Story of the Irish Church Missions*, passim; Bowen, *Souperism*, 67–149; Bowen, *Protestant Crusade in Ireland*, chap. 5.
8 Bowen, *Protestant Crusade in Ireland*, 218–29.
9 Ibid., 220.
10 Bowen, *Souperism*, 138.
11 Ibid.
12 One informant knew of Young as a "tract dropper" who dropped religious tracts along the road for people to collect. See MS 1758/179–80, Irish Folklore Commission, Department of Irish Folklore, University College, Dublin (hereafter cited as IFC).
13 Leslie, *Armagh Clergy and Parishes*, 227.
14 Bowen, *Protestant Crusade in Ireland*, 221–2.
15 Ibid.
16 Michael J. Murphy, a collector for the Irish Folklore Commission in the 1940s, noted that a "Doui [Douay] bible" had been found in Larkin's public house in a chest of old papers (MS 1752/51, IFC).
17 Secretary of the Primate to Meredith Chambré, 13 February 1855, Chambré MS 7035/11/14, National Archives of Ireland (NAI).
18 Hempton and Hill, *Evangelical Protestantism in Ulster Society*, 92–4.
19 *Newry Telegraph* (NT), 16 December 1854.
20 The Chambrés were unpopular landlords in the neighbouring parish of Killeavy (James Keating, "Art Bennett and the Bible," passim).
21 Reverend Young's speech was reported in the *Weekly Northern Whig*, 19 July 1873 (quoted in Wright, *Two Lands on One Soil*, 428).
22 *NT*, 24 June 1852.
23 The full set of correspondence and testimonials concerning the alleged conversion of Hugh Gartlany was printed in the *Newry Telegraph* on 10 March 1853.
24 Statement of Patrick Gartlany (18 February 1853), *NT*, 10 March 1853; statement of Terence Muckian (18 February 1853), *NT*, 10 March 1853; Reverend McShane to the Editor (18 February 1853), *NT*, 10 March 1853.
25 Statement of Terence Muckian (18 February 1853), ibid.
26 Reverend McShane to the Editor (18 February 1853), ibid.
27 Hugh Gartlany to the Editor (14 February 1853), ibid.
28 Statement of Hugh Gartlany (24 February 1853), ibid. Young dismissed the statement of Gartlany's daughter, Mary Muckian, on the grounds that she was a "rejected Irish teacher" whose word could not

be trusted. See letter of Reverend Young (3 March 1853), *NT*, 10 March 1853.

29 Letter of Reverend Young (24 February 1853), ibid.

30 Letter of Reverend Young (3 March 1853), ibid. Hugh Gartlany was not the only Catholic who responded to Young's overtures. The register of marriages for the Church of Ireland in Forkhill records the union of Terence McCoy and Mary Hollywood on 26 December 1854; both the McCoys and the Hollywoods were Catholic families in the townland of Tiffcrum.

31 Transcribed letter of Art Bennett to Father Patrick Lamb, 27 April 1853, MS G428, National Library of Ireland. There is some dispute over Bennett's association with the Irish Society. In *Hidden Ulster*, Peadar O'Snodaigh stated that Bennett had been employed in the Bible schools under the supervision of Hugh McDonnell, who was a teacher with the Home Mission. When the Home Mission faltered and McDonnell lost his job, McDonnell moved to Belfast to work as an assistant to the Gaelic scholar Robert MacAdam, copying and annotating Irish manuscripts, and he later introduced Bennett to MacAdam (O'Snodaigh, *Hidden Ulster*, 74). The south Armagh historian and biographer of Bennett, Séamas Céitinn, also reported that the scribe worked as a Bible reader (Céitinn, *Art Bennett and His Poetry*, 6). A more recent biography of MacAdam, which describes Bennett at some length, does not identify him as a Bible reader, though it mentions that his father, John Bennett, was an Irish teacher (Hughes, *Robert Shipboy MacAdam*, 44–6).

32 Translation of verses in Céitinn, *Art Bennett and His Poetry*, 20–1. I am grateful to Séamas Cregg for providing a translation of the poem.

33 *NT*, 20 August 1853.

34 13 January 1836, Outrage Papers (Armagh, 1836), NAI.

35 8 March 1842, Outrage Papers (Armagh, 1842), 2/4287, NAI; 28 March 1842, Outrage Papers (Armagh, 1842), 2/5591, NAI.

36 *Armagh Guardian*, 10 March 1846. Clashes between Bible teachers and their opponents in the 1850s inspired incidents of Bible burning. In June 1854 a Londonderry man quarrelled with a Scripture reader, seized his Bible, and threw it into the fire; in another case, a Bible was set alight and flung at the door of a man who supported the Bible societies (*NT*, 24 June 1854).

37 The trial was reported in the *Dundalk Democrat (DD)*, 24 December 1853.

38 *DD*, 24 December 1853.

39 *DD*, 6 September 1856.

40 Ibid.

41 *DD*, 13 September 1856.

42 Ibid.
43 Public theological controversies had been popular during the 1820s. Protestant and Catholic orators, usually clergymen, engaged in lengthy debates on doctrinal matters and points of theology, combined with polemical comments on contemporary issues. The disputes could last for hours or even days.
44 Keating, "Art Bennett and the Bible."
45 DD, 31 January 1857.
46 Reverend Young left his post at Forkhill in 1858 but remained an active agent of the ICM. In 1868 he sent a report to Reverend Dallas from his mission station in Ardee, commenting on the success of his mission, where the "greed, selfishness, turbulence, and dirt," of the young people had been replaced by "qualities of an opposite character" (Bowen, *Protestant Crusade in Ireland*, 253).
47 The Protestant church at Forkhill was erected in 1767. The Catholic chapel at Faughart was several miles from Forkhill village. "An Tagra an Da Theampall" is printed in Carpenter, ed. *Verse in English from Eighteenth-Century Ireland*, 323–6.
48 Ibid.
49 There were 418 members of the established church and 61 Presbyterians in Forkhill in 1834 ("Returns of Religious Denominations in the several parishes of the county of Armagh in 1834," Tenison-Groves MS, T808/14943, PRONI). These figures match those provided in a statistical return of the diocese in 1836, which reported 6,582 Catholics, 436 Episcopalians, and 45 Presbyterians in Forkhill (O'Kane, "A Statistical Return of Armagh Diocese in 1836," 181–9).
50 In 1861 there were 248 Protestants living in the parish (*Census of Ireland for the Year 1861, Part V, General Report*, [3204–IV] HC 1863, 61:1).
51 Edward Hudson to Charlemont, 7 December 1789, Charlemont MS 12 R15, no. 67, Royal Irish Academy (RIA).
52 This selection is printed in O'Mordha, "Arthur Bennett's Correspondence with MacAdam," 382–3. According to Céitinn, the work was written in 1857–58; the original manuscript was discovered in 1978 (Céitinn, *Art Bennett and His Poetry*, 9).
53 Hughes, *Robert Shipboy MacAdam*, 45.
54 Ibid.
55 Art Bennett to Robert MacAdam, 20 March 1850, in O'Mordha, "Arthur Bennett's Correspondence with MacAdam," 384, quoted in Hughes, *Robert Shipboy MacAdam*, 46.
56 Hughes, *Robert Shipboy MacAdam*, 46.
57 Céitinn, *Art Bennett and His Poetry*, passim.
58 Quoted in Morash, *Writing the Irish Famine*, 60–1.

59 Keller, *Feminization of Famine*, 1–11 and passim.

60 Larkin, "The Devotional Revolution in Ireland," 625–52; Rafferty, *Catholicism in Ulster*, chap. 4.

61 By 1900, there was one priest for every 900 Catholics (Rafferty, *Catholicism in Ulster*, 141; Larkin, "The Devotional Revolution in Ireland," 626–7).

62 Papers of Most Reverend Joseph Dixon, 1852–1856, folder no. 7, O'Fiaich Library and Archive.

63 *DD*, 26 May 1855.

64 An entry in the minute books of the Forkhill trustees reads thus: "That the trustees are not empowered under the will of the late Mr Jackson to make any grant of money for the purpose set forth in the memorial of the 'Roman Catholic Clergymen and the Building Committee of the Roman Catholic Church at Mullabawn,' and that a copy of this resolution be communicated by Mr Murdock to Memorialists" (2 May 1864, Minutes of the Forkhill Trustees, vol. 3).

65 *DD*, 19 October 1862.

66 Bridget Hughes was the niece of the Reverend Nicholas McIvor and was married to Michael Hughes. Upon the expiry of his lease in 1822, McIvor transferred the lease of his lands in Longfield and Carnally to Bridget and Michael Hughes. In return, they agreed to provide him with necessary board, lodging, clothing, and washing (Chambré Papers, D/294/85, PRONI).

CHAPTER NINE

1 MS 1758/171–4, Irish Folklore Commission, Department of Irish Folklore, University College, Dublin (hereafter cited as IFC).

2 *Orangeism in Ireland*, 276–7.

3 Musgrave, *Memoirs of the Different Rebellions*, 51–3.

4 Colonel Ogle to Dublin Castle, 14 November 1796, Rebellion Papers, 620/26/50, National Archives of Ireland (NAI). A military barracks, known as Belmont Barracks, had been established in the parish in 1795. It was financed partly by Susanna Barton, sister of Richard Jackson and mother-in-law of Colonel Ogle (*Belfast News-letter*, 25 May 1795).

5 12 April 1803, Forkhill Vestry Minute Book, 1793–1846 (in private collection).

6 Affidavit sworn before Hunt Walsh Chambré, 22 June 1832, Chief Secretary's Office Registered Papers, 1832/1124 (Private Index), NAI.

7 For an alternative explanation of the stirrings in the countryside late at night, see the description of "nightly meetings" in the memoir of Hugh Dorian, a labourer in nineteenth-century Donegal. At these meetings,

often held during the winter months, the men of the locality would gather at the cabin of one of their number for several hours of conversation and debate. On a typical night, the meeting house would be overcrowded, with standing room only. Politics, religion, the wars in Europe, the Book of Revelation, and contemporary Irish affairs were discussed, and the atmosphere often became highly charged. "During the greater part of the time ... the speakers would agree very well, at other times the dispute would run so high that they would be ready to throttle each other and in the heat of passion would actually rise to their feet ... and by words insult and point their sticks at one another." The meetings were kept up "night after night during the long winter season ... from house to house and from village to village; at twelve, one, or two o'clock in the mornings," when the men roused themselves to make their way home in the pitch dark (Mac Suibhne and Dickson, eds., *The Outer Edge of Ulster*, chap. 5).

8 Stewart, *Shape of Irish History*, 33.

9 Contrary to all expectations, the Reverend Edward Hudson found himself speaking out against Orangeism in the wake of the 1798 rebellion. Marianne Elliott quotes from a letter written by Hudson, who was then rector of the parish of Portglenone in County Antrim. He complained of the spread of "the Orange mania," which had been introduced to his area by the yeomanry. Those who tried to stop it, including himself, "were denounced as 'Catholic lovers'" (Hudson, quoted in Elliott, *Catholics of Ulster*, 262).

10 Walsh and Murphy, eds., *Kick Any Stone: Townlands, People, and Stories of Forkhill Parish*, 45.

11 MS 1758/179–80, IFC.

12 Application for grant-in-aid from the Board of Commissioners for National Education and related correspondence, ED/1/11/22, Public Record Office of Northern Ireland (PRONI).

13 Walsh and Murphy, eds., *Kick Any Stone*, 46.

14 Will of Richard Jackson, 1776, printed in Miller, ed., *Peep O'Day Boys and Defenders*, 92. See also 1 August 1818 and 1 May 1823, Minutes of the Forkhill Trustees, vol. 1; Poor Inquiry, appendix B, 32:209–11 and supplement, 32:104.

15 Will of Richard Jackson, 1776, printed in Miller, ed., *Peep O'Day Boys and Defenders*, 91–3.

16 1 November 1791 and 1 February 1810, Minutes of the Forkhill Trustees, vol. 1. At most meetings of the trustees in the 1820s, the names of "old, decayed farmers" were added to the list and the names of the deceased were struck off (Minutes of the Forkhill Trustees, vol. 1, passim).

17 1 August 1817, Minutes of the Forkhill Trustees, vol. 1.

18 1 February 1837, Minutes of the Forkhill Trustees, vol. 1.

19 Will of Richard Jackson, 1776, printed in Miller, ed., *Peep O'Day Boys and Defenders*, 92.

20 Petition of the Tenants of Forkhill (1844), Minutes of the Forkhill Trustees, vol. 2.

21 The trustees were divided on this question. Several of them felt that they did not have the authority to alter the terms of Jackson's original bequest. They had solicited a legal opinion on a similar matter the previous year and had been informed that they were not authorized to set up a fund for agricultural improvements using income from the estate (Case of the Forkhill Estate, with Mr Sergeant Warren's opinion thereon, 14 December 1843, Papers of the Jackson Trust, Forkhill). They put the matter before the high chancellor of Ireland in 1844, proposing a scheme in which the surplus funds would be used to distribute premiums of money, agricultural implements, and clothing among deserving and industrious tenants. As usual, the trustees' benevolence was leavened by their business sense. They noted in their application that "by the improvement of [the] estate, the fund applicable to the trusts would be gradually increased," as the land would be valued at a higher rate and could be leased more profitably. The chancellor agreed that such a scheme was desirable, though he stipulated that the sum must not exceed £200 annually (Petition of the Trustees of the Charitable Donations of Richard Jackson of Forkhill to the Lord High Chancellor of Ireland [1844]; reply of 22 June 1844, Papers of the Jackson Trust, Forkhill, in private collection).

22 Chambré Papers, D/294, PRONI.

APPENDIX

1 Ribbon oath, c.1835, Ribbon Documents, 1835–36, Howard Bury Papers, T/3069/D/5, PRONI.

Bibliography

MANUSCRIPT SOURCES

Armagh Public Library

Beresford Correspondence, vols. 1–11
County Armagh Crown Book (Indictments) General Assizes, 1737–97

Cardinal Tomas O'Fiaich Memorial Library and Archive, Armagh

Papers of the Most Reverend Joseph Dixon, 1852–56

Department of Irish Folklore, University College, Dublin

Manuscripts of the Irish Folklore Commission

National Archives of Ireland, Dublin

Board of Commissioners for National Education. Correspondence files
Chambré MSS
Chief Secretary's Office Registered Papers
Distress Papers. CSORP Z Series
Frazer MSS
Official Papers. First and Second Series
Outrage Papers, 1835–52
Rebellion Papers
Relief Commission Papers, 1845–47
State of the Country Papers

National Library of Ireland, Dublin

Letters of General Lake, MS 56
Transcribed letter of Art Bennett to Father Patrick Lamb, April 1853, MS G428

Private Collections

Manuscript Census for the parish of Forkhill, 1821
Minute Book of the Forkhill Vestry, 1793–1846
Minutes of the Proceedings of the Trustees of the Charitable Donations of Richard Jackson of Forkill, Esq., vol. 1 (1789–1830), vol. 2 (1830–45), vol. 3 (1845–76)
Register of Marriages for the Parish of Forkhill, 1845–1932 (Church of Ireland)

Public Record Office of Northern Ireland, Belfast

Abercorn Papers
Armagh Diocesan Registry Papers
Armstrong, William. Map of Barony of Upper Orior. 1827
Bell, H.E. "Notes of Three Tours in Ireland in 1824 and 1826"
Carlisle Correspondence. James Carlisle and his wife Kate Carlisle to his mother and family in Forkhill, County Armagh, and Newry, County Down, 1851–92
Chambré Papers
County Armagh Crown Book (Indictments) General Assizes, 1797–1822
County Armagh National Schools Register, vol. 1
Downshire Papers
Gosford Papers
Howard Bury Papers
National Board of Education files
Newry Board of Guardians records
Patterson, T.G.F. Notes on Richard Jackson and the Forkhill Estate
Pelham Transcripts
Register of Baptisms for Forkhill, 1845–77 (Roman Catholic Church)
Register of Marriages for Forkhill, 1844–77 (Roman Catholic Church)
Stevenson, Robert. "View of County Armagh." 1795
Tenison Groves Transcripts
Tithe Composition Book for the Parish of Forkhill, 1828

Royal Irish Academy, Dublin

Charlemont Correspondence, MS 12 R, vols. 14–27

PARLIAMENTARY PAPERS

Abstract of Answers and Returns, Pursuant to Act 55 Geo. 3, for Taking an Account of the Population of Ireland in 1821, HC 1824 (577), vol. 22

Census of Ireland for 1851. Part I. Province of Ulster. County of Armagh, [1547] HC 1852–53, vol. 92

– *Part V. Tables of Deaths. Vol. II*, [2087-II]. HC 1856, vol. 30

– *Part VI. General Report*, [2134], HC 1856, vol. 31

Census of Ireland for the Year 1861. Part IV. Report of Tables relating to the Religious Professions, Education, and Occupations of the People, [3204-III] HC 1863, vol. 60

– *Part V. General Report*, [3204-IV] HC 1863, vol. 61

Census of Ireland for the Year 1901. Part I. Area, Houses, and Population, also the Ages, Civil or Conjugal Condition, Occupations, Birthplaces, Religion and Education of the People in Each County, and Summary Tables for Each Province. Part III, Province of Ulster, [Cd 1123] HC 1902, vols. 126, 127

Copies of the Depositions Taken by the Coroner of Armagh County at the Inquest Held on the Body of the Late Mr Mauleverer, HC 1850 (566), vol. 51

Copy of the Proceedings of an Investigation Held at Armagh, of the Transaction Which Took Place in the Neighbourhood of Keady, between the Police and Country People, on Collecting an Arrear of Tithe Due to the Reverend James Blacker, Wherein One Man Was Killed and Several Wounded; with a Copy of the Inquest, and All Other Documents Connected with That Transaction, HC 1835 (179), vol. 47

First Report of Inquiry into the Condition of the Poorer Classes in Ireland. Appendix (A) and Supplement (Deserted and Orphan Children, Bastardy and Vagrancy), [369] HC 1835, vol. 32; *Appendix (B) and Supplement (Public Medical Relief, Dispensaries, Fever Hospitals, Lunatic Asylums)*, [369] HC 1835, vol. 32, part 2; *Appendix D: Baronial Examinations Relative to Earnings of Labourers, Cottier Tenants, Employment of Women and Children, Expenditure; Appendix E: Baronial Examinations Relative to Food, Cottages and Cabins, Clothing and Furniture, Pawnbroking and Savings, Banks, Drinking; Appendix F: Baronial Examinations Relative to Con-acre, Quarter or Score Ground; Small Tenantry; Consolidation of Farms; Emigration; Landlord and Tenant; Agriculture; Taxation; Roads*, [36], [37], [38], [38], [39], [40], [41], [42], HC 1836, vols. 30–4

Papers Relating to Proceedings for the Relief of the Distress, and State of Unions and Workhouses in Ireland. Eighth Series, 1849, [1042] HC 1849, vol. 48

Relief of the Distress in Ireland. Correspondence, from July 1846 to January 1847, Relating to the Measures Adopted for the Relief of the Distress in Ireland, [764] HC 1847, vol. 50, and [761] HC 1847, vol. 51

– *Correspondence from January to March 1847, relating to the Measures Adopted for the Relief of the Distress in Ireland (Board of Works Series), Second Part*, [797] HC 1847, vol. 52

Report from Her Majesty's Commissioners of Inquiry into the State of the Law and Practice in Respect to the Occupation of Land in Ireland, Minutes of Evidence. Part I, [606] HC 1845, vol. 19

Report from the Commissioners of the Board of Education in Ireland, 1809–1812. Thirteenth Report: English Schools of Private Foundation, HC 1813–14 (47), vol. 1

Report from the Select Committee Appointed to Inquire into the Nature, Character, Extent, and Tendency of Orange Lodges, Associations, or Societies in Ireland, with the Minutes of Evidence and Appendix, [377] HC 1835, vol. 15

Report from the Select Committee of the House of Lords Appointed to Enquire into the State of Ireland in Respect of Crime, HC 1839 (486-II), vol. 72

Report from the Select Committee on Outrages (Ireland), HC 1852, (438), vol. 14

Report of the Commissioners Appointed to Take the Census of Ireland for the Year 1841, HC 1843 (504), vol. 24

Report on the Status of Disease in Ireland, [1765] HC 1854, vol. 58

Reports from the Select Committees on Foundation Schools and Education in Ireland. Part I, HC 1835 (630), vol. 13

A Return of the Name and Residence of Each Person in Ireland, to Whom Licenses Have Been Granted to Keep Arms, by the Magistrates at Quarter Sessions ... since 1st August 1832, HC 1836 (255), vol. 47

A Return of the Number of Murders, Waylayings, Assaults, Threatening Notices, Incendiary Fires, or other Crimes of an Agrarian Character, Reported by the Constabulary within the Counties of Louth, Armagh, and Monaghan, since the 1st day of January 1849, HC 1852 (448), vol. 47

Royal Commission on Irish Education. Second Report, Appendix (Parochial Abstracts), HC 1826–27, vol. 12, app. 12

Sixth Report of the Commissioners of National Education in Ireland, for the Year 1839, [246] HC 1840, vol. 28

NEWSPAPERS

Armagh Guardian
Belfast News-letter
Dundalk Democrat
Faulkner's Dublin Journal
Freeman's Journal
Hibernian Journal
Irish Volunteer
Newry Examiner

Newry Reporter
Newry Telegraph
Northern Star

SECONDARY SOURCES

Adams, J.R.R. *The Printed Word and the Common Man: Popular Culture in Ulster, 1700–1900*. Belfast: Institute of Irish Studies, 1987

Akenson, D.H. *Between Two Revolutions: Islandmagee, County Antrim, 1798–1920*. Hamden: Archon Books, 1979

– *The Church of Ireland: Ecclesiastical Reform and Revolution, 1800–1885*. New Haven and London: Yale University Press, 1971

– *God's Peoples: Covenant and Land in South Africa, Israel, and Ulster.* Montreal and Kingston: McGill-Queen's University Press, 1991

– *The Irish Education Experiment: The National System of Education in the Nineteenth Century.* Toronto: University of Toronto Press, 1970

– "The Population of the United States, 1790: A Symposium." *William and Mary Quarterly*, 3rd series, 41 (1984): 127–9

– "Pre-University Education, 1870–1921." In Vaughan, ed., *A New History of Ireland*. Vol. 6: *Ireland under the Union, 1870–1921*, 523–38

– *Small Differences: Irish Catholics and Irish Protestants, 1815–1922. An International Perspective*. Montreal and Kingston: McGill-Queen's University Press, 1988

– ed. *Canadian Papers in Rural History*, 10. Gananoque: Langdale Press, 1996

Bartlett, Thomas. "Defence, Counter-Insurgency, and Rebellion." In Bartlett and Jeffery, eds., *A Military History of Ireland*, 247–93

– "Defenders and Defenderism in 1795." Select Documents 38. *Irish Historical Studies* 24 (1985): 373–94

– "An End to Moral Economy: The Irish Militia Disturbances of 1793." In Philpin, ed., *Nationalism and Popular Protest in Ireland*, 191–218

Bartlett, Thomas, and Keith Jeffery, eds. *A Military History of Ireland*. Cambridge: Cambridge University Press, 1996

Beames, M.R. *Peasants and Power: The Whiteboy Movements and Their Control in Pre-Famine Ireland*. New York: St Martin's Press, 1983

– "The Ribbon Societies: Lower-Class Nationalism in Pre-Famine Ireland." In Philpin, ed., *Nationalism and Popular Protest in Ireland*, 245–63

Belchem, John. "'Freedom and Friendship to Ireland': Ribbonism in Early Nineteenth-Century Liverpool." *International Review of Social History* 39 (1994): 33–56

Bourke, P.M.A. *"The Visitation of God"? The Potato and the Great Irish Famine*. Dublin: Lilliput Press, 1993

Bowen, Desmond. *The Protestant Crusade in Ireland, 1800–1870*. Montreal and Kingston: McGill-Queen's University Press, 1978

– *Souperism: Myth or Reality. A Study in Souperism*. Cork: Mercier Press, 1970

Brown, Stewart J. "The New Reformation Movement in the Church of Ireland, 1801–1829." In Brown and Miller, eds., *Piety and Power in Ireland, 1760–1960*, 180–208

Brown, Stewart J., and David W. Miller, eds. *Piety and Power in Ireland, 1760–1960*. Belfast and Notre Dame: Institute of Irish Studies and University of Notre Dame Press, 2000

Brozyna, Andrea Ebel. "Female Virtue and Chastity in Pre-Famine Ireland: Kenneth Hugh Connell Revisited." In Akenson, ed., *Canadian Papers in Rural History* 10: 117–26

Budd, John W., and Timothy Guinnane. "Intentional Age-Misreporting, Age-Heaping, and the 1908 Old Age Pensions Act in Ireland." *Population Studies* 45 (1991): 497–518

Burke, Helen. *The People and the Poor Law in Nineteenth-Century Ireland*. London: Argus Press, 1987

Byrne, J. "An Impartial Account of the Late Disturbances in the County of Armagh." 1792. In Miller, ed., *Peep O'Day Boys and Defenders*, 11–108

Carleton, William. *The Autobiography of William Carleton*. London: MacGibbon and Kee, 1968

Carney, F.J. "Aspects of Pre-Famine Irish Household Size: Composition and Differentials." In Cullen and Smout, eds., *Comparative Aspects of Scottish and Irish Economic and Social History, 1600–1900*, 32–46

Carpenter, Andrew, ed. *Verse in English from Eighteenth-Century Ireland*. Cork: Cork University Press, 1998

Céitinn, Séamas. *Art Bennett and His Poetry*. Dublin: Éigse Oirialla, 1979

Chart, D.A., ed. *The Drennan Letters*. Belfast: His Majesty's Stationery Office, 1931

Clark, Samuel, and J.S. Donnelly, Jr, eds. *Irish Peasants: Violence and Political Unrest, 1780–1914*. Wisconsin: University of Wisconsin Press, 1983

– "The Unreaped Harvest." In Clark and Donnelly, eds., *Irish Peasants: Violence and Political Unrest, 1780–1914*, 419–33

Clarke, Brian P. *Piety and Nationalism: Lay Voluntary Associations and the Creation of an Irish-Catholic Community in Toronto, 1850–1895*. Montreal and Kingston: McGill-Queen's University Press, 1993

Clarkson, L.A. "Household and Family Structure in Armagh City, 1770." *Local Population Studies* 20 (1978): 20–3

– "Irish Population Revisited, 1687–1821." In Goldstrom and Clarkson, eds., *Irish Population, Economy, and Society*, 13–36

Coigly, James. *Life of the Reverend James Coigly*. London, 1798

Collins, Peter. *Pathways to Ulster's Past: Sources and Resources for Local Studies*. Belfast: Institute of Irish Studies, 1998

Conley, Caroline. *Melancholy Accidents: The Meaning of Violence in Post-Famine Ireland*. Lanham: Lexington Books, 1999

Connell, K.H. *The Population of Ireland, 1750–1845*. Oxford: Clarendon Press, 1950

Connell, Paul. *Parson, Priest, and Master: National Education in Co. Meath, 1824–41*. Dublin: Irish Academic Press, 1995

Connell, Paul, Denis Cronin, and Brian O Dalaigh, eds. *Irish Townlands: Studies in Local History*. Dublin: Four Courts Press, 1998

Connolly, S.J. *Priests and People in Pre-famine Ireland, 1780–1845*. New York: St Martin's Press, 1982

Coote, Charles. *Statistical Survey of the County of Armagh, with Observation on the Means of Improvement, Drawn up in the Years 1802, and 1803, for the Consideration, and under the Direction of the Dublin Society*. Dublin, 1804

Corry, John. *Odes and Elegies Descriptive and Sentimental with The Patriot: A Poem*. Newry, 1797

Crawford, E. Margaret. "Dietary Considerations in Pre-Famine Louth and Its Environs." In Gillespie and O'Sullivan, eds., *The Borderlands*, 107–27

Crawford, W.H. *The Handloom Weavers and the Ulster Linen Industry*. Belfast: Ulster Historical Foundation, 1994

– "The Linen Triangle in the 1790s." In *The Turbulent Decade*, 43–53

– "The Reshaping of the Borderlands, 1700–1840." In Gillespie and O'Sullivan, eds., *The Borderlands*, 93–105

Crawford, W.H., and R.H. Foy, ed. *Townlands in Ulster: Local History Studies*. Belfast: Ulster Historical Foundation, 1998

Cullen, L.M. "Late Eighteenth-Century Politicization in Ireland." In *Culture et pratiques politiques en France et en Irlande, XVIe–XVIIIe siècle*

– "The Political Structures of the Defenders." In Gough and Dickson, eds., *Ireland and the French Revolution*, 117–38

– "The Political Troubles of County Armagh: A Comment." *Irish Economic and Social History* 23 (1996): 18–23

– "The United Irishmen: Problems and Issues of the 1790s." In *The Turbulent Decade*, 7–27

Cullen, L.M., and T.C. Smout, eds., *Comparative Aspects of Scottish and Irish Economic and Social History, 1600–1900*. Edinburgh: John Donald Publishers, 1977

Culture et pratiques politiques en France et en Irlande, XVIe–XVIIIe siècle: actes du colloque de Marseille, 28 septembre – 2 octobre 1988. Paris: Centre de Recherches Historiques, 1988

Curtin, Nancy. *The United Irishmen: Popular Politics in Ulster and Dublin, 1791–1798*. Oxford: Clarendon Press, 1994

Dallas, Alexander. *The Story of the Irish Church Missions*. London, 1867

Danaher, Kevin. *The Year in Ireland: Irish Calendar Customs*. Dublin: Mercier Press, 1972

Darroch, A. Gordon, and Michael D. Ornstein. "Ethnicity and Occupational Structure in Canada in 1871: The Vertical Mosaic in Historical Perspective." *Canadian Historical Review* 61 (1980): 305–33

Davies, Simon. "The *Northern Star* and the Propagation of Enlightened Ideas." *Eighteenth-Century Ireland* 5 (1990): 143–52

Day, Angélique, and Patrick McWilliams, eds. *Ordnance Survey Memoirs of Ireland: Parishes of County Armagh, 1835–8*. Belfast: Institute of Irish Studies, 1990

de Ris, Sean. *Peadar O'Doirnin: a bheatha agus a shaothar.* Baile Atha Cliath: Oifig an tSolathair, 1969

Dewar, M.W. *Orangeism: A New Historical Appreciation.* Vol. 1. Belfast: Grand Orange Lodge of Ireland, 1969

Dickson, David. "Taxation and Disaffection in Late Eighteenth-Century Ireland." In Clark and Donnelly, eds., *Irish Peasants: Violence and Political Unrest*, 37–63

Dickson, David, Daire Keogh, and Kevin Whelan, eds. *The United Irishmen: Republicanism, Radicalism, and Rebellion.* Dublin: Lilliput Press, 1993

Digest of Evidence Taken before Her Majesty's Commissioners of Inquiry into the State of the Law and Practice in Respect of the Occupation of Land in Ireland. Vol. 1. Dublin: Alexander Thom, 1847

Donaldson, J. *Historical and Statistical Account of the Barony of Upper Fews.* Dundalk, 1844

Donnelly Jr., J.S. "Excess Mortality and Emigration." In Vaughan, ed., *A New History of Ireland.* Vol. 5: *Ireland Under the Union*, 350–71

– "Pastorini and Captain Rock: Millenarianism and Sectarianism in the Rockite Movement of 1821–4." In Clark and Donnelly, *Irish Peasants: Violence and Political Unrest*, 102–39

Dowling, P.J. *The Hedge Schools of Ireland.* Cork: Mercier Press, 1968

Duffy, R. Quinn. "Redmond O'Hanlon and the Outlaws of Ulster." *History Today* 32 (August 1982): 12–13

Edwards, R. Dudley, and T. Desmond Williams, eds. *The Great Famine: Studies in Irish History, 1845–52*. Dublin: Lilliput Press, 1994

Elliott, Marianne. *The Catholics of Ulster: A History.* London: Penguin, 2000

– "The Defenders in Ulster." In Dickson, Keogh, and Whelan, eds., *The United Irishmen*, 222–33

– *Partners in Revolution: The United Irishmen and France.* New Haven: Yale University Press, 1982

Farrell, Sean. *Rituals and Riots: Sectarian Violence and Political Culture in Ulster, 1784–1886*. Kentucky: University Press of Kentucky, 2000

Foster, R.F. *The Irish Story: Telling Tales and Making It Up in Ireland.* London: Allen Lane, 2001

– *Modern Ireland, 1600–1972*. London: Viking Penguin, 1988

Gamble, John. *Sketches of History, Politics, and Manners, in Dublin, and the North of Ireland, in 1810*. London: Baldwin, Craddock and Joy, 1826

Garnham, Neal. "How Violent Was Eighteenth-Century Ireland?" *Irish Historical Studies* 30 (1997): 377–92

Garvin, Tom. "Defenders, Ribbonmen, and Others: Underground Political Networks in Pre-Famine Ireland." In Philpin, ed., *Nationalism and Popular Protest in Ireland*, 219–44

– *Nationalist Revolutionaries in Ireland, 1858 to 1928*. Oxford: Clarendon Press, 1987

Gillespie, Raymond. "An Historian and the Locality." In Gillespie and Hill, eds. *Doing Irish Local History*, 7–23

– "The Transformation of the Borderlands, 1600–1700." In Gillespie and O'Sullivan, eds., *The Borderlands*, 75–92

Gillespie, Raymond, and Harold O'Sullivan, eds. *The Borderlands: Essays on the History of the Ulster-Leinster Border.* Belfast: Institute of Irish Studies, 1989

Gillespie, Raymond, and Myrtle Hill, eds. *Doing Irish Local History: Pursuit and Practice.* Belfast: Institute of Irish Studies, 1998

Glass, D.V., and P.A.M. Taylor. *Population and Emigration: Government and Society in Nineteenth-Century Britain. Commentaries on British Parliamentary Papers.* Dublin: Irish University Press, 1976

Goldstrom, J.M., and L.A. Clarkson, eds. *Irish Population, Economy, and Society: Essays in Honour of the Late K.H. Connell.* Oxford: Clarendon Press, 1981

Gough, Hugh, and David Dickson, eds. *Ireland and the French Revolution.* Dublin: Irish Academic Press, 1990

Gowan, Ogle Robert. *Orangeism: Its Origin and History.* Toronto, 1859

Gray, Jane. "Rural Industry and Uneven Development: The Significance of Gender in the Irish Linen Industry." *Journal of Peasant Studies* 20 (1993): 590–611

Gregory, Brad S. "*Is* Small Beautiful? Microhistory and the History of Everyday Life. A Review Essay." *History and Theory* 28, no. 1 (1999): 100–10

Guinnane, Timothy W. *The Vanishing Irish: Households, Migration, and the Rural Economy in Ireland, 1850–1914*. Princeton: Princeton University Press, 1997

Hammel, E.A., and Peter Laslett. "Comparing Household Structure over Time and between Cultures: A Suggested Scheme for Representation and Classification with a Provision for Handling by Computer." *Comparative Studies in Society and History* 16 (1974): 80–103

Harnden, Toby. *Bandit Country: The IRA and South Armagh*. London: Hodder and Stoughton, 1999

Hempton, David, and Myrtle Hill. *Evangelical Protestantism in Ulster Society, 1740–1890*. London and New York: Routledge, 1992

Henderson, Reverend Henry. *The True Heir of Ballymore*. n.p., n.d

Hill, George. *The Plantation in Ulster, 1608–1620*. Belfast, 1877

Hirst, Catherine. *Religion, Politics, and Violence in Nineteenth-Century Belfast: The Pound and Sandy Row.* Dublin: Four Courts Press, 2002

Hobsbawm, Eric. *Bandits*. Middlesex: Penguin Books, 1985

Hollingsworth, T.H. *Historical Demography*. Ithaca: Cornell University Press, 1969

Hoppen, K. Theodore. *Elections, Politics, and Society in Ireland, 1832–1885*. Oxford: Clarendon Press, 1984

Hoskins, W.G. *Local History in England*. London: William Clowes, 1959

Hughes, A.J. "Anecdotes Relating to Peadar O Doirnin and Cormac na gCeann." *Seanchas Ardmhacha: Journal of the Armagh Diocesan Historical Society* 12 (1987): 128–37

– "Gaelic Poets and Scribes of the South Armagh Hinterland in the Eighteenth and Nineteenth Centuries." In Hughes and Nolan, eds. *Armagh: History and Society*

– *Robert Shipboy MacAdam (1808–95): His Life and Gaelic Proverb Collection*. Belfast: Institute of Irish Studies, 1998

Hughes, A.J., and William Nolan, eds. *Armagh: History and Society. Interdisciplinary Essays on the History of an Irish County*. Dublin: Geography Publications, 2001

Jordan, Donald. *Land and Popular Politics in Ireland: County Mayo from the Plantation to the Land War*. Cambridge: Cambridge University Press, 1994

Keating, James. "Art Bennett and the Bible." *Mullaghbawn Historical and Folklore Society Journal* 2 (1974)

Kelleher, Margaret. *The Feminization of Famine: Expressions of the Inexpressible?* Cork: Cork University Press, 1997

Keneally, Christine, and Trevor Parkhill, eds. *The Famine in Ulster: The Regional Impact*. Belfast: Ulster Historical Foundation, 1997

Kennedy, Liam, Paul S. Ell, E.M. Crawford, and L.A. Clarkson. *Mapping the Great Irish Famine*. Dublin: Four Courts Press, 1999

Keogh, Daire. *A Patriot Priest: The Life of Father James Coigly, 1761–1798*. Cork: Cork University Press, 1998

Larkin, Emmet. "The Devotional Revolution in Ireland, 1850–75." *American Historical Review* 77 (1972): 625–52

Larkin, Emmet, and Herman Freudenberger, ed. *A Redemptorist Missionary in Ireland, 1851–1854: Memoirs by Joseph Prost*. Cork: Cork University Press, 1998

Lecky, W.E.H. *A History of Ireland in the Eighteenth Century*. London: Longmans, Green, 1892

Lee, Joseph. "On the Accuracy of the Pre-Famine Irish Censuses." In Goldstrom and Clarkson, eds., *Irish Population, Economy, and Society*, 37–56

– "The Ribbonmen." In Williams, ed., *Secret Societies in Ireland*, 26–35

Leslie, J.B. *Armagh Clergy and Parishes*. Dundalk: William Tempest, 1911

Lewis, George Cornewall. *On Local Disturbances in Ireland*. London: B. Fellowes, 1836

Lewis, Samuel. *Topographical Dictionary of Ireland*. London, 1849

Lyons, F.S.L. *Ireland since the Famine.* London: Fontana Press, 1985

MacAtasney, Gerard. *The Famine in Lurgan/Portadown.* Belfast: Beyond the Pale Publications, 1997

– *"This Dreadful Visitation": The Famine in Lurgan/Portadown.* Belfast: Beyond the Pale Publications, 1997

McBride, Ian, ed. *History and Memory in Modern Ireland.* New York: Cambridge University Press, 2001

MacDonagh, Oliver. "The Economy and Society, 1830–45." In Vaughan, ed., *A New History of Ireland.* Vol. 5: *Ireland under the Union, 1801–1870,* 218–41

– "Politics, 1830–45." In Vaughan, ed., *A New History of Ireland.* Vol. 5: *Ireland under the Union, 1801–1870,* 169–92

McDowell, R.B. *The Irish Administration, 1801–1914.* London: Routledge and Kegan Paul, 1964

McEvoy, Brendan. "Father James Quigley: Priest of Armagh and United Irishman." *Seanchas Ardmhacha: Journal of the Armagh Diocesan Historical Society* 5, no. 2 (1970): 247–68

– "The Peep of Day Boys and Defenders in County Armagh." *Seanchas Ardmhacha: Journal of the Armagh Diocesan Historical Society* 12 (1986–87)

Mac Giolla Choille, Breandan. "Fenians, Rice, and Ribbonmen in County Monaghan, 1864–67." *Clogher Record* 6 (1967): 221–52

McHugh, Roger. "The Famine in Irish Oral Tradition." In Edwards and Williams, eds., *The Great Famine,* 391–436

McKeown, Thomas. "The Wounding of Meredith Chambré." *Mullaghbawn Historical and Folklore Society Journal* (Newry), 3 (1979)

McMahon, Kevin. "Agrarian Disturbances around Crossmaglen, 1835–1855." *Seanchas Ardmhacha: Journal of the Armagh Diocesan Historical Society* 9 (1979): 302–32

"The 'Crossmaglen Conspiracy' Case, Part I." *Seanchas Ardmhacha: Journal of the Armagh Diocesan Historical Society* 6, no. 2 (1972): 251–86; 7, no. 1 (1973): 65–107; 7, no. 2 (1974): 326–59

– "The O'Hanlon Letter." *Seanchas Ardmhacha: Journal of the Armagh Diocesan Historical Society* 10, no.1 (1980–81): 37–41

McManus, Antonia. *The Irish Hedge School and Its Books, 1695–1831.* Dublin: Four Courts Press, 2002

Mac Suibhne, Breandan, and David Dickson, eds. *The Outer Edge of Ulster: A Memoir of Social Life in Nineteenth-Century Donegal.* Dublin: Lilliput Press, 2000

Madden, R.R. *Antrim and Down in '98.* London, 1860

Magennis, Eoin. "A 'Presbyterian Insurrection'? Reconsidering the Hearts of Oak Disturbances of July 1763." *Irish Historical Studies* 31 (1998): 165–87

Mason, William Shaw. *A Statistical Account or Parochial Survey of Ireland.* Vol. 2. Dublin, 1814–1819

M.-F., W.T., ed. *Irish Rural Life and Industry, with Suggestions for the Future.* Dublin: Hely's, 1907

Miller, David. "The Armagh Troubles, 1784–95." In Clark and Donnelly, eds., *Irish Peasants: Violence and Political Unrest*, 155–91

– *Peep O'Day Boys and Defenders: Selected Documents on the County Armagh Disturbances, 1784–96*. Belfast: Public Records Office of Northern Ireland, 1990

– "Politicisation in Revolutionary Ireland: The Case of the Armagh Troubles." *Irish Economic and Social History* 23 (1996): 1–17

Morash, Christopher. *Writing the Irish Famine*. Oxford: Clarendon Press, 1995

Murray, A.C. "Agrarian Violence and Nationalism in Nineteenth-Century Ireland: The Myth of Ribbonism." *Irish Economic and Social History* 13 (1986): 56–73

Murray, L.P. "Shanroe Barrack, Mullaghbawn (1795–1821)." *Journal of the County Louth Archaeological Society* 9, no. 1 (1937)

Musgrave, Richard. *Memoirs of the Different Rebellions in Ireland*. Dublin, 1801

Nicholas, Stephen, and Richard H. Steckel. "Tall but Poor: The Living Standards of Men and Women in Pre-Famine Ireland." *Journal of European Economic History* 26 (1997): 105–34

Nolan, William. *Fassidinin: Land, Settlement, and Society in Southeast Ireland, 1600–1850*. Dublin: Geography Publications, 1979

Nolan, William, and Kevin Whelan, eds. *Kilkenny: History and Society. Interdisciplinary Essays on the History of an Irish County*. Dublin: Geography Publications, 1980

O'Ciardha, Eamonn. "Toryism and Rappareeism in County Armagh in the Late Seventeenth Century." In Hughes and Nolan, eds., *Armagh: History and Society*

O'Ciosain, Niall. "Famine Memory and the Popular Representation of Scarcity." In McBride, ed., *History and Memory in Modern Ireland*, 95–117

– *Print and Popular Culture in Ireland, 1750–1850*. London: Macmillan, 1997

O Cuiv, Brian. "Irish Language and Literature, 1845–1921." In Vaughan, ed. *A New History of Ireland*. Vol. 6. *Ireland under the Union, 1870–1921*, 385–435

O'Dea, Kevin, and Kevin Whelan, eds. *Nations and Nationalisms: France, Britain, Ireland, and the Eighteenth-Century Context*. Oxford: Voltaire Foundation, 1995

O'Fiaich, Thomas. "Parish Priests of Mullaghbawn." *Mullaghbawn Historical and Folklore Society Journal* (Newry), 2 (1974)

O'Grada, Cormac. *Black '47 and Beyond: The Great Irish Famine in History, Economy, and Memory*. New Jersey: Princeton University Press, 1999

O'Hanrahan, Michael. "The Tithe War in County Kilkenny, 1830–1834." In Nolan and Whelan, eds., *Kilkenny: History and Society*, 481–505

O'Kane, David, ed. *Statistical Report of the Parishes of Ballinascreen, Kilcronaghan, Desertmartin, Banagher, Dungiven and Boveva in the County of Londonderry by John Mac Closkey, 1821*. Ballinascreen: Ballinascreen Historical Society, 1983

O'Kane, Louis. *Lower Killevy, Ireland. Outlines of Their History*. Newry: Edward Hodgett, 1955

– "A Statistical Return of Armagh Diocese in 1836." *Seanchas Ardmhacha: Journal of the Armagh Diocesan Historical Society* 3 (1958): 181–9

O'Mordha, Seamus. "Arthur Bennett's Correspondence with Robert S. MacAdam." *Seanchas Ardmhacha: Journal of the Armagh Diocesan Historical Society* 2 (1957)

O'Muiri, Reamonn. "Rural Deanery of Creggan, 1798." *Creggan* 1 (1989)

O'Neill, Kevin. *Family and Farm in Pre-Famine Ireland: The Parish of Killashandra*. Wisconsin: University of Wisconsin Press, 1984

Orangeism in Ireland and Throughout the Empire. Vol. 1. London: Thynne, 193–

O'Snodaigh, Peadar. *Hidden Ulster: Protestants and the Irish Language*. Belfast: Lagan Press, 1995

O'Sullivan, Harold. "Land Confiscations and Plantations in County Armagh." In Hughes and Nolan, eds., *Armagh: History and Society*, 333–80

O'Tuathail, Eamonn. "The Bennett Family of Forkhill, Co. Armagh." *The Irish Book Lover* 22 (1934)

Philpin, C.H.E., ed. *Nationalism and Popular Protest in Ireland*. Cambridge: Cambridge University Press, 1987

Pollard, H.B. *The Secret Societies of Ireland, Their Rise and Progress*. London: P. Allan, 1922

Quinlan, Tom. "The Registered Papers of the Chief Secretary's Office." *Irish Archives* (Autumn 1994): 5–21

Rafferty, Oliver P. *Catholicism in Ulster, 1603–1983*. London: Hurst and Company, 1994

Repealer Repulsed! A Correct Narrative of the Rise and Progress of the Repeal Invasion of Ulster. Belfast: William McComb, 1841

Report of the Trial of Richard Jones, Who Was Charged with Being a Member of an Illegal Society ... Taken in Shorthand by Andrew Bourne. Dublin: Hodges and Smith, 1840

Roberts, Paul E.W. "Caravats and Shanavests: Whiteboyism and Faction Fighting in East Munster, 1802–11." In Clark and Donnelly, eds., *Irish Peasants: Violence and Political Unrest*, 64–101

Robinson, Philip. *The Plantation of Ulster: British Settlement in an Irish Landscape, 1600–1670*. Dublin: Gill and Macmillan, 1984

Scally, Robert. *The End of Hidden Ireland: Rebellion, Famine, and Emigration.* Oxford: Oxford University Press, 1995

Seaver, George. *History of the Seaver Family.* Dundalk: Dundalgan Press, 1950

Secret Committee of the Lords. *Statement of the Origins and Progress of the Societies of United Irishmen.* Dublin, 1798

Senior, Hereward. *Orangeism in Ireland and Britain, 1795–1836.* London: Routledge, 1966

Sherry, Bryan, ed. *Along the Black Pig's Dyke: Folklore from Monaghan and South Armagh.* Castleblayney: Castle Printing, 1993

Simmons, D.A. *A List of Peculiar Words and Phrases (Armagh and Donegal).* Dublin, n.d.

Smyth, Jim. *The Men of No Property: Irish Radicals and Popular Politics in the Late Eighteenth-Century.* London: Macmillan, 1992

Sobek, Matthew. "Work, Status, and Income: Men in the Occupational Structure in the Late Nineteenth Century." *Social Science History* 20, no. 2 (1996): 169–208

Soltow, Lee. "Age and Economic Achievement in an Irish Barony in 1821." *Explorations in Economic History* 18 (1981): 389–98

Stewart, A.T.Q. *The Narrow Ground: Aspects of Ulster, 1609–1969.* London: Faber and Faber, 1977

– *The Shape of Irish History.* Montreal and Kingston: McGill-Queen's University Press, 2001

Story, George. *An Impartial History of the Wars of Ireland.* London, 1693

Study Committee of the Office of the Foreign Secretary of the National Academy of Sciences. *Rapid Population Growth: Consequences and Policy Implications.* Vol. 2: *Research Papers.* Baltimore: Johns Hopkins Press, 1971

Sullivan, A.M. *New Ireland.* London: Low, Marston, Searle, & Rivington, 1877

Trench, William Steuart. *Realities of Irish Life.* London: Longmans, Green, 1870

The Turbulent Decade: Ulster in the 1790s. Belfast: Federation of Ulster Local Studies, 1997

Vaughan, W.E. *Landlords and Tenants in Mid-Victorian Ireland.* Oxford: Clarendon Press, 1994

– ed., *A New History of Ireland.* Vol. 5. *Ireland under the Union, 1801–1870.* Oxford: Clarendon Press, 1989

– *A New History of Ireland.* Vol. 6. *Ireland under the Union, 1870–1921.* Oxford: Clarendon Press, 1996

Vaughan, W.E., and A.E. Fitzpatrick, eds. *Irish Historical Statistics: Population, 1821–1971.* Dublin: Royal Irish Academy, 1978

Walsh, Una, and Kevin Murphy, eds. *Kick Any Stone: Townlands, People, and Stories of Forkhill Parish.* Jordanstown: O'Donnell Press, 2003

Whelan, Kevin. *The Tree of Liberty: Radicalism, Catholicism, and the Construction of Irish Identity, 1760–1830.* Cork: Cork University Press, 1996

– "United and Disunited Irishmen: The Discourse of Sectarianism in the 1790s." In O'Dea and Whelan, eds., *Nations and Nationalisms*, 231–47

Williams, T.D, ed. *Secret Societies in Ireland*. Dublin: Gill and Macmillan, 1973

Wilson, David A. *United Irishmen, United States: Immigrant Radicals in the Early Republic*. Ithaca: Cornell University Press, 1998

Wright, Frank. *Two Lands on One Soil: Ulster Politics before Home Rule*. Dublin: Gill and Macmillan, 1996

Young, Robert M. *Ulster in '98: Episodes and Anecdotes*. Belfast: Marcus Ward, 1893

Index

Act of Union (1800), 28
agriculture, 52–62. *See also* occupations
Alexander, Henry, 117, 127, 129–30, 135
Alexander, Nathaniel, 103
Ancient British Fencibles, 38–9
Armagh (county), 3–5, 10–11, 18–19, 26, 31–43, 54, 73–4, 80–1, 86–7, 90, 99–100, 103, 126, 133, 145
– south: Defenders, 19, 21, 28; disturbances, 3–5, 82–3, 91–3, 104–7, 110–13, 115–17, 147–8; education, 65–6, 70, 77; famine, 121, 126–8, 135–6, 138; language, 80–1; mission, 155; social conditions, 123–5
Armagh Disturbances, 3–5, 13–14, 18–19, 23–4, 28, 42, 54, 67, 170n41
Armagh (town), 86, 132, 160
Atkinson, Rev. Charles, 99, 142, 160
Aughadanove, 67
Aughanduff, 90

Balleek, 82
Ballykeel, 117, 139
Balmer, Robert, 46–7, 59
Barton, Susanna, 12, 15, 37, 39, 43, 161
Begley, Andrew, 102–3
Belfast, 12, 13, 29, 34, 40, 86, 103, 134
Belmont Barracks, 21, 37–8, 43, 175n51, 188n9, 215n4
Bennet, John, 17–18
Bennett, Arthur, 117, 127, 139–40, 146–7, 151–4, 211n137, 213n31
Beresford, J.G., 78
Berkley, Alexander: attack on (1791), 2–5, 23–7, 34, 37, 67, 111, 156–9, 172n70, 173n79; and Defenders, 17, 24–7; pension, 173n78; as schoolmaster, 2, 24, 67
Bernard, Maj. Arthur A., 89, 100, 106, 123–6, 133
Berry, Francis, 111–12, 201n212–13
Best, Robert, 17, 21, 22
Bourke, P.M.A., 123
brat Bríde, 96–7
Brooks, Thomas, 117–18
Brunswick Clubs, 73–4
Burgess, John, 35, 68
Byrne, J., 12, 23–4, 67, 96

Camlough, 99, 112
Campbell, Rev. James, 61, 102, 144, 182n51; and famine relief, 129, 133; national schools dispute, 75–8; rent strike, 103–4; tithe agitation, 89–91
Carrickasticken, 92, 109
Carriff, 59, 92
Catholic Committee, 29–30
Catholic convention (1792), 29–30, 34
Catholic emancipation (1829), 73–4, 89
Catholics/Catholicism, 3–9, 18–19, 41–2, 83–5, 99–100, 144–55; baptisms, 133; Catholic chapel, 101, 155, 215n64; clergy, 33–5, 61, 64, 71, 75–8, 114, 145–6; education, 64–78; experience of famine, 133–7, 139–40; faction fighting, 101; family size, 48–52, 62, 158; farm size, 52–4, 62, 158;

literacy, 78–80; marriages, 134; missions, 113–14, 154–5; occupations, 54–8, 60–1; penal laws, 29–30, 65–6, 73–4; population, 7, 47–8, 152, 214n49–50; settlement of estate (1790s), 13–16; social profile, 48–64; souperism, 135–7, 142–5, 159–60. *See also* disturbances; sectarianism; tithe agitation
census (1821): of Forkhill, 8, 45–63, 109, 161, 178n13; of Ireland, 45–8
Chambré, Hunt Walsh, 74–5, 84–5, 89, 100, 110–11, 117, 145, 201n209, 210n108
Chambré, Meredith, 110–12, 136, 201n206, 201n211
Charlemont, Earl of, 3, 4, 13–14, 15, 32, 34
cholera, 138–9
Church Missionary Society, 142
Church of Ireland. *See* Protestants/Protestantism
Cloghinny, 108, 109
Coigly, Rev. James, 24, 32, 34–5, 39
Connell, K.H., 122
Connory, Laurence, 17–18, 25
County Armagh. *See* Armagh (county)
Creggan: Catholic mission, 155; disturbances, 20, 83, 99, 106, 116, 147; education, 66, 70; and famine, 124, 128; language, 80
Crossmaglen, 5, 97, 112, 124, 135, 155
Cullaville, 36
Cullen, L.M., 9, 18–19, 24, 34–5, 170n45
Cullen, Rev. William, 34
Curtin, Nancy, 35

Dallas, Rev. Alexander, 143–4
Dawson, James, 36, 61, 82–4, 182n50
Dawson, Walter, 105, 136
Defenders: in Forkhill, 2–5, 13–14, 17–18, 21–7, 38, 43, 152, 156–8; historiography of, 18–19, 41–2, 114–15; nature and aims, 19–21, 31, 86, 96; origins, 18–19; politicization of, 29–30, 34; Regenerated Defenders, 82, 157, 188n2; and United Irishmen, 29–34, 41–2
Derry, Valentine, 34
Devon Commission, 104–6, 198n174
Dick, John, 17–18, 21–3
Dickson, Samuel, 35, 67–8
diet, 122–4, 127–8
disease. *See* health
disturbances: estate settlement (1790s), 2–5, 13–14, 16–27, 34, 67, 152, 157, 169n31, 172n70, 173n79, 183n16, 188n1; faction fights, 100–3; famine-related, 128, 132–3; historiography of, 114–15, 170n45; land-related, 103–9, 115; post-famine, 109–14, 200n204; and ribbonism, 85–8, 95–8, 102–3, 108–9, 112–14, 116–17; and Scripture readers, 147–8, 213n36; and tithe agitation, 84–5, 88–100, 157; and United Irish movement, 36–43, 147, 157
Dixon, Rev. Dr Joseph, 78, 155
Dixon, William Steele, 35
Donaldson, William, 40
Donnelly, Michael, 17–18, 24, 25
Drennan, William, 4, 29, 35
Drumintee, 110–11, 114, 149
Dublin, 86, 103, 134
Duncan, William, 17, 21–5
Dundalk, 4, 12, 23, 40, 41, 74

education, 64–81; Catholic grievances, 71–2, 75–6; Forkhill charity schools, 12, 61, 64–71, 75, 77–8, 81, 158–60; hedge schools, 65–6; inquiry into (1806–14), 69; national schools, 64, 75–8; and penal laws, 65–6; royal commission (1824), 69–71
emigration, 51, 125, 206n38
English language. *See* language

faction fighting, 96, 100–3, 108, 195n133–4
family size, 48–52, 62, 158. *See also* household structure
famine (1845–49), 109, 111, 121–41, 143–4, 154, 159; and birth rate, 133–4; deaths, 128, 137–8, 210n114; and diseases, 130–1, 137–9; disturbances, 128, 132–3; evictions, 135; popular response to, 131–5, 154; population decline, 121, 137–9; public works, 129–30; relief efforts, 127–31, 142, 159, 209n102; social dislocation, 134–5; souperism, 135–7; soup kitchens, 131–2

farming. *See* occupations
farm size, 52–5, 62, 158
Fews, Upper and Lower, 40, 65–6, 83, 128, 133
Fine Morning. *See* faction fighting
Finnegan, Rev. James, 145, 151,
folklore, 103, 111, 135–8, 156, 159, 204n1, 210n114, 212n16. *See also* songs
Forkhill: baptisms, 133–4; Belmont Barracks, 21, 37–8, 43, 188n9; Catholic chapel and church, 155; census (1821), 8, 45–63, 109, 161, 178n13; charity schools, 12, 61, 64–71, 75, 77–8, 81, 158–60; and Church of Ireland, 12, 42, 61, 142, 144, 147, 150–2; clothing, 125; constabulary, 90–1, 127, 133; diet, 122–4, 127–8; dispensary, 61, 124–5, 128; education, 64–81; famine, 121–41, 154, 159–60; Forkhill Lodge, 42; housing, 125; land system, 48–55, 103–9; loan society, 160; manor court, 118; market, 11–12; marriages, 133–4; petty sessions court, 117–19, 145, 204n241; population, 7, 15, 47–8, 109, 152, 214n49–50; religious disputes, 142–55; social conditions, 10, 123–6; social profile, 48–64; yeomanry, 36–7, 42, 157
Forkhill charities. *See* Jackson, Richard
Forkhill estate: improvements, 11–13; leasing of lands, 3, 13–16, 21, 53–4, 104; legal disputes, 103, 197n158, 197n160; purchase by Richard Jackson, 8–10; rents, 104–5, 123, 135; settlement, 3, 7, 13–16, 21, 152, 158; trustees of, 3–4, 12–13, 35, 44, 67, 69, 75, 77, 90, 128, 129, 131, 135, 160, 209n102, 215n64, 217n21
Forkhill Relief Committee, 126–7, 128–31, 136, 207n46, 210n113
fosterage, 51, 60, 62, 124
Foxall, John, 100, 117, 127
Foxall, Powell, 100
French Revolution, 28–9, 31–2

Gartlany, Hugh, 146
Gillespie, Raymond, 7
Gosford, Earl of, 18, 83, 97
Gracey, Thomas, 89–91, 94
Hamilton, Alexander, 37
Hanlon, John, 17–18
Hanlon, Redmond, 101
Hanratty, Felix, 76
Hanratty, Loughlin, 102
health: disease, 127–8, 130–1, 137–9; Forkhill dispensary, 61, 124–5; Jackson charitable trust and, 12, 160, 205n24; medical ailments, 124–5, 133–4; women's, 55, 125, 133–4
Hearts of Oak. *See* Oakboys
hedge schools. *See* education
Hobsbawm, Eric, 20–1
Hoey, John, 41
Hope, James, 33
household structure, 48–51. *See also* family size
Hudson, Rev. Edward: and Alexander Berkley, 2–4, 27, 157; and charity schools, 24, 67; and James Coigly, 177n75; life, 165n1; and Defenders, 17–22; and Orangeism, 216n9; and political agitation, 32–4, 41; settlement of estate, 12–16, 152
Hughes, Rev. Nicholas, 61, 114, 155

illegitimacy, 59, 182n41
informers, 22, 25–7, 41, 43, 85, 88, 176n67
Irish Folklore Commission, 111, 135–8
Irish language. *See* language
Irish Society, 142–7
Irish Volunteers, 19, 21, 28, 30

Jackson, Richard: charitable trust, 12, 45, 56, 124, 129, 135, 152, 158–61, 181n39, 205n24, 216n16; charity schools, 12, 61, 64–71, 75, 77–8, 81, 158–60; Church of Ireland, 150–1, 214n47; and Forkhill estate, 10–13, 19, 21, 43–4; life of, 167n7; will of, 12, 24, 67, 75
Johnston, Arthur, 76, 89, 99, 191n57
Jonesborough, 19, 32, 35, 93, 135
Jordan, Christopher, 118–19

Keady, 92–3, 94, 96, 97, 147
Kelly, Edward, 102–3
Kildare Place Society, 70, 71–3, 77, 80, 142, 184n33

Killeavy: Chambré family, 74, 110, 112, 145; disturbances, 82, 85, 93, 117, 147; education, 66, 70; famine, 124, 135; Heath Hall, 140; land, 104–5
Knox, Gen., 36–7, 39, 41

Lake, Gen. Gerard, 32, 36, 38
Lamb, Rev. Patrick, 146, 153
land: inheritance patterns, 49–51; landholding system, 48–55, 103–9, 123; leases (1790s), 13–16; leases (1830s), 105; and outrages, 103–9, 115. *See also* Devon Commission; disturbances; Forkhill estate; occupations; outrages; ribbonism
language: English, 12, 24, 80–1, 118; Irish, 24, 77, 80–1, 119, 139, 142–3, 147, 151, 153, 187n94
Lappin, Thomas, 38
Lecky, W.E.H., 18, 22, 94
Lennon, Rev. Michael, 104–5, 124, 128, 198n167, 201n207
Lewis, George Cornewall, 20, 22, 25–6, 87, 94, 98
Lewis, Samuel, 7, 182n53
linen industry: in Armagh, 18–19, 54; in Forkhill, 12, 15–16, 54, 56–8, 62, 123–4, 158, 182n53
literacy, 78–80, 187n85
London Hibernian Society, 72, 142
Longfield, 61, 68
Loughgall, 31, 132
Loughgilly, 34, 36

MacAdam, Robert, 127, 139, 153–4, 213n31
Macan, Catherine, 91–2
Macan, Owen, 90–2, 94, 102, 196n148
MacCumaigh, Art, 150
MacDonagh, Rev. Paul, 34
McElevy, Ferdinand, 17–18, 21
McElevy, Patrick, 17–18
McGill, Hugh and Peter, 85, 88, 93, 95, 102–3, 108–9, 119–20, 189n22, 200n196
McIvor, Rev. Nicholas, 61, 155, 186n60, 215n66
McNeal, Archibald, 102–3
McParlan, Rev., 130, 140
McShane, Rev. Charles, 146, 151
Madden, R.R., 33
Maginnis, Edward Augustus, 154
Malone, Rev. James, 114
Maphoner, 89; national school at, 76–7
Marmion, Anthony, 41
medicine. *See* health
Meigh, 118, 124
Methodist chapel, 7, 59, 149, 159
Miller, David, 18–19, 54
Mitchel, John, 140, 154
Morris, James, 93–5. *See also* tithe
Mullaghbawn: Catholic chapel at, 101, 155; Catholic mission (1864), 114; disturbances, 23–4, 92, 117, 133, 136; schools, 67–8, 77–8; public house, 102
Mulligan, Rev. Hugh, 78, 140, 149, 186n60
Murdock, Alexander, 118
Murdock, Archibald, 89–90
Murphy, Laurence, 25, 27
Murphy, Michael J., 103, 156, 159, 204n1, 210n114, 212n16
Murphy, Peter, 25, 27
Murphy, Thomas, 25, 27
Musgrave, Richard, 4, 16, 21, 23, 156–7

national schools. *See* education
Newry, 43, 76, 82, 96, 132, 140; and United Irishmen, 36, 37, 39; workhouse, 126, 130–1, 138
Newry Telegraph, 90, 93, 95, 102, 111, 146
Newtownhamilton, 33, 35, 37, 39, 82–3, 126, 127, 132
Northern Star, 30, 32–3, 36
Nugent, Gen., 40

Oakboys, 20, 22, 43, 88
O'Callaghan, James, 113
occupations, 54–62, 181n38; agricultural industry, 52–7, 60; household service, 59–60; linen industry, 12, 15–16, 18–19, 54, 56–8, 62, 123–4, 158; professions, 60–1; Protestants and Catholics, 56–8, 60, 182n46; trades, 60–1
O'Ciosain, Niall, 136
O'Connell, Daniel, 72–3, 140, 211n135
O'Doirnin, Peadar, 65–6
Ogle, Col. John, 34, 36–9, 42, 157, 177n80

Ogle, Julia Eliza (née Barton), 12, 37
O'Rafferty, Rev. Daniel, 64, 75–7, 123–6, 186n60
Orange Order, 4–5, 19, 31, 41, 86–7, 95, 98, 145, 156–7
Orior, Upper, 10, 22, 46, 80–1, 83, 128, 130, 133, 151
outrages, 82–120; sectarianism and, 83–4, 107–8, 113, 115. *See also* disturbances

Paine, Thomas, 29
Peep O'Day Boys, 3, 18–19, 31, 33, 42
penal laws, 29–30, 65–6, 73–4, 153
petty sessions court, 117–19
Poor Inquiry (1835), 118, 123–6
population, 7, 15, 47–8, 109, 152, 214n49–50; ages, 55, 60, 62, 181n36; decrease, 121, 133–4; increase, 103, 123, 126
Presbyterians, 7, 10, 29, 33, 41, 43, 166n19
proselytism. *See* souperism
Protestants/Protestantism, 3–5, 7–9, 12, 14–16, 17, 21, 23–4, 33, 35, 82–5, 87–8, 99–100, 113, 115–16, 142–55; Church of Ireland, 42, 61, 142, 144, 147, 150–2, 214n47; education, 66–71, 75, 77–8; family size, 48–52, 62, 158; famine relief effort, 126–7, 129–31, 135–7; farm size, 52–5, 62, 158; literacy, 78–80; marriages, 209n100, 213n30; occupations, 54–8, 60–1; population of, 7, 15, 47–8, 152, 214n49–50; "Protestant Defence Association," 85; Second Reformation, 72–3, 142–3; settlement of estate (1789–92), 14–16; social profile, 48–63; souperism, 135–7, 142–9, 159–60; tithe agitation, 99–100. *See also* Methodist chapel; Presbyterians; religious controversy; sectarianism
public houses, 102–3, 182n47
Pyar, Peter, 90, 93, 97

Rafferty, Charles, 92
Rafferty, Pat, 108
Rebellion of 1798, 28–44. *See also* Defenders; Society of United Irishmen
Red the Roads/Rednecks. *See* faction fighting
Regenerated Defenders, 82, 157, 188n2
Relief Commission, 121, 129–31
religion. *See* Catholics/Catholicism; Protestants/Protestantism; religious controversy; Scripture reading; Second Reformation; sectarianism
religious controversy, 71–5, 144–55, 166n19
repeal, 140
ribbonism: Catholic Church and, 113–14; faction fighting, 102–3, 108; in Forkhill, 85, 88, 91–7, 100, 102–3, 108–14, 115–16, 158, 200n196–7; in Ireland, 86–8, 94–8, 103, 115–16, 189n27, 194n114; land, 108–9, 112–13, 115, 141; mock trials, 88, 94, 116; oaths, 87–8, 163–4, 202n225; prosecutions, 86–7; sectarianism, 107–8, 111, 113, 115, 203n233; social mores, 116, 203n238; tithe agitation, 88–95, 99–100; wearing ribbons, 95–7
Richardson, Rev. William, 83–4
Rightboys, 87–8, 114
Rising of 1797. *See* Society of United Irishmen
Roman Catholic Church. *See* Catholics/Catholicism

Saint Bridget, 96–7
schools. *See* education
Scripture reading, 70–2, 74–6, 80, 142–3, 145, 147–8, 213n36
seasonal migration, 51, 60, 62, 70, 98, 123
Seaver, Jonathan, 82, 84, 100, 201n210
Seaver, Thomas, 105, 140
Second Reformation, 72–3, 142–3
sectarianism, 4–9, 87–8, 99–100, 107–8, 113–16, 137, 157–62; and Armagh Disturbances, 18–19; in Forkhill, 4–5, 13–17, 21–3, 27, 71–8, 83–5, 150–2; historiography, 5–9, 115, 162, 166n14–15, 203n234; Rebellion of 1798, 29–31, 41–2. *See also* Catholics; Protestants; Defenders; disturbances; education; Orange Order; religious controversy; ribbonism; tithe
Shanroe, 61, 91
Shean, 59, 67, 109, 117–18, 133

Smith, Bernard, 102–3, 117, 196n145, 196n148
Smith, Thomas, 84
Smith, Rev. William, 123–6, 129
Smyth, Jim, 42
social conditions, 45–63, 104–6
Society of Irish Church Missions, 143–4, 147–9
Society of United Irishmen, 24, 28–43, 86; in south Armagh, 28, 33–42
songs: "The Boys of Mullaghbawn," 43–4; "The Carrive Blacksmith," 38; "The Market Stone," 40, 42
souperism: charges of, 135–7, 142–9, 159–60, 210n110
spinning. *See* linen industry; occupations
Steelboys, 20, 22, 87
Stewart, A.T.Q., 5, 158

Tandragee, 74–5
taxation, 20, 22, 43, 115–16. *See also* tithe
threatening letters, 94, 99, 110, 116–17
Threshers, 82–3, 96
Tiffcrum, 46, 85, 102, 109, 119
tithe, 88–9, 190n46; agitation (1830s), 74, 85, 88–95, 99–100, 108, 116, 141, 157, 191n51, 191n57, 195n25; and Oakboys, 43; tithe proctors, 17, 20, 22, 83, 86, 89–90, 93–5
Tone, Theobald Wolfe, 29, 35
Trainor, James, 92
Trainor, Philip, 91–2
Trench, William Steuart, 94–5, 108, 200n195
Tuft, James, 91
Tullymacreeve, 101, 117
Turner, Samuel, 37, 39, 175n50

Ulster (1790s), 28, 36, 39, 41–2
United Irishmen. *See* Society of United Irishmen

Verner, William, 4, 157

weaving. *See* linen industry; occupations
Whiteboys, 20, 22, 26, 66, 87–8, 98, 114
women: education, 68, 70; health, 55, 125, 134; occupations, 56–60; role of, 58–60
workhouse. *See* famine

Young, Rev. Henry Wray, 142, 144–52, 154–5, 159, 161, 212n12, 214n46

Printed in the USA
CPSIA information can be obtained
at www.ICGtesting.com
JSHW082345100524
62661JS00011B/27